The Heart of Healing

Jeffrey A. Kottler
Thomas L. Sexton
Susan C. Whiston

The Heart of Healing

Relationships in Therapy

Jossey-Bass Publishers • San Francisco

Substantial discounts on bulk quantities of Jossey-Bass books are available to corporations, professional associations, and other organizations. For details and discount information, contact the special sales department at Jossey-Bass Inc., Publishers. (415) 433–1740; Fax (415) 433–0499.

For sales outside the United States, please contact your local Paramount Publishing International Office.

Manufactured in the United States of America. Nearly all Jossey-Bass books and jackets are printed on recycled paper that contains at least 50 percent recycled waste, including 10 percent postconsumer waste. Many of our materials are printed with either soy- or vegetable-based ink; during the printing process these inks emit fewer volatile organic compounds (VOCs) than petroleum-based inks. VOCs contribute to the formation of smog.

Library of Congress Cataloging-in-Publication Data

Kottler, Jeffrey A.
  The heart of healing : relationships in therapy / Jeffrey A. Kottler, Thomas L. Sexton, Susan C. Whiston.
    p.   cm.—(The Jossey-Bass social and behavioral science series)
  Includes bibliographical references and index.
  ISBN 0-7879-0026-5
  1. Psychotherapist and patient. 2. Psychotherapy. I. Sexton, Thomas L., date. II. Whiston, Susan C., date. III. Title. IV. Series.
RC480.8.K684   1994
616.89'14—dc20   94–17755
                                                            CIP

FIRST EDITION
HB Printing   10 9 8 7 6 5 4 3 2 1   *Code 94117*

The Jossey-Bass

Social and Behavioral Science Series

To our children
Cary Jay Kottler, Jennifer Whiston Kimble,
Michael Whiston Kimble,
Matthew Whiston Sexton

Contents

Preface

If there are three people who each think as differently as we do about therapeutic relationships, we would like to meet them. The ambitious project that we have undertaken, to write a comprehensive work on the nature of human relationships in the helping process, is daunting enough. Our task has been made even more difficult by the fact that, as researchers, educators, and practitioners, we operate in such divergent ways.

This book was born during a series of morning runs in the desert. Several times per week, we would meet in the early dawn, running though neighborhoods and dry river beds, dodging lizards and cacti, talking to distract ourselves from the pain. Since we are practitioners, we spoke a lot about what we do and how we do it. Because we are also educators, we tried to convince one another that each of us had more accurate and righteous perceptions than the others. Our thinking started from very different places. Our conceptions were so divergent that reconciliation seemed out of reach.

Eventually, with the help of fatigue and the inevitability that we would have to find different running partners if we did not come to some agreement, we realized that, although we use different words to describe our actions, in the end, we do the same things with our clients. Some of our differences were more apparent than real; others were, and are, irreconcilable. We also realized that our discussions paralleled the debates happening in the field at large. Whereas some practitioners might go to their respective corners and pout, we stayed to resolve our differences, asking, In spite of the divergences in our styles, values, preferences, experiences, and goals, what is it that we can agree on?

The dimension that seemed to bond us together, as friends as well as colleagues, was the realization that it is the therapeutic relationship that holds the key to our work. We may not be able to agree which facets of this human connection are most significant or what names should be used to describe it, but we are unanimous in our belief that something important is operating within this phenomenon. In the discussions underlying this book, we called one another a lot of names—"fuzzy-headed," "rigid," "sanctimonious," and others a lot more visceral. Interestingly, our conflicts over what a therapeutic relationship consists of, what its components are, and what role it plays in therapy are what led us to search for an integrative perspective, one that almost all practitioners would agree with, yet one that would acknowledge the incredible diversity among those practitioners.

Therapists may argue about a lot of issues in their field—whether quantitative methods are superior to qualitative investigations or whether cognitive strategies work better than systemic interventions—but one thing that most everyone believes is that, in varying degrees and forms, the relationship between people plays a significant role in the therapeutic process. This relationship may be viewed as the primary operative ingredient, as a necessary but insufficient condition for change, or as a desirable means to a more important end, but all therapists harness its powers in some way.

Audience

We have tried to make *The Heart of Healing* accessible for practitioners of therapy, students in the field, and interested observers. We are hopeful that it will be used in a number of different ways—as a stimulus for further research about the therapeutic relationship, generating hypotheses to be further tested; as a text for advanced students, particularly in those courses that work toward integration of knowledge for the purposes of clinical application; as a resource for practitioners meeting in study groups, trying to sort out the mysteries of their relationships with clients; and as a synthesis for the solitary practitioner wanting especially to know more about the state of the art, which practitioners may take for granted. Ultimately, this is a book intended to help professionals get unstuck from the ways they think about relationships and expand the ways they employ these human alliances to reach desired goals.

Overview of the Contents

Five major threads—personal, cultural, conceptual, empirical, and clinical—undergird much of what we have to say. Each major thread represents a theme to be addressed in considering the therapeutic relationship and each thread is made up of a number of subordinate threads. Whereas some treatments of the client-therapist relationship have been primarily empirically based, theoretically driven, or even profoundly personal statements, we have sought to include all this subject's facets in a book practitioners will find useful as a resource, an inspiration, and most of all, a stimulus to think and function more effectively.

Moreover, several unique features are lodged in the five distinct threads that structure our discussions: an interdisciplinary approach that combines material from diverse fields; a cross-cultural perspective that addresses cultural differences in how relationships are constructed; a solid conceptual foundation that includes several innovative as well as integrative models of relationships; a comprehensive review of the empirical and anecdotal literature; and an emphasis on clinical applications of ideas to particular situations with clients.

The Heart of Healing is divided into three sections, the first of which is devoted to introducing the subject of the therapeutic relationship in a way that retains all of its complexity and magic.

We thus begin, in Chapter One, with a discussion of the inherent paradoxes of our subject under investigation. We suggest that this seemingly clear-cut and professional relationship is, by its very nature, fraught with complexity, sparking confusion in both client *and* therapist. In Chapter Two, we review the conceptual framework that we adopt throughout, one that emphasizes the integration of diverse theoretical models through incorporating a multicultural and multidisciplinary approach, considering the differential needs of various clients over time, and letting go of some of practitioners' most cherished assumptions and models in the search for a more encompassing model of what takes place during healing encounters.

Following these chapters that address some of the conceptual threads of healing, Chapter Three moves into the realm of the personal. How does the work of healing impact the relationships in a therapist's personal life? Conversely, how do therapists' interactions with significant people in their personal lives affect what they do with their clients? This personal dimension remains at the core of every clinical decision therapists make, each intervention they select, and every relationship they participate in, whether in the filtered air of their offices or the fresh air of their own backyards.

Chapter Four continues laying the foundation for what will follow by discussing cross-cultural perspectives in therapeutic relationships. If practitioners and researchers alike are to build on a broad base of knowledge, it is imperative that they put aside their differences to search for universals across cultures and time. By gaining this global perspective (literally and metaphorically), they will be better equipped to make sense out of a human phenomenon so complex that it has so far defied adequate description and explanation. Thus, in our discussion, we attempt to retain all the nuances of the varied healing alliances that are active in diverse disciplines from medicine and religion to social work and nursing. Yet we also examine some of the universal factors that operate across the various cultures and contexts in which healing takes place.

Part Two of this book provides the concepts for understanding various models of healing relationships. We have attempted no less than to review some of the major theoretical explanations for how and why human relationships are, in fact, potentially helpful in therapy. Some of these explanations are traditional while others represent new perspectives that have received scant attention.

Chapter Five reviews the range of traditional and contemporary theoretical models and current empirical findings, and offers a unique multidimensional model of therapeutic relationships. This multidimensional model is considered in the contexts of the five threads. Then each of the remaining chapters in this section provides a more detailed analysis of the complexities of the multiple dimensions in the model. Chapter Six discusses existing conceptual models that describe the authentic nature of the relationship, emphasizing caring. Chapter Seven borrows some ideas from colleagues in the social sciences, presenting a social psychological perspective on what takes place between client and therapist. Chapter Eight examines the dimension of projection and the existing models for understanding "ghosts" in the room. Chapter Nine closes the section with an exploration of the interactional dynamics that occur during therapeutic encounters.

Part Three is devoted to the final and most important thread, applying the concepts presented previously to a number of clinical challenges. Chapter Ten provides a synthesis for the practitioner, a model of the therapeutic relationship that incorporates most of what is known about this complex phenomenon. Chapter Eleven thoroughly explores how the relationship can be used advantageously in various therapeutic scenarios, and Chapter Twelve looks at the limitations of the relationship as a healing force and suggests what to do when the relationship is not enough to produce desired results. In the final chapter, we come full circle and once again turn our attention to all five threads of healing in therapeutic relationships, focusing on the future and what is to come in this ever-changing journey of discovery.

Conclusion

During the three years in which we undertook this project, our own relationships changed indelibly, for better and for worse. There has been conflict. Coalitions among the three of us have changed over time. There was even a marriage between two of the authors (Sexton and Whiston) during the tenure of our collaboration. Just as in all intense human collaborations, our relationships have been healing for each of us to the extent that we have been willing to follow what it is that we claim to understand. We wish you the best in your own efforts to do the same.

Las Vegas, Nevada   Jeffrey A. Kottler
August 1994   Thomas L. Sexton
                                                                    Susan C. Whiston

The Authors

Jeffrey A. Kottler is a professor of counseling and educational psychology at the University of Nevada, Las Vegas. He has studied at Oakland University, Harvard University, Wayne State University, and the University of Stockholm, and received his Ph.D. degree from the University of Virginia. He has worked as a therapist in a variety of settings including hospitals, mental health centers, schools, clinics, universities, corporations, and private practice.

Kottler is the author or coauthor of the books *Ethical and Legal Issues in Counseling and Psychotherapy* (1977, with William Van Hoose), *Pragmatic Group Leadership* (1983), *On Being a Therapist* (1986), *The Imperfect Therapist: Learning from Failure in Therapeutic Practice* (1989, with Diane Blau), *Private Moments, Secret Selves: Enriching Our Time Alone* (1990), *The Compleat Therapist* (1991), *Introduction to Therapeutic Counseling* (1992, 2nd edition, with Robert Brown), *Compassionate Therapy: Working with Difficult Clients* (1992), *On Being a Teacher* (1993, with Stan Zehm), *Advanced Group Leadership* (1993), *Teacher as Counselor* (1993, with Ellen Kottler), *From Dreams to Realities: The Emerging Professional Counselor* (1994, with Richard Hazler), and *Beyond Blame: A New Way of Resolving Conflicts in Relationships* (1994).

Thomas L. Sexton is associate professor of counseling and educational psychology at the University of Nevada, Las Vegas. He received his Ph.D. degree from Florida State University. He has been a therapist at a variety of centers, working with juvenile delinquents, mental health clients, and university students. He has authored or coauthored a number of articles investigating the common elements of therapy that most influence successful outcomes. In addition, he has written about the systemic nature of interactional counseling. He serves on the editorial board of *Counselor Education and Supervision* and is also book section editor for that journal.

Susan C. Whiston is associate professor of counseling and educational psychology at the University of Nevada, Las Vegas. She grew up in the "wilds" of Wyoming and received her doctoral degree from the University of Wyoming. Currently, she serves on the editorial board of the *Journal of Counseling and Development*. Whiston is investigating the empirical basis for therapeutic practice and researching aspects of career development. She has published numerous articles about incorporating therapy research into practice.

The Heart of Healing

Part One

Understanding Healing Relationships

Chapter One

Paradoxes in Therapy

A new client enters your office, naïve and uncertain about what it is that you do and exactly how therapy works. This is a gentleman from Missouri, the "show me" state. Furthermore, he is a chemical engineer, comfortable in the world of substances that can be measured and controlled. As you begin your standard introduction and orientation to the process that he is about to undertake, you can see that he is becoming more and more skeptical, more confused about what sort of experience he is bargaining for. As you get to your favorite section, the part where you talk about the kind of relationship that is likely to develop between the two of you and what form it will take, the man's impatience gets the best of him, and he interrupts you.

Wait a minute! Wait one minute! Let me get this straight. Let me see if I understand what you have been saying. I am going to be participating in some kind of relationship with you. I am supposed to trust you, but I have to do that on faith because I know next to nothing about who you are. You said this will be an equal relationship, one in which we are both partners, but it seems to me that you are clearly the one in charge. You mentioned that we will become close to one another, intimate and personal, where I have to spill my guts and you listen. Then, you said it will be spontaneous, that we will deal with whatever comes up, yet you will also be directing and prescribing things. You told me that this is a safe place to open up, but you also said that things could get a little dicey, even dangerous, because I will be taking risks and changing. Finally, you said that the object is to help me become more independent; that's all very fine, but you also indicated that I am likely to become dependent on you during the interim. You will pardon me if I am confused, but almost everything you have described will happen during this experience seems contradictory.

This client from Missouri is not far off. Much of what we explain to clients about the nature of therapy is contradictory. That they go along with the plan anyway is a testimony to our persuasiveness, to our confidence that the paradoxes and polarities inherent in this healing process do eventually work themselves out and blend together beautifully along the way.

Paradox is at the core of therapy and permeates many facets of relationships designed to be healing. A paradox implies a contradiction that refutes logic, a state of affairs that is not necessarily incompatible with the work that therapists do, because, as much as therapists might enjoy discovering logical causes and effects, the irrational, unpredictable, and serendipitous are at the heart of human relationships. Unless both therapists and their clients are willing to suspend a degree of belief, to honor that which is inexplicable, the journey they take together is likely to be frustrating and unsatisfying.

Every day therapists live with compelling evidence of the paradoxes in their relationships—when they foster dependency in order to promote independence; when they advertise themselves as trustworthy and genuine yet resort to manipulation as a means to reach desired goals; when they care deeply about a certain client—until the moment the client leaves the room; when they try to create an atmosphere of safety and security that is actually quite dangerous in its potential for doing good or harm to the client; and even when they accept a fee (or salary) in exchange for their "authentic" caring.

Faced with each of these apparent contradictions, we have learned to live with paradox. While the following pages will attempt to reconcile some of these discrepancies, the ideas presented here also acknowledge the importance of honoring the irra-tional. There is at the core of the therapeutic relationship an essence that is so complex, so utterly mysterious and baffling, that it defies complete description, much less human understanding. We offer this admission not as an excuse for our own limited vision but as an accurate representation of this phenomenon.

Practitioners, students, and interested observers of therapy have already seen much about this subject, yet not nearly enough to explain adequately what takes place between human beings during healing encounters. To some extent, many of us take our relation-ships with clients for granted, as if this process will simply unfold all by itself if we simply stay out of the way. At other times, we believe we have a definite idea of the kind of relationship we wish to create, one that has worked for us a hundred times before. The paradox is that we are creating a human connection that appears similar to almost any other relationship yet is substantially differ-ent enough to produce effects that are often quite extraordinary.

The intent in describing the following paradoxes is to create a temporary state of increased dissonance and confusion in the reader. Of course, you hardly picked up this book in order to feel even more uncertain about what you are doing, any more than a client actually wants to encounter more pain before the hold of the existing pain can be loosened. But it is perhaps the ultimate para-dox of human change and influence, whether in a therapy session, classroom, or book, that the world must first be turned upside down before it can be set right again, in a way that provides more solid footing. Such contradictions as described here can be confusing, but they can also be rich, stimulating, and provocative, residing at the heart of the change process that takes place.

Equal and Democratic Yet Unequal and Authoritarian

Most relationships, whether between friends, colleagues, or lovers, are based on principles of reciprocity and symmetry. In therapy relationships as well, there is a kind of interdependence, but one in which the degree of risking and disclosure is hardly equal. On first glance, the therapeutic relationship may very well appear to be like a friendship in that the participants are intimately involved. However, they hardly bring equal power and resources to the relationship. The therapist is perceived as an expert, a sanctioned healer who is endowed with certain attributes, skills, knowledge, and power. The client thus functions in a one-down position, deferring to the professional's position as a healer.

The therapist, as authority, determines the kind of relationship that will be most profitable for the client, whether it is friendly and informal or more highly structured. The expert also decides where they will meet, how often this will take place, and how much time they will spend together. Furthermore, the professional defines the nature of the collaboration and what needs to be done in order to address the client's concerns. In short, in spite of therapists' pronouncements about how egalitarian therapeutic relationships are supposed to be ("We are partners in this process"), these relationships are actually asymmetrical in terms of who is in charge.

We often promote and perpetuate this paradox. On the one hand, we talk about the importance of trust and closeness; on the other, we deliberately attempt to distance ourselves. We speak of the relationship as a collaboration but we are the director. We simulate symmetry by dressing as a friend rather than sporting the white lab coat of an expert. We create a friendly atmosphere by the way we arrange our offices like living rooms yet use our diplomas and books to proclaim our credentials. We tell individuals that they know what is best for themselves, yet we subtly guide them in directions that we think would be in their best interests. For example, when we say, "You keep asking me what you should do, but *you* are the one who must live with your decisions. You will have to make your own choices. I can't tell you what to do, but I think it would be wise for you take your time, study the options, and then consider the likely consequences of quitting your job," we are sending the message "I think it is stupid for you to quit your job before you have something else lined up."

One of the outcomes of this paradox of our proclaiming egalitarianism while enacting authoritarianism is that our clients are confused about our roles. Do therapists function more as doctors or friends? Is their job to give direction or support? Clients express their uncertainty when they say to therapists, "I have told you so much about me and my life. I have shared my dreams with you, and my fears. I have trusted you with my deepest secrets. Why can't you tell me something about you?"

Therapists suffer doubts and uncertainties about their roles as well. Since therapeutic relationships so closely resemble other human affiliations, we are often caught in dilemmas that test the boundaries and limits of what constitutes professional work. We develop strong attachment to many of our clients; we feel great affection, regard, and even love for some of them. It becomes difficult to separate professional from personal interests, to respond objectively to the thought, *Am I asking this question because it is related to the client's treatment, or because I have a personal interest in knowing the answer?*

The existence of dual and multiple relationships continually challenges us to define our professional roles. When does the supervision of other practitioners become therapy? To what extent do our relationships with interns or students become like relationships with friends or clients or colleagues? When, if ever, does a client stop being a client? If I go out for lunch with a student, is this a breach of appropriate conduct? What if I write a reference letter for a client? Am I permitted to see an ex-student as a client? What about an ex-client as a student? These questions are among those most often debated in staff lounges, case conferences, professional journals, and ethics committees. And for good reason! On the one hand, we are doing our best to appear authentic and engaging; on the other hand, we attempt to enforce rigid boundaries in which our genuine caring may be expressed.

It is no wonder that the paradoxical way the therapeutic relationship is defined creates problems for clients and therapists in
deciding how a relationship can be both democratic and authoritarian, collaborative and asymmetrical, equal and quite unequal in
power. And contradictory elements are also evident in other
dimensions of this peculiar kind of human relationship.

Intimate and Personal Yet Professional and Distant

Across all of the various arenas in which they occur, therapeutic
relationships seem to consist of two inseparable but paradoxical
parts: overt intimacy and hidden authority (Hardesty, 1986). First
of all, the therapist embodies characteristics of intimacy, empathy,
caring, and concern. Yet this closeness exists in a context in which
the therapist remains apart and separate from the client, unwilling
to meet personal needs or to indulge in extended sharing of self.
This aloof role stands in stark contrast to the overt role of a loving
and supportive confidant. In fact, one of the great paradoxes of the
healing relationship is that, while it is supposedly built on complete
honesty, genuineness, openness, and authenticity, it is actually quite
deceptive and contrived.

Clients, therefore, are presented with a conundrum. They must
relate to therapists both as experts, to whom they defer, and as nur-
turers, to whom they come for support. On the one hand, both
therapist and client act as if they are in an egalitarian encounter:
they are polite, respectful, and take turns speaking. The therapist
even says something like this: "You are the boss here. This is your
time to talk about whatever you wish. You are the one responsible
for whether this treatment succeeds."

On the other hand, it is quite clear that both structural and
interpersonal dimensions are mostly controlled by the therapist.
When the client is nodding his head, acknowledging the therapist's
definition of rules and roles that say that the client chooses content and direction, he is already happily ensconced in a deferential

position ("Tell me what to do." "What do you think the problem is?" "How long will this take, and how often should I come?" "Do you think that you can help me?").

One of the areas in which this paradox of the intimate and personal yet professional and distant relationship is most evident is the way payment is handled. For those therapists who are compensated directly by their clients (or the clients' insurance carriers), money issues complicate the relationship even further. In her essay on how money pollutes the therapeutic relationship, Mellan (1992) describes how payment touches the deepest unresolved issues of both client and clinician. In interviewing practitioners, she found that many felt like prostitutes, charging strangers for an hour of intimacy. They also felt quite hypocritical in belonging to the materialistic middle class yet espousing values of altruism and service. In the words of one therapist, who speaks for many of us who have been in private practice:

> Money pollutes doing therapy for me. No matter how hard I try to convince myself that this is a profession, it feels more like a business. When a client decides to leave treatment, my first reaction, before concern, hope, pride, or disappointment, is how am I going to fill this time slot? I feel guilty taking money for what I do, as if I am not doing enough to earn it. Yet with several of my clients who are paying me only what they can afford, I feel resentful, as if I am being taken advantage of.
>
> Many issues permeate, or I should say infect, every facet of this process. Time is measured in dollars clicked off a meter. I hear it running in my head—ten minutes gone, that's another $20 I earned. Then I have a hard time reconciling this heartfelt, moving, incredibly intimate encounter we have just completed with the client's writing me a check. I feel dirty."

Of course, therapists recognize that payment for professional services has its advantages as well. There is nothing that says that the contradictory elements of an intimate, professional relationship are somehow inherently bad. Many clients respond quite well to a contractual arrangement with clear rules and boundaries. Just because we are being paid for our services does not mean that we do not care.

These are just some of the concerns therapists have about the paradox of taking money in exchange for a supposedly authentic, open, and trusting relationship. Clients also have their own issues related to this perplexing, contractually professional and interactionally personal arrangement, in which they are essentially renting a friend as they might lease a parking space or regular court time to play tennis.

The consequences of this paradox are that clients often expect things from us that we are unable or unwilling to give. Clients may then feel frustrated and deprived, a familiar state of affairs in their lives and one that led them to seek help in the first place. We, in turn, feel guilty and uneasy about not reciprocating on a more equal level; yet we also feel uncomfortable when we do cross some invisible boundary, becoming more friendly or personal than would seem appropriate.

Real and Genuine Yet Manipulative and Projective

One of the guiding principles of intimate relationships is that they have as their foundation a real and genuine involvement by both parties. It is this honest and open communication that invites continued sharing by both parties. By its very definition, intimacy is the presence of an authentic caring for one another that is honestly and genuinely expressed.

Even though we advertise therapeutic relationships as meeting these criteria, even going so far as to proclaim that they are the most genuine of all human connections, with the safeguards they provide, there are aspects of these affiliations that are quite contrived, if not downright phony. Both therapist and client enter the therapeutic process with their own hidden agendas about what they hope will take place. The client comes to the meetings with a number of expectations and beliefs that are usually not shared aloud.

I want you to fix me.

I don't really want to change; I want everyone else to act differently.

Even though I am acting contrite, I resent your authority and control.

I am going to get you to see things my way.

All I really care about is that I want you to like me and approve of what I am doing.

To make matters even more contrived, we have our own hidden agendas and genuine reactions, which are rarely disclosed explicitly.

I don't really care for you as much as I pretend to.

When I tell you that it does not matter to me what you decide, I am really lying because I do have some strong beliefs about what is best.

I want you to improve according to my pace, usually faster than you might prefer.

Even though I tell you that you are in charge of what we do, I will be the one who really decides the direction things take.

You don't end this until I decide you are ready.

As much as we might feel a certain amount of resistance to, even resentment of, acknowledging our own deceptions and disingenuous remarks, it is often the case that, while we might pretend to be best buddies with our clients during the session, if we saw certain clients coming down the street, we might very well turn and run the other way. There are clients we spend much time with, locked in intimate sharing, who, unless we were paid to be with them, would be some of the last folks on the planet we would choose as company. As much as this may be unpleasant to admit, we may act sincere and caring when the client is in our presence (and even genuinely feel this way as we adopt our professional stance), but once the client is out the door, those feelings of good-will may very well melt in the short time it takes us to sit down and reflect on what took place.

An additional factor that confuses the intimate and genuine nature of therapeutic relationships is even more difficult to pin-point. When clients talk about their troubles, the discussion may have several possible effects on our internal states. First, we may be intensely interested in what the client is saying, focused with all our attention and energy, hanging on every word. Our reflections of feeling, interpretations of content, verbal and nonverbal acknowledgments are thus genuine and sincere expressions of what we are thinking and feeling inside. While this state of functioning is preferable, we all operate on this level far less frequently than we are willing to admit.

Second, although we may very well be interested in the client as a person, the present discussion may not be in the least appeal-ing to us. What is being talked about may be digressive, irrelevant, or just downright boring. If you doubt this, spend a day monitoring the amount of time in any given session that you spend attending fully to what your client is saying. Compare this to how often you lapse into fantasy or distracting thoughts that float through your awareness all the while you are pretending to be intensely interested.

Third, boredom is not the only reason we may have difficulty pretending interest. The subject matter at hand may be a little too close to our hearts. Unresolved issues in our own lives crop up con-tinuously. Projected identification and transference processes may also be operating in both client and therapist, so that they relate to one another not as they actually appear in reality but as figments of each other's imagination, memories, or distorted perceptions.

Thus, one profoundly paradoxical aspect of therapeutic relationships is that, although they appear to be based on genuine, or "real" intimate behaviors, they may frequently or occasionally (depending on conceptual beliefs) reflect very little of what is taking place in the present. Clients sometimes see and react to us not as we really are (after all, clients know us in one-dimensional ways) but as they perceive/imagine/distort/project us to be. How many times, for example, have you had the experience of feeling completely misunderstood or unappreciated by a client with whom you have been doing your absolute best to make contact? No matter what you say, no matter how diplomatically and cautiously you handle matters, the client reacts to you as if you were some sort of insensitive bully. Yet, as you examine your own behavior, you can find no evidence that you have been anything other than compassionate and empathic.

Likewise, there are times that we may overreact to what clients say and do, responding to them in "unreal" ways, or in what analytic theories describe as countertransference. How many times have you caught yourself treating clients not as they are, but as others in your life, whom the clients remind you of? How often have you noticed yourself overreacting to a particular client or to an issue she is presenting? How frequently have you conveyed the idea that you are helping a client with a thorny dilemma you believe he is struggling with when you notice that you are speaking as much to yourself as to him?

It is clear that although we may see (and market) therapeutic relationships as natural, intimate, and close collaborations involving honest and authentic disclosure and responsiveness, they also have elements that are quite contradictory. On one level, the parties interact with all the characteristics one would normally associate with authentic intimacy. On another level, the client and therapist each attempt to manipulate, control, and influence one another, while also entertaining a number of hidden agendas. The shape of the relationship becomes even more elusive when both client and therapist are distorting what is taking place, reacting as if they are talking to one another when they are actually relating to someone else.

Independent Yet Dependent

Therapeutic relationships are successful when clients become more independent, when they take charge of their lives, when they make better decisions and take action. Promoting greater independence and autonomy is thus a frequently espoused goal in the form of therapeutic healing most prevalent in our culture. We attempt to aid clients in searching for personal identity, in separating from their families of origin, in formulating their own unique visions for their lives, and in being able to support themselves emotionally and financially.

Independence is a major theme that runs throughout much of what we do, and there are sound reasons for this emphasis, given the value placed in our U.S. culture on self-sufficiency. Paradoxically, this independence results from a relationship that is developmental and therefore involves a great deal of dependence. A client thus receives a mixed message from a therapist: "I want to help you to grow up and separate from others whom you have been leaning on, *but* I want you to lean on me for awhile." In other words, "Dependence is generally a bad thing, *except* when you feel that way toward me."

This tension between independence and dependence presents some interesting challenges for the participants in these relationships. On the one hand, we work feverishly to prevent clients' overdependence ("Thank you for your compliment, but it was *you* who did the work"); on the other hand, we deliberately encourage clients to depend on us in the short run ("I would like to meet with you on a regular basis, and I suggest that you not make any major decisions without discussing them with me first"). Naturally, clients become confused. They are often struggling for independence in other relationships all the while they are working so hard to gain our approval. In time, they will eventually wean themselves of their need for our validation as well, but that transitional period can be quite trying for both parties, just as is the case in the developing relationship between parents and children.

The unique feature of therapeutic relationships is that they exist only as transitional states; they are neither intended nor designed to operate indefinitely. The paradox is that it seems that we cannot help clients to become more independent unless we can create the conditions that lead to trust, and thus dependence, as a temporary state. The two ends of the independence-dependence polarity are linked in such a way that you cannot have one without the other.

Spontaneous Yet Prescribed

The next chapter builds a case that intimate personal relationships of all kinds are part of the very fabric of human existence. There are few things more natural or spontaneous than striking up a conversation with someone or making contact with a loved one. Yet with the evolution of certain technological and cultural imperatives, much of the natural spontaneity in relationships has diminished. The advent of single-family dwellings, high walls, and strong doors, with locks, have reduced the possibilities for informal interaction. With the elimination of sidewalks, front porches, and central meeting places, opportunities are further reduced. Families have dispersed to faraway places. The main ways individuals reach out and touch one another are by telephone, or increasingly, by fax machines, electronic mail, and answering machines. Add to this situation people's preference for (and necessity of) driving in insulated, fast-moving objects instead of walking as their primary means of transportation, and one can further appreciate how rare it has become for people to spend time together in spontaneous encounters.

Although people come to us often hungering for intimacy, therapy is anything but a spontaneous enterprise. There are rules and regulations regarding almost every facet of the encounter: where the meetings take place, who sits where, who does what, how long the sessions last, and when conversation may take place outside of this context. The paradox is that, within the rigid parameters of this controlled relationship, we aspire to teach people to be more spontaneous and natural in their lives. It is a strange kind of model that we present, concerned as we are with controlling every facet of the exchange.

"Yes, it would be good to talk about that."
"No, it would be better if we saved that for later."

"Yes, you can squeeze my arm affectionately in gratitude."
"No, you may not hug me."
"Yes, you can hug me, but no sustained body contact."

"Repeat after me: 'I am in control of my life.'"
"I notice that you are repeating my words. Express yourself in your own language."

"You have got to stay in reality."
"Now what I would like you to do is to sit over there and pretend . . ."

"I think it is crucial that you make every appointment."
"Let's skip the next session. I will not be able to see you next week."

"Say whatever you feel."
"Rather than saying 'must,' say 'prefer.'"

"Tell me what is happening."
"Don't talk to me; tell your daughter."

Clearly, therapists exhibit quite a lot of control over the proceedings, with respect to language that is used, behavior that is practiced, and even the seating arrangements and appointment schedules. Yet it is within this closely monitored environment that clients are encouraged to be spontaneous.

"Tell me whatever is going through your mind."

"What are you feeling right now? Show me with your hands."

"Don't *tell* me. *Act out* the way the interaction might proceed."

There is yet another paradox related to control, one that particularly embodies the complexity of the therapeutic relationship. Sheltzer (1986) suggested that all therapies are inherently paradoxical in that each endeavors to help clients comprehend the voluntariness and controllability of behaviors and emotions that seem to clients to be uncontrollable. Thus, establishing a therapeutic relationship is synonymous with taking control. The therapist gains control by giving it up, by being indirectly direct, by structuring a process of spontaneous compliance and healing (Haley, 1973) and exercising control over the process without seeming to do so ("It is amazing what you have been able to do in such a short period of time! That was quite brilliant how you thought up that plan last week and put it into action with so little help from anyone but yourself").

The view that change occurs in a relationship that is based on the creation of spontaneous compliance is seemingly contradictory and certainly paradoxical. But this type of alliance is more universal than anyone might imagine, since people rarely make direct requests of others (Weeks, 1989). When individuals wish to get somebody to do something that they think might be good for that person (or for the individuals themselves), they typically frame it as a request rather than an order for compliance. In a similar manner, we invite clients to take control in a relationship in which we intend to stay in the driver's seat for awhile. And then, when we have been instrumental in facilitating desired change, we attribute the success to the client's actions.

Natural Yet Requiring Professional Training

It is relatively recently in human history that professionals other than clergy have been delegated to act as healers. It is only in Western culture that societies have developed so-called relationship experts, trained in the art and science of relating to others, and on some level, this seems absurd, like developing a training school to teach pigeons to coo, ducks to swim, or eagles to fly. There is something incongruent, even paradoxical, about teaching people to do something that is supposed to be so natural—relating to someone else. If Efran, Lukens, and Lukens (1990) are correct in saying that human relations skills are the main operative ingredient in healing, then why must these skills be taught? Are they not natural behaviors of humans, these *human* relations? There is, after all, some evidence to indicate that such "therapists" as hairdressers and taxi drivers, who have not received any training, can be quite effective (Cowen, 1982). So, why bother with training at all?

There will obviously be debate among any group of professionals as to how much they value natural inclinations (intuition, altruistic attitudes, compassion, and so forth) versus skills that can be taught. Similarly, one question that has prevailed in the helping field for some time is whether therapists are essentially "trained" or "grown." One answer to this question is reflected in the ways potential therapists are recruited. Which criteria are considered to be the best predictors of future performance as a helper? The profession has tried test scores, undergraduate grade point averages, interviews, references, work histories, skill demonstrations, and essays, none of them very good indicators by themselves. It is the combination of a number of these criteria that seems to be most useful in selecting and retaining future helpers. In fact, many therapists first enter the field because they believe they already possess something to offer others, a kind of raw talent that needs developing.

The paradox with which we are confronted is that we are attempting to learn something that is supposed to be natural by very unnatural means. We have trained ourselves in how to influence people within the context of human relationships. We have attempted to connect with others in a natural way by remaining separate through professional training.

Open to Technology Yet Responsive to Human Contact

Contributing to the state of confusion (or at least lack of consensus) in the field is the fact that future therapists are prepared in fairly diverse institutions and programs. Some of these programs are designed around structured classes emphasizing content, replete with lectures, examinations, and a high level of academic proficiency. Some excellent practitioners have emerged from such environments, although they may have certain weaknesses in pragmatic areas of application once they get into the field. Other training programs emphasize skill development above all else. As the discrete behaviors that good therapists engage in are identified, trainees are taught to observe, imitate, and practice these skills. They receive feedback on their performances and reach high levels of mastery. When these graduates obtain jobs, they also do quite well, although they have limitations in conceptual understanding of what they are doing and why. Some institutions "grow" therapists through experiential learning opportunities. The learners work on their personal issues, direct their own studies, interact with peers, engage in authentic relationships with staff members, and practice *being* therapists. This also works quite well as a means of preparing clinicians, although these beginners were limited in their mastery of basic skills.

Each of these three models of therapist preparation follows distinctly different roads to clinical competence, emphasizing content, skill development, or experiential learning. There seems to be no definitive evidence that indicates the superiority of one model over another, although it seems fairly obvious that a combination approach hits all the important areas. Moreover, these different approaches share a common ground in that they all believe that professionals require some form of education/training/growth in order to help people. Relationships may be natural among our species, but most people are not very good at maintaining them, at least when it comes to helping others.

In a study of clinical relationships between lawyers, physicians, teachers, psychologists, and their clients, Sarason (1985) described an alarming trend in which technical innovation is superseding caring and compassion in treatment. The ideals of Hippocrates, Plato, Socrates, and Aristotle, which valued sensitive understanding, human contact, and responsiveness, are slowly being replaced in the fields of medicine, education, and psychology by an emphasis on techniques, procedures, interventions, and computer-assisted assessments. The meaningful encounter, the therapeutic relationship between client and helper, is being discarded as cost ineffective. Thus, many people who are hurting are yearning for intimacy and closeness with others. They not only want their problems solved, their diseases cured, and their educational goals attained, but they want to be respected, understood, and valued.

In spite of our search for the answers to the questions that befuddle us as therapists, one of the most baffling paradoxes of all is how we can reconcile so many discrepant sources of information and thus figure out what it is about some relationships that is so potentially helpful to people in trouble. One movement would have us believe that it is the technology of helping that holds the future: as we refine our models; develop more reliable methods of measurement, prediction, and control; and apply consistent methods that are empirically supported for particular situations and problems, we can expect greater success. Another movement, also compelling, emphasizes the spiritual aspects of human connections as the most healing: if we could operate more from our hearts than our heads, reach out to people in a loving way, and concentrate on the quality of their connection to their clients, then we would be best serving others.

The resolution of this contradiction, as is the case with so many paradoxes, is to abandon an either/or mentality. It is hardly necessary to be either technologically proficient or compassionate. Both the empirically based methodologies and the intuitively originated ways of being are necessary if we are not only to make contact with clients but sustain a type of relationship likely to be useful in reaching goals.

Safe and Predictable Yet Dangerous and Changing

One reason clients come to us in the first place is that they believe we offer a safe environment that they cannot find elsewhere. Confidentiality ensures their privacy. Our training and expertise are supposed to protect clients from hurting themselves further, and even to help with the healing process. Clients also hope that by seeking professional assistance they can make needed changes with a minimum of pain or inconvenience. However, if we were to supply an accurate statement of informed consent, it might read something like this:

Consumer Beware!

There are a number of dangers and risks associated with the treatment that you are about to undergo. Please read this warning carefully before you proceed any further.

1. You will be subjected to intense scrutiny, resulting in a diagnostic label that will be entered into your records as well as into an unknown number of data banks that may be accessible by other parties.

2. Although claims will be made that what you disclose is confidential, actually that is not strictly so. Anything you tell your therapist may indeed be kept private, unless:

It is believed that you may doing something that is harmful, in which case the authorities will be notified.

It is considered necessary to talk about your case to other colleagues and supervisors; also, *anyone* in the agency can look up your record any time he or she wishes and read the sordid details that have been logged therein.

Your therapist makes a mistake and inadvertently lets slip the details of your life in such a way that you might be identified by someone who knows you and has been looking for ways to "get" you for some time.

You are involved in litigation, and the opposing party finds out that you have been in therapy and decides to subpoena your records.

3. Although your therapist will appear confident and expert, he or she may very well not have much experience with the issues you are struggling with. Unlike drivers in training, beginning therapists are not required to wear signs warning people to keep their distance until the new drivers can figure out how to negotiate the road without hurting anyone else.

4. Even so-called experts may be using procedures or interventions that are considered experimental. Your therapist may have attended a workshop during the past weekend and is all excited to try out a few of the new things he or she learned. Although there is no consistent scientifically verified evidence to indicate that this procedure is indeed helpful, and it may, in fact, lead to brain damage, you will be relieved to know that the workshop presenter swears by this strategy.

5. Do not be fooled by the comfortable setting and the folksy

manner of your therapist. You are about to experience one of the most wrenching, excruciatingly difficult, and intensely painful times of your life. You will hear your therapist justify this with the statement, "You may have to get worse before you can get better." This is the same sort of warning your doctor gives when she says to you just before she jabs you with a needle the length of a medium-sized canoe paddle, "You may feel a little pinch." You will be forced to look at things about yourself that you would prefer to leave alone. Secrets in your life, long tucked away in neat little holes, will be uncovered. You will be asked to do some things that you would prefer not to do; your therapist is *very* persistent and is not likely to take no for an answer.

6. Any group of more than half a dozen professionals in the field cannot agree on how this mysterious process works nor the best way that it should be done. That is why you are so confused when you consult with a number of different practitioners—they all tell you that you have a different problem and require a quite different treatment.

7. There is a possibility that, despite the trouble you go to, you may end up much worse after this relationship is over. Although most people do get something out of therapy, some do indeed deteriorate because the therapist was inept, incompetent, or just had a bad day. Try not to schedule appointments at three o'clock in the afternoon (that is when mammals have low biorhythms and when most industrial accidents take place and lions like to take naps).

As cynical as this proclamation might seem, the intent is to drive home the point that although we advertise to others that we are providing a safe environment in which to change, there are actually quite a number of risks that are involved with what we do. Predictability, comfort, and safety are the hallmarks that people usually associate with therapeutic relationships. Unfortunately, since we are in the business of promoting change, these minor, and sometimes major, alterations do not come without a certain degree of effort, risk, and pain.

Universal Principles and Cultural Relativism

One of the threads discussed throughout this book has to do with reconciling the general guidelines of our profession with unique cultural guidelines for relationships. The concept of structure, for example, is central to most of what therapists do in their work. Any number of theories, empirical studies, and clinical experiences clearly document that therapeutic relationships should be *generally* structured to include certain parameters and elements. Yet the individual experiences of each client, as well as his or her cultural context, will affect the likelihood that some structures will work better than others. This cultural context determines the preferred narrative language and underlying cognitive organization of the client as well as the client's perceptions of the relationship and appropriate roles within it (White & Epston, 1990).

Look only at how time is treated within relationships in different cultures to have a sense of how dramatically different things can unfold, especially if the term *culture* is expanded to include not only ethnic, religious, and national origins but also gender, class, and age variables. Thus, the seventeen-year-old son of a New York stockbroker is likely to demand a much faster pace to his relationships than an eighty-eight-year-old Yakima Indian. Certain Native-American tribes, such as the Algonquins, who believe that when people are awake they are really dreaming and that reality takes place in dreams—have a quite different texture to the structure of their relationships than other groups.

Even some of the most cherished assumptions of our profession, such as the primacy of talking about feelings in therapy, are not universal across the cultures with which therapists in the United States may come into contact. It would be hardly appropriate, for example, to invite many South Pacific Islanders to talk about their feelings in therapy sessions. Among the Maori of New Zealand, asking people what they are feeling is a gross breach of etiquette. Doing so would communicate the therapist's ignorance not only of social conduct but of relationships, since emotions cannot be dissociated from physical states. It should be immediately apparent what people are feeling, and hardly necessary to ask, because the feelings are clearly written on their faces. For example, the Maori word *pukuriri* (anger) contains the root *puku* (stomach). Anger is felt in the stomach. Since feelings are lodged in the body, it is an insult to state the obvious. At Maori funerals, one would never *say* what one is feeling ("I am so sorry for your loss"). One is expected to *show* what one is feeling through one's tears.

If one wished to conduct therapy with a Maori family, as with any other business conducted, one would have to honor certain relationship procedures. Paradoxically, many of these would violate the universal conventions of our profession. The relationship would begin with certain formal rituals involving welcoming speeches by each family member, each one linked to a "song of relish" to embellish the spoken words. The therapist would be expected to reciprocate. All of this would take place in the family *marae* (meeting place) attended by the family's *eiwi* (tribe). Next, there would be an exchange of gifts, followed by the most important ritual of all—the *hongi*, in which life breath is shared by pressing noses together. This signifies that those about to begin this new relationship are friends, not enemies, a familiarity that is enhanced by sharing food together.

Once everyone was on an equal footing, trust had been established, and rituals observed, the therapeutic work could begin. Whatever started out as universal principles of the profession have now been so adapted to the particular setting that their original forms are all but unrecognizable.

Reconciling the Contradictory

It is truly amazing that the therapeutic relationship can work at all, given the number of contradictions that are part of its foundation, and that is not a cynical observation. After all, there are many aspects of life that work quite well in spite of, or maybe even because of, their paradoxical nature. For example, how is it that everyone accepts that all solid matter is actually made up of intangible energy, or that the seeming chaos of many events is actually highly structured and that this chaos may be the natural order of our universe (Gleick, 1987), or even more stunning, that the symmetry that underlies all life may be best expressed as polarity? In his work on the contradictory nature of reality, Murchie (1978) explains that, from the opposite poles of our planet, which keep things spinning in balanced rotation, to the nature of freedom, which cannot exist unless people are fighting against constraints, paradox is a part of daily life. It may well be that the contradictory polarities of therapeutic relationships, like other paradoxes, are not problematic but instead are part of the way that things work.

Certainly we are no strangers to paradox. We all learned long ago that our profession is riddled with mysterious contradictions— that by doing less we can do more; that clients say they want one thing but do quite another; that the client who comes in for treatment is not necessarily the member of the family with the problem; and, the ultimate paradox, that by ordering clients to do one thing we can produce spontaneous recovery when our order, as we had hoped, causes them to do the opposite.

The problem lies not in reconciling contradictory elements but in explaining how these elements work together to create a powerful and influential relationship. In order to arrive at this explanation, it is necessary to weave together each of the threads that will be presented throughout this book, beginning with the personal elements that both client and therapist get out of their encounters.

Chapter Two

Personal and Therapeutic Relationships

Molly is a tremendously efficient woman in her forties. She is a successful executive who also manages her home and four children as a single parent. Years previously, she had been married to an abusive husband, who was repeatedly hospitalized for a bipolar disorder. After twelve years of being battered around, thrown down stairs and out of windows, she evicted the man for the safety of her children. Another dozen years elapsed, and during this time, Molly had not been able to relate well to men except in her professional capacity. In her own mind, her recurrent fears of violence became associated with sex, since the two became inexorably linked during her marriage. She feared getting close to any man because of her vow never to be vulnerable again to the threat of abuse.

Enter a male therapist. Molly contracted for a brief treatment of six weeks since she was unwilling to risk becoming dependent on him. He readily agreed, and they began intensive work, looking at the patterns of her life in the past and where she wished to be in the future. Within this relatively brief period of time, a mere six hours of contact, they ended the therapy as agreed. Molly felt she had a better understanding of the issues involved. She felt more willing to risk getting closer to men and had already initiated a few "friendships." She reported feeling more in control of her life.

Although we will probably never really know what made the greatest difference to Molly in helping her to change a life-long self-defeating pattern, both she and her therapist formulated their own hypotheses. He felt quite strongly that, although his confrontations and cognitive challenges seemed quite helpful in pushing her along,

27

there appeared to be something about their relationship that promoted healing. It was as if Molly's being able to let herself get close to this man, her therapist, without suffering betrayal, made it possible for her to have similar experiences that could be just as satisfying with other men.

Six weeks after her treatment ended, she wrote this letter to her therapist.

> I thought you might be interested in knowing how a little time has affected some of the thoughts which I shared with you in our sessions together. I think that so much of what I discussed with you had been worked through so much in my own mind that I really needed only to be open to complete the work.
>
> I find it hard to articulate the changes that have taken place, especially around my own sexual thoughts and feelings. I know that I no longer associate sex and violence, that for the first time I can visualize sex as a gentle possibility. This is so new for me that I am just beginning to feel comfortable with the idea.
>
> I think most of what you did for me is give me permission to talk about things that I had never before said out loud. I think that I am typical of a nation full of single mothers who have carried so much and been such a source of strength—out of necessity, not choice. Everyone I know who turns to me, who leans on me, sets up expectations that I can do it all and carry it all. So I don't admit, even to myself, my own needs and my incredible loneliness. I gained so much just by having you listen to me, without judging me or wanting anything back.

The Mysterious Process of Change

This case is hardly an unusual occurrence. Almost every month, if not every week, therapists see direct and irrefutable evidence of change that takes place in their offices—healing that occurred as a direct result of the relationships they have been able to create with their clients. Yet to the outside observer, much of what takes place between the therapist and client may seem to be very much like any social conversation—two or more people engaged with one another, often in an intense and emotional context, but quite often discussing matters in a relatively calm manner.

As professionals, we view these encounters as part of a complex interactional process called therapy. We believe that the relationship between Molly and her therapist was qualitatively and substantially different than any other encounter she had yet experienced, so much so that it provided leverage to initiate changes that previously had seemed out of reach for her. Yet in spite of our belief, we still face the same perplexing questions that have followed our profession since its inception: What is the mechanism of change? How is it that the encounter between client and therapist is helpful? and, What are the dimensions of these therapeutic encounters that contribute to successful work with clients?

We begin the journey of understanding and reconciling the paradoxes of therapeutic relationships by asking you to consider both the personal *and* therapeutic aspects of that which is healing in relationships. Josselson (1992) argues that studying healing relationships only within the confines of therapy blinds us in a number of ways. Since this peculiar type of relationship is unequal in power, nonmutual in input, and largely focused on abnormal experiences, it is hardly representative of a person's complete life. It is a relationship skewed heavily in the direction of negativity, dependence, inequity, and artificial boundaries, often bearing little resemblance to more authentic encounters outside these secret chambers. Until we examine healing interactions within a larger context of human relatedness, we will never understand what is both unique and universal about this phenomenon.

One confounding fact about therapeutic relationships is that, in many ways, they look and act similarly to other close personal relationships. But, unfortunately, therapists often fail to look at this most basic level of the relationship: the personal value inherent in human contact, from which *both* therapist and client benefit.

Evolution of the Therapeutic Relationship

Much of the way we and other therapists think about our relationships with clients has its roots in the history of our profession. Therapeutic relationships were designed first by leaders of the early Roman Catholic Church and later by physicians, philosophers, teachers, and the first therapists to help the afflicted through a variety of structures that were sometimes benevolent and other times quite Machiavellian. Modern-day psychotherapy has continued the search begun by our ancestors. One approach has been to determine the differences in effectiveness between various therapeutic methods. Distinct schools of thought number in the hundreds, if not thousands. Each of them posits a different mechanism to explain change; each offers a different process for conducting the helping procedure. The curious fact remains that, despite varied content and divergent opinions about what procedures and practices are most important, in the end, each of these methods seems to be about equally helpful (Orlinsky, Grawe, & Parks, 1994). Thus, theoretical orientation does not seem to provide useful information about which aspects of the helping process account for the changes that clients make.

A more pragmatic approach to struggling with these questions of effectiveness begins with the assumption that it is possible to identify certain kinds of treatments for particular clients, with certain problems, in specific circumstances (Paul, 1967). While certainly an ambitious undertaking, the results of these investigations have been disappointing (Bergin & Lambert, 1978). However compelling the medical model might be, suggesting the possibility of tailoring interventions according to specific disorders and diseases, just as an internist or neurologist does, there has not been much empirical support thus far for replicating therapeutic prescriptions (see Goldstein & Stein, 1976; Sexton & Whiston, 1991; Shapiro & Shapiro, 1982; Smith, Glass, & Miller, 1980).

Quite another approach recommends that we should be iden-

tifying "non-specific factors" that are active in all methods of treatment (Garfield & Bergin, 1986), rather than seeking particular
prescriptions for specific client complaints, à la the physician.
Unfortunately, because of the complexity of the therapeutic
process, as well as the infinite number of factors involved, it has
been difficult to identify those elements that are most powerful and
common to virtually all approaches. A number of "universal" ingredients, to which most practitioners, theoreticians, and researchers
would agree, have been identified, including elements such as role
induction, catharsis, altered states of consciousness, opportunities
for rehearsal, structured risk taking, and most of all, the trusting
relationship that develops between client and therapist (Kottler,
1991). Unfortunately, without a model that ties these elements
together, implementation is extremely difficult.

Therapeutic Relationship as the Unifying Thread

John is a thirty-seven-year-old professional. He complains of an
inability to sleep, difficulty concentrating, and a melancholic mood.
Within the therapeutic community, John might receive a stagger-
ing diversity of treatments for these symptoms. A behavioral therapist might have John monitor his moods, activities, diet, and
sleeping patterns and later manage the contingencies in his life in
order to help increase target behaviors. A humanistic therapist
might provide a safe environment for John to discuss his most personal feelings, letting him sort out his concerns in the safety of a
trusting relationship. A family therapist might ask John to bring
his wife to counseling and focus on his relationship with her, within
the context of his family of origin. There is considerable evidence
that each of these treatment methods might be equally successful
with symptoms such as those expressed by John. However, each
method appears to take a quite different path, focusing on varied
dimensions of human experience.

Nevertheless, within the diverse field of therapy, there is

remarkable agreement that the one thread that seems to weave through the fabric of almost every helping approach is the relationship that develops between client and therapist. Look closely enough at most any helping strategy, from the chants of a Bolivian *curandero* or the incantations of a strategic therapist to the ministrations of an intensive care nurse, and the human relationship emerges as a central component. Within our profession alone, some approaches consider the relationship between therapist and client as central, the core of all work that is completed, while others treat the relationship as an ancillary bridge between elements that are perceived to be more important. But all approaches do consider the relationship.

For many years, humanistic, psychoanalytic, behavioral, and other single-theory practitioners proposed that their respective visions of the relationship were superior to the others. Psychoanalysts designed relationships that capitalized on transference and projective elements. Rogers (1957) argued that the facilitative conditions of empathy, warmth, and genuineness were the key. Strong (1968) argued that relationships that were credible and trustworthy were likely to be most influential. Behaviorists quite passionately stated that the best sort of relationship is one that is designed to ensure compliance to therapeutic tasks, a position later adopted by strategic practitioners.

Although most practitioners would hardly dispute that their relationships with clients are indeed important—whether as a central ingredient of their work or as a means to another end— these affiliations are often designed in remarkably different ways, as loose, friendly, informal engagements or as quite structured arrangements with clearly defined tasks and roles. This is, of course, what makes understanding this complex phenomenon so challenging.

One fact that seems clear is that the therapeutic relationship is much more than a dialogue between two people wherein one person agrees to be influenced by the other. It is an interaction in the truest sense of what that means—an inter-action, or exchange, of influence that travels in many ways, weaving, spinning, branching out in all directions, touching many others along its path.

When Amateurs Do Good Work

The picture of what is therapeutic in relationships is also complicated by the fact that healing, or influence between individuals, is hardly restricted to professional contexts alone. Whatever curative elements operate in healing encounters also operate as part of other human relationships, such as those between friends or lovers, or those within the contexts of teaching, hairdressing, taxi driving, or bartending.

We have all had experiences in which our interactions with other people had a profound influence on our lives. A waitress makes an offhand remark that echoes inside the patron's head for weeks afterwards. A neighbor offers some advice on a matter, information that proves critical in making an important decision. We are impacted by friends, by the media, by an assortment of different kinds of professionals. There is even some evidence that relationships with animals can precipitate breakthroughs in otherwise hopeless cases (Beck & Katcher, 1983; Levinger, 1979; Peacock, 1986). In one particularly dramatic example, an eleven-year-old boy who had been hit by a car lay in a coma for weeks, showing no response to any medical intervention. When the boy's beloved dog was brought to his bedside and began licking his face, he immediately woke up.

What is it about these interactions that seems to work such magical wonders? How is it that a relationship, a series of interrelated behaviors between two people, can influence and affect each participant in ways that may make either a positive and or negative difference in his or her life? What is it that occurs in these interactions that has such a strong influence on an individual's present and future behavior, thoughts, or feelings? How can a phenomenon fraught with so many contradictions and paradoxes be capitalized on for some ultimate good?

Interdisciplinary and Multicultural Threads

Throughout, this book takes the position that healing relationships are not the sole province of modern therapy. The study of these relationships must, of necessity, be interdisciplinary, since no single field covers the depth, breadth, and complexity of what takes place during helping encounters. Certainly social, clinical, and counseling psychology have contributed significantly to the literature on the subject. However, anthropology and sociology have also investigated curative phenomena that take place between people in cultures other than our own. Similarly, the medical sciences, nursing, dentistry, osteopathy, homeopathy, and allied disciplines have also contributed much research and clinical experience to explaining the nature of healing relationships. Religious scholars, spiritual healers, counselors, marriage and family therapists, social workers, psychiatrists, psychologists, speech and occupational therapists, nurses, physicians, lawyers, and practitioners of all allegiances and persuasions have studied the effects and impact of the healing relationship on therapeutic outcomes. Curiously, much of the healing that occurs in the relationships people have with this range of helpers occurs without many of the characteristics that the Western therapeutic community has defined as necessary and sufficient.

Cultural contexts also play a crucial role in the ways people make sense of the healing nature of relationships. Culture influences what things are determined to be problems, the manner in which these problems are approached, and who practices the art of helping, whether that professional is a priest, doctor, midwife, pharmacist, sorcerer, or counselor. Among the indigenous peoples of any continent, healers are viewed much differently than the dominant culture views its healers. Even within the cultural jurisdictions represented by each state and province of North America, different professionals are sanctioned as the primary mental healers. In some regions, psychologists may be designated as the primary providers, whereas a few miles away, across an imaginary boundary, another legislature has deputized professional counselors or marital and family therapists as eligible professionals.

Take the case of a young man complaining of anxiety and stress who walks into place where he expects to receive help. The clinician's professional affiliation, as a physician, social worker, psychologist, family therapist, accountant, or even acupuncturist, will influence the choice of treatment program selected—medication; family, group, or individual therapy; or vengeful litigation against an imagined enemy. Each of these approaches has its prescribed "treatment" appropriate for symptoms of stress and anxiety.

A physician may be extremely helpful to this patient without exhibiting any of the behaviors that the psychological community would define as an appropriate chairside manner. After listening to his patient for less than two minutes, jotting notes in a chart and making eye contact once in the beginning and once at the end, the physician offers the patient a prescription for Xanax and sends him on his way. If this man was to consult his minister instead, he might be directed to read some scripture, to pray for deliverance, to attend church more regularly, and to have faith that God will provide relief. If this man sought the counsel of his neighborhood bartender, he would receive quite different treatment, perhaps an attentive ear as long as business was slow and a continuous flow of liquid sedatives. An interaction with a bartender might also produce significant relief in that, while tidying the counter and listening halfheartedly, the bartender seems unconcerned with what the man is saying, thereby normalizing the situational pressures the man may be experiencing. In each of these cases, a relationship has been created that may very well produce results similar to those of the other relationships.

Consider the important role played by either a physician or an attorney. There is little in the training of these professionals that prepares them for the healing relationships that accompany their care of patients and clients. The physician learns about conducting physical exams and performing surgical procedures. The lawyer learns to write contracts, to research precedents, to negotiate settlements, and to argue against opponents. Yet in many instances in which a person seeks the services of a lawyer or doctor, it is not only important to have her problems solved but to tell her story. In fact, in many cases in which a person sees a doctor, no diagnosable medical condition can be found; the person just needs to talk to somebody. Almost half the time family practice attorneys spend with their clients involves listening to their personal problems.

The importance of a relationship between patient/client and helper does not end with doctors and lawyers. The therapeutic relationship is an integral part of nursing practice, even though it is less well defined than the kind of encounter that takes place in psychotherapy. Relationships can be superficial ("How are you doing today?"), intimate (getting to know the patient's family and providing personal support in difficult times), confrontive ("You must follow the medical orders"), or mutual and reciprocal (sharing personal details of life). All of these permutations fall within the bounds not only of acceptable behavior but also of required professional conduct (Morse, 1991). Clients' desire for more than just "treatment" may also be the reason such professionals as midwives are making a comeback. Midwives, for example, pride themselves on creating a relationship with the mother as part of their birthing services.

Seyster (1987) writes about her experience as a student nurse taking care of a stroke-paralyzed seventy-five-year-old woman. Although her assignment involved mostly routine physical care of the patient, she noticed that the friendship she offered became just as crucial. The woman had been unresponsive and passively allowed the medical staff to poke, clean, and feed her, and change the sheets as she indifferently waited for her death. Yet the student nurse made a concerted effort to talk to her: "I took time to greet her as I would greet a personal friend, by looking into her eyes and asking her how she was, not perfunctorily but sincerely" (p. 57). Before long, the patient was drawn out of her shell, and began to improve. All the medical care in the world was useless to her without the healing relationship that accompanied it.

Personal Threads in Therapeutic Relationships

The wide ranging existence of healing relationships suggests that something therapeutic exists within the natural and basic fabric of human interaction. Since our goal is to grasp fully what it is about human relationships that is healing, it is important to investigate more closely what happens not only in professional alliances but also in the interpersonal connections between *any* two people.

It is certainly not unknown for someone experiencing distress to consult a family member, colleague, or friend for support and advice. Indeed, it is considerably more likely that the distressed person will take such action rather than seek the services of a professional. Quite often, these close personal relationships do supply sufficient elements of whatever is soothing and constructive, providing the person with much the same relief that he might find from work with a therapist. During times of grief, or stress, or hopelessness, it feels good to reach out to others who care about us. Quite often, whatever they offer in terms of advice or interventions is somewhat less useful than just the feeling of support we feel, the belief that we are not alone, that other people do care about us, that our lives will indeed continue on as before. It is for this very reason that people usually seek therapists' services only as a last resort, when everything else they have tried has failed.

The Value of Human Contact

Relationships are basic units of human life. Blessed neither with blazing speed nor formidable strength, our species has survived against creatures who can outrun or outfight us because we are clever, but also because we cooperate in our efforts to find and prepare food and shelter. Close, intimate relationships have evolved between people; not only do we often mate for life, but we also retain permanent affiliations with those who are not of our direct bloodline. Relationships have become the basis for our successful growth and development. They are the source of our greatest pleasures, but also the origin of our most heartfelt personal anguish.

It is not surprising that many consider that life and happiness are integrally related to the nature and quality of our relationship with others. For example, Klinger (1977) found that when asked what makes life meaningful, most people indicated that it was feeling loved and desired by friends, parents/siblings, or a partner. In one survey, Campbell, Converse, and Rodgers (1976) found that what is considered most important in life is a happy marriage, a stable family, and good friends. Mentioned as relatively less important were work, housing, money, and religion.

Indeed, the need for human contact is so great among members of our species that people will literally die from loneliness. In a review of the relevant findings, Bloom, Asher, and White (1978) concluded that there is an unequivocal association between marital disruption and physical and emotional disorders. Divorced white males under the age of sixty-five have twice the chance of strokes and lung cancer, ten times the rate of tuberculosis, seven times the rate of cirrhosis of the liver, and twice the rate of stomach cancer when compared to their married counterparts. They also are more prone to accidents, and have a significantly higher likelihood of suffering a heart attack (Lynch, 1977). People who lack companionship are also more prone to depression, anxiety, sleep disorders, headaches, life dissatisfaction, and a variety of physical complaints (Duck, 1983; Rook & Pietromonaco, 1987; Rubenstein & Shaver, 1982). This point is further illustrated by the reports from hostages and other captives that exile and solitary confinement are excruciating tortures.

The Hunger for Close Relationships

It is curious that although most North Americans interact with about two thousand acquaintances during a typical month, the average person has only four or five friends. Even among those who have double that number of close confidantes, the vast majority feel they are suffering some deprivation in not having more (Fischer, 1982). Over 70 percent of people consider their lack of enough friends to be among the most serious voids in their lives (Yankelovich, 1981). Pogrebin (1987) describes a number of reasons for this problem, most notably the mobility in U.S. society, in which stable relationships are challenged by geographical distance. In order for intimacy to flourish, friends must be in close physical proximity. Yet many long-standing relationships become strained, or at least neglected, when people relocate in the pursuit of a better job or life-style.

Another factor is the ethic of competition that has developed in recent years as people attempt to attain higher status at the expense of cooperation. People of Asian or South Pacific heritage are somewhat befuddled by the emphasis North Americans place on individuality at the expense of teamwork. For example, baseball and football, the consummate American sports, emphasize the performance of a few superstars on each team, whereas cricket and rugby, their counterparts in the Pacific Rim, downplay individual effort in favor of cooperative responsibility and performance. In Pacific Rim countries, a competitive atmosphere, whether in the arena of sports, business, or social situations, is not conducive to developing closeness and mutual trust.

The hunger for closeness to others is certainly not unique to North American or Western peoples. However, other societies seem to value the healing powers of friendships by structuring more opportunities for interaction. After working with the African Bangwa society, Brain (1976) reported that within that culture friendships are considered as important as marriages! Community elders assign children "best friends" early in life. These affiliations carry with them certain formal role requirements and an acknowledged public legitimacy with clearly understood rights and rituals.

In Western cultures, friendships are treated quite differently. Outside of marriage or becoming godparents, we have few ceremonies or rituals to honor or acknowledge close relationships like friendships. Suttles (1970) suggests that, in fact, friendships are the least programmed of all social relationships in our culture. The manner in which these types of interpersonal relationships are treated within our culture is curious given their central role as a dependable source of benefits and social rewards (Hayes, 1988). In his classic work on the role of therapy in society, Schofield (1964) implies that maybe if we assigned more importance to friendships people would not have to "purchase" them.

Biological/Evolutionary Perspectives

It is simplistic to conceptualize relationships only in terms of satisfying psychological needs, since humans are very much biologically driven creatures as well. In fact, there may be an innate biological or evolutionary need to affiliate with others in close personal relationships, such as friendships, love relationships, or in some cases, psychotherapeutic relationships.

Early work on biological needs focused on the attachment between infant and caregiver. Bowlby (1958, 1969, 1982) proposed that an intimate connection between child and parent was essential to survival and psychological development. Bailey (1988) confirmed this premise by suggesting that there is a biological predisposition for attachment behavior—individuals are born into the world prepared to form relationships in order to survive. Such instinctual behavior as the smiling reflex in infants is designed, for example, to "seduce" adults other than parents to feel committed to help care for this vulnerable being should the need arise.

In an alternative and quite compelling conception, Glantz and Pearce (1989) have constructed an evolutionary model for understanding how and why relationships (including therapeutic ones) produce beneficial results. Throughout most of human existence, until the last few thousand years, individuals lived as part of hunter-gatherer tribes. Everyone in these tight-knit social units was responsible for everyone else. Parenting responsibilities were shared by all adults for all children, regardless of biological connections. People spent their lives with friends and relatives, never venturing more than a hundred miles from home, and then always in the company of companions. Being successful as a citizen of a tribe was equated with success in relationships with others. We can still find evidence of this way of life when we observe the cultures of indigenous peoples. Many Native American tribes, for example, believe community responsibility takes precedence over any individual achievement. Healing occurs within the context of tribal intervention and the interconnected relationships among people who all care for one another.

A mere several hundred years ago many human tribes disbanded. Most people no longer live in the immediate vicinity of their extended families or ancestral homes. Given this migration across the globe and disconnection from our tribes, Glantz and Pearce reason that human biological development has not caught up with the social evolution that has changed the way we live. Although our bodies are tuned to function as part of a tribe, these communities no longer exist. Yet humans still crave close connections to others and intimate relationships that help them feel safe and supported.

If human relationships are the lifeblood of our species, then kinship is the primary organizing principle. *Kinship* may include not only biological relatedness but also relationship by nature and other qualities. In their discussion of psychological kinship, Bailey, Wood, and Nava (1992) contend that people who are experiencing stress feel a need to extend their concept of "family" to encompass others with whom they are interpersonally connected. According to this theory (Bailey, 1987, 1988; Bailey & Nava, 1989), clients are searching for a surrogate family member in their therapist, one who provides the kind of emotional support and intimacy that is typically associated with a loved one. The therapeutic relationship is thus seen as a kinship relationship in which a simulated family is temporarily created. This supposition explains why clients may strive for more closeness than their therapists do. While professionals attempt to maintain a degree of detachment and objectivity, clients follow their biologically driven urges to form kinship bonds of intimacy. The more stress they are experiencing, the more likely they will be to revert to emotionally dependent relationships (House, Landis, & Uberson, 1988; Jackson, 1990; MacLean, 1978).

Just as Glantz and Pearce speak of the biological imperative to find a tribe, Bailey talks about finding the smaller kinship unit as the great motive of life, especially for people who are troubled. Both these models stress how therapeutic relationships resemble other close personal affiliations but have added dimensions. Therapeutic relationships exhibit many of the characteristics often associated with other personal relationships, including freedom and permissiveness, yet paradoxically, they also supply a degree of structure that precipitates permanent changes in the way people feel, think, and act.

Listening to Clients

This book advocates a very simple premise: that the personal dimension of human relationships is one thread at the core of healing, a premise consistent with what clients have been saying for many decades even though few scholars have been listening. Clients have consistently attributed success in therapy to relationship factors, whereas their therapists have associated outcomes with their own techniques and skill (Sloane, Staples, Cristol, Yorkston, & Whipple, 1975). Even today, if you were systematically to interview all the clients in your caseload and ask them what it is about their therapy experience that seems most powerful, it is likely that you will hear some mention of the relationship.

Lazarus (1971) noted some time ago, in a follow-up study of clients' therapy experiences, that clients cited characteristics such as sensitivity, gentleness, and honesty as the significant factors related to improvement. Clients clearly felt that the personal qualities of the therapist were more important than technical expertise. Sloane, Staples, Cristol, Yorkston, and Whipple (1975) also found that clients emphasized the personal qualities of their therapists. In this latter study, regardless of whether they were treated by behavioral or psychoanalytic therapy, clients rated the same items as important in the progress they made: the personality of the therapist, the therapist's efforts to help promote understanding of the problems, opportunities provided to practice facing whatever is perceived as disturbing, and being able to speak with someone who appears to be caring and understanding. It is a bit disconcerting to acknowledge that therapists ask clients to tell them what is important and the clients do, yet often the relationship itself, which clients see as important, is seen by therapists mainly as icing on the cake.

Practitioners preferred models for understanding the active ingredients in therapy may have influenced the neglect in the study of the therapeutic relationship. In many ways, the search for specific psychotherapeutic treatment guidelines has been dictated by the history of the field. It is important to remember that psychotherapy began as a medical specialty. Nineteenth-century physicians were trained to believe that what mattered most was the treatment administered to the patient. Factors outside the "prescription" were important only under the heading of "bedside manner." However, mental disorders and interpersonal living problems cannot be diagnosed with the degree of accuracy and reliability that physical diseases have been diagnosed, and treated.

It is becoming increasingly clear that the key to understanding the essence of healing relationships, with all of their complex, paradoxical features, lies in taking a broad interdisciplinary and multicultural perspective, one that breaks the bounds of the traditional theoretical models of therapy. It is a perspective that considers the personal, cultural, conceptual, and clinical threads of therapy. It is the authors' view that all of us, as therapists, can no longer take a limited approach to understanding what we do and why it works. Our theoretical models and clinical practices are often based on simplistic and sometimes limited views of what the human relationship can and cannot do. Without a comprehensive model, we are left to flounder, doomed to search for the "magic" in techniques when in fact that power may very well be lodged in our interactions with clients and the characteristics of our personalities. That, after all, is what clients have been telling us all along.

Chapter Three

Relationships in the Life of the Therapist

In the first two chapters, therapeutic relationships were viewed primarily from the perspective of the client. Yet the therapist is also a partner in this interaction, often in a profoundly personal way. If we practitioners of psychotherapy are to understand the complex process that takes place in therapy, we must delve into our world as well as that of the client.

Perhaps more than any other professionals, we are afforded numerous opportunities to integrate what we do in our work with our personal lives. As relationship specialists, all our skills that are useful in making sense of human behavior—in decoding why people act the way they do, in responding to others sensitively, in maintaining connections to those who are often working hard to push us away—also make us uniquely qualified to apply what we know to our own life. Who is better suited to inviting intimacy? Who else knows better how to flourish in relationships?

Since relationships are our business, we put ourselves on the line with every therapeutic encounter. Just as clients may be dramatically affected by the therapeutic experience, so too do therapists sometimes leave sessions with their heads spinning and their hearts aching. We are also not the only ones affected; we take this stuff home. Directly and indirectly, the relationships we have with family members, friends, colleagues, and even with ourselves are irrevocably changed as a result of our contacts with clients. So too does each of these significant affiliations in our lives shape the ways we perceive and react to others, including our clients.

Personal and Professional Dimensions
of Practicing Therapy

There is little doubt that our experiences growing up as well as our daily encounters provide the basis for much of what we do as practitioners. Our training rarely began in graduate school; instead, some of us were recruited early into the profession by family members looking for a mediator, and we still rely as much on our early understandings of conflict as we do on our clinical skills.

We also enjoy tremendous personal satisfaction as a result of our professional encounters. After serving stints as a civil rights activist, Peace Corps volunteer, community action lawyer in Harlem, and head of an alcohol treatment facility, Luks (1991) concluded that therapeutic relationships clearly have reciprocal effects on both parties. Other attempts (Guy, 1987; Kottler, 1993) to document the ways in which therapists are significantly affected by their interactions with clients have brought out a number of both positive and negative experiences.

Luks researched the benefits of therapeutic relationships for helpers, surveying over 5,000 professional and volunteer helpers. A vast majority of the respondents (95 percent) reported that a number of spiritual and physical benefits accrued to them as a result of their helping endeavors, benefits most often summed up as a "helper's high." As a result of their participation in therapeutic relationships, helpers reported definite feelings of euphoria, increased energy, increased self-worth, and inner tranquillity. Citing a number of studies on the biochemistry of endorphin reactions to emotional bonds and the healing benefits of intimate relationships, Luks investigated the mechanisms by which helpers experience an increased sense of well-being from their work. It is his belief that altruism triggers the body's immune system to protect it against stress and illness.

The bad news is that our own relationships are often affected as a result of the intimate work we do, sometimes in unpredictable, less desirable ways. You see an elderly couple who remind you of your own grandparents or parents, and not in a way that you would prefer. Another couple complain that they do not spend enough quality time together. They absolutely demand that they each arrive home every evening by five o'clock so that they can be with one another. As you hear yourself tell them that they might be a bit unrealistic in their expectations, you freeze inside as you realize how infrequently you share a meal with your own family or friends because of an overloaded schedule. Many clients whom we see remind us, in some way, form, or shape, of our own experiences as human beings as well as our experiences as trained experts in therapeutic intervention. A young child complains of feeling helpless and triggers our remembrances of feeling much the same way. As we stand by and watch members of a family take verbal shots at one another, trying their best to do some damage, we are often reminded of times when we were caught in similar conflicts. When an elderly couple appear to despise one another so much that each literally wants to kill the other, it sparks a number of complex feelings in us that are not altogether pleasant.

The process of mutual influence that takes place in therapy works in several directions simultaneously. Just as we are constantly being reminded of our own unresolved issues as we join hundreds of other families as surrogate parents and siblings, we are constantly drawing upon our experience as children, parents, friends, spouses, and lovers to understand what others are living through. Our own families have taught us much about how systems can be both dysfunctional and healthy. The choices we have made about how we choose to work, the theoretical approaches with which we align ourselves, and the style in which we seek to promote changes are all strongly affected by our personal experiences as well as our professional training.

The implications of this premise, that the personal and professional dimensions of our lives are inextricably linked, spark the following conclusions.

Family of Origin and Experiences Growing Up Affect Our Relationships

If the ideas of Murray Bowen, Ivan Boszormenyi-Nagi, and James Framo have merit for our clients' families, then certainly they are applicable to our own. We each carry within us a collection of family legacies, of multigenerational transmission processes, of introjects that we not only impose on our spouses, but on the families that we work with. These influences have both positive and negative impacts. Most of us understand firsthand what it is like to feel "scapegoated," "triangulated," "enmeshed," "disengaged," "punctuated," "symmetrically escalated," and all the other behaviors that we look for in the family systems we work with. Our having experienced life as a child, sibling, parent, "distancer," or "distracter," and in other roles we have played, allows us to recognize more easily when our clients engage in similar behaviors. Those of us who were subjected to some form of physical, sexual, or verbal abuse, who suffered neglect or fused relationships, understand even better what it is like for the families we work with. Once we have come to terms with the experiences that often initially trained us as helpers, we are able to draw on them as easily as we would our most favored clinical interventions. Consider this case in point from Jeffrey Kottler:

> When an elderly couple ran through their repertoire of favorite forms of verbal and physical abuse, I tried everything that I knew how to do as a professional. After sixty years of practice, and more years experience in family therapy than I ever hoped to have, this couple successfully countered my most vigorous and creative attempts to break their cycle of abuse. Sculpturing, paradoxical directives, pretending, circular questioning—they had seen and tried it all before. Finally, it occurred to me that I knew as much about this pattern as they did, and that source of personal knowledge became the key for us to restructure the ways they related to one another and to me.

Such family of origin issues not only provide us with our greatest resources but are also the source of our largest blind spots. One therapist who lost her mother to cancer when she was a young child helps every family she sees to understand their difficulties in terms of maternal deprivation. Another therapist, herself an ongoing sufferer of sexual abuse, specializes in working with victims who have yet to express their rage toward their perpetrators, an act that she has not yet been able to complete. Still another therapist was so smothered and overprotected within his family as the youngest child of eight siblings that he helps the members of all the families he works with to disengage from one another to the point that autonomy is always emphasized over cooperation, regardless of the individuals' ethnic, cultural, or personal values. Finally, a therapist who did not receive sufficient physical contact during his childhood, insists that all his group therapy clients join together in a collective hug, whether they wish to or not.

Thus, our ability to help clients differentiate themselves from their families of origin is directly related to the extent to which we have separated from our own enmeshments (Bowen, 1978). The families from which we were spawned have shaped the choices we have made regarding our profession, our specialties, the ways in which we work, and our clinical decisions. For better and worse, our own families of origin join us during every session we conduct with others.

Current Relationships Influence Our Work

A number of investigative teams (Guy, Poelstra, & Stark 1988; Pope & Bouhoutsos, 1986; Thoreson, Miller, & Krauskopf, 1989) have conducted research on which therapists are most likely to engage in inappropriate sexual relationships with their clients. It is clear from such studies that professionals who are undergoing divorce or separation from their spouses are more likely than their peers to act out unprofessionally. Similarly, therapists impaired by addictions, debilitating depression, life crises, and other traumatic family problems are less able to attend to their work with the same degree of clarity and competence than they would have if their personal lives were in order.

When we have fights with our children, conflicts with our partners, or other major problems in our relationships, it is very difficult for us to insulate ourselves from these difficulties in such a way that they will not affect our responses to those who come to us for help. Remember a recent time that somebody was "on your case" in a major way, especially someone in a supervisory role. You felt distracted, perhaps even lost sleep and considerable peace over the situation. Your very sense of professional competence and personal worth felt in doubt. Now recall the sessions that you conducted during those times when you felt most disturbed and distracted. In what ways did your personal conflict affect your relationships with your clients? How did your relationship troubles affect what you did and how you did it?

One therapist answers these questions in a vein that may be similar to your own experiences:

> I like to think that I can insulate my personal life from what I do in my sessions. I know that, to some extent, this is impossible. I have noticed hundreds of ways that these two parts of my life sometimes blend together, no matter how careful I am. One time I was having some problems with another therapist in my office whom I was supposed to be reporting to. I resented the hell out of this arrangement because I felt that I knew far more than he did. I found myself, almost every day, spending more time thinking about him than I did my clients. I would play over and over in my head conversations we had just had or those that might take place in the future.
>
> Until this time, I thought of myself as a very good therapist. There was something about this relationship, though, that was starting to affect my confidence. I started doubting myself, second-guessing the decisions I was making. I began to hear his voice haunting

me when I would try to fall asleep at night. Sometimes his voice would even invade my session, admonishing me to do something that, ordinarily, I would never do. There is no doubt my relationships with my clients were affected by this very unsatisfactory relationship in my own life.

I have noticed the same pattern at other times when I have had a fight with my son, when I am angry with my husband, or when my parents come to stay with us for awhile. I "fish" for more compliments than usual from my clients. [When I had the poor relationship with the supervisor] it was as if I was looking for them to take my side, to reassure me that I was right and my supervisor was wrong. I also become more impatient with their progress, needing some quick result to prove my potency. There were even times it was like I wasn't even talking to my client at all, but to my supervisor, telling him things that I wished I could say to his face.

This disclosure illustrates the myriad ways that all the relationships in our lives, with our colleagues, friends, and family members, are affected by and, in turn, have an impact upon our relationships with clients. In spite of our best efforts to keep our professional and personal lives separate, they blend together constantly. Is it possible for professionals to be highly skilled and successful therapists when they are unable to apply what they know to their own lives? There are few things more bothersome to us than hearing "crazy shrink" stories about members of our profession who are purportedly teaching others to lead more fully functioning lives but cannot do what they ask their clients to do. As they preach the value of conducting family conferences, of facing conflicts rather than avoiding them, of showing compassion rather than exploiting others through power, there is ample evidence to indicate that they operate in quite a different manner in their own personal relationships. How many professors and supervisors have you had in your life, supposed models for you to emulate, who espoused the importance of empathy and kindness while you observed them being rude and insensitive to others? How many therapists have you known who cannot manage to sustain love relationships in their own lives? To what extent do you practice in your own relationships, with those you care the most about, what you advocate to your clients?

Conducting Therapeutic Relationships Affects Our Own Relationships

There is simply no way that we could spend intimate, intense, dramatic moments with people in excruciating pain and not be significantly affected by these experiences. It is virtually impossible for us to avoid being profoundly moved by some of the changes that we become part of. On each day we complete as therapists, we review a host of new things that we have learned about the people we work with, about how they function, and about ourselves. For better or for worse, we change in ways we could never have anticipated as a result of entering into the private worlds of our clients. In some ways, we become more battle scarred, more cynical and suspicious, more cut off from our feelings in an effort to protect ourselves, and our families, from human inhumanity. After all, we see people at their worst, when they are angry and wounded, when they are lashing out, when they feel helpless. Sometimes, these experiences get the best of us. We bring stuff home that is best left in the garbage, or at least at the office. All day long, and sometimes well into the night, we see people being cruel to one another. The effects are sometimes more contagious than we would like to admit. You spend the day watching several adolescents demonstrate remarkable inventiveness in their defiance toward their parents. Then you come home and your own child refuses to do the chores. You react way out of proportion to the incident. You listen to clients complain how their spouses are oblivious to the clients' discontent. When the clients file for divorce, their husbands or wives will be shocked that they had no idea how bad things had become.

You accuse your own spouse of feeling similarly dissatisfied with your relationship. "What brought that on?" he or she wisely remembers to ask. "You saw several couples today, huh?"

There are so many ways that our personal and professional lives merge together that it is difficult to determine where one ends and the other begins. Yet we are also able to enhance our relationships as a result of what we learn as therapists. Nobody else has greater access to what makes relationships work or fail than we do. No one knows as much as we do about how to recognize problems before they get out of hand and how to do something constructive to change the patterns of mediocrity. But the personal and professional dimensions of being a therapist remain inseparable, just as the sum total of all our relationships, in the past and present, joins us in every session we conduct. Until we are able to capitalize more fully on our personal experiences to enhance our professional effectiveness, we will continue to feel crippled by what we have lived through. Until we can better insulate ourselves from the pressure and strain we encounter every day as we live with people in crisis, our own loved ones will suffer as a result.

Specific Areas of Professional and Personal Vulnerability

There are many specific areas in which we may find the relationships from our professional lives influencing or being influenced by other relationships. A look at the most common areas in which we are vulnerable also shows how important relationships are in all parts of our lives.

Never Off Duty

Guy's investigations of the personal life and relationships of therapists (Guy & Liaboe, 1986; Guy, 1987; Guy, Poelstra, & Stark, 1988) highlight how the work that we do has a significant impact on our daily worlds. Not only do the majority of us operate thera-peutically when in social situations (72 percent according to a study by Farber, 1983), but for many of us it is difficult to separate our relationships with clients from those with our friends and family. We are accused of "shrinking" people when we are off duty, and although we may vehemently deny it, we cannot help but apply what we know and understand to all the situations in our lives. We pay attention to underlying motives. We attempt to make sense of why people act the way they do. And yes, on occasion, we do automatically begin to offer an interpretation, clarification, or reflection of feeling. Guy suggests that these tendencies put a damper on the spontaneity of our relationships; we may also be per-ceived suspiciously by others because of fears that we may be exer-cising subliminal control owing to our training and experience. Those who suspect us are not far off base—we *are* better than most at controlling emotions and getting others to do our bidding.

The isolation that we work in also affects our relationships with others. Unlike our friends, we are inaccessible throughout the day, locked in session where we can not be interrupted. We keep secrets for a living. And it is hard for others to understand the pressure and stress that we live with. Jeffrey Kottler's experience exemplifies this.

> One of the reasons I left private practice for the public sector is that I got tired of trying to separate whether I was a professional or run-ning a business. Of course, I had gone into private practice in the first place because I was frustrated dealing with the bureaucratic and political restraints on doing good therapy, so I suppose there are comparable pressures in any setting.
>
> I would come home exhausted each night at 9:30, working late because that is when clients preferred to schedule. I never devel-oped the restraint to set limits that are so crucial to a healthy pro-fessional life-style. I never lost my fear that if I turned away a single case, if I didn't accommodate every client who came my way, I might live to regret it during leaner times. As I would try to unwind,

my brain would play back the faces I had seen and the voices I had heard that day. My wife would ask me how things were going. I didn't know where to start, so I muttered, "fine," meaning, "don't ask." I tried to concentrate on the cases I felt most excited about, the clients I cared the most for, to offset the tough ones that challenged and frustrated me. I had a good support system around me— loving colleagues I could go to for hugs, an excellent supervisor who confronted and nurtured me, but it was never enough.

I worried too much. I worried about whether a few of my clients would ever return. Then I worried that a few others might return whom I wished would not. I worried about some holes in my schedule that I needed to fill if I was going to pay my bills; then I worried that I was working too hard and was in danger of burning out. I worried about a client who seemed to be at risk of hurting himself. I worried about another who was developing a dependency on me that was starting to feel stifling. I worried about the overdue accounts of some clients who had promised to pay but had, as yet, not done so. I worried that I had some problems with money issues. I worried about whether I was doing enough for my clients . . . or maybe I was doing too much. I worried that I would always be this worried and that even therapy wouldn't help.

The stresses and strains associated with therapeutic relationships are among the greatest sources of career dissatisfaction among practitioners. These stresses are especially strong when we try to evaluate our effectiveness even though confronted with ambiguous, uncertain outcomes. We feel responsible for the results of our work in the face of clients who are emotionally troubled and sometimes uncooperative with our efforts (Farber & Heifetz, 1981).

Emotional Depletion

Whereas being an expert in human relationships certainly equips us with skills that are helpful in our personal lives, we also pay a price for this privilege. Oftentimes, we are so depleted at the end of the day we have nothing left over to give to family and friends. We feel a decreased desire to listen and respond empathetically to the people we love the most (see Burton, 1975; Cray & Cray, 1977; Farber, 1983; Kottler, 1993; Maeder, 1989; Tryon, 1983 for a discussion of other dangers).

It is not uncommon for therapists to feel overwhelmed with the intensity of human experience that they encounter during any working day. A therapist working in a community agency might begin the day by seeing a mother and her four-year-old child. Both are malnourished and lethargic, without hope. The therapist offers what feeble support he can and then tries once again to help the mother negotiate through the system so that she can become eligible for financial assistance. He next moves into a group for battered women. Each of the clients tells a story of physical, emotional, and/or sexual abuse that began when she was a child and continues until this moment. Most of these women currently lack the resources and strength to break loose from the chains of codependent relationships, so they use the group to release their pent-up feelings of frustration and rage. It would be exhausting for any therapist to manage such a group, but, because he has a string of other appointments scheduled after lunch, there is no time to examine his feelings. Right after lunch, he sees a person, or actually several people simultaneously in the form of a multiple personality disorder. Because he knows how stressful this case is, he has scheduled a supervision conference immediately afterwards. This gives him some relief but at the expense of uncovering raw nerves. He sees a couple of children in the afternoon, an eight-year-old who wets his bed and an adolescent who is hostile and belligerent, and then he rounds off the day with a combative couple who, if he does not watch carefully, will start throwing things at one another during their fights. The therapist arrives home physically exhausted and emotionally depleted. His spouse meets him with an expectant smile, looking forward to telling him about her day. His response? "I don't feel like talking or listening right now; I have been doing that all day."

Narcissism

Therapists have been known to entertain illusions of grandeur and self-importance, even pomposity and arrogance. They sometimes believe that what they have to say is more important than what anyone else has to offer. Needless to say, such an attitude radically affects a therapist's personal relationships. Two therapists, married to one another, struggle more than most over control issues. Each is used to being in charge of relationships at work, accustomed to getting his or her way. Yet when they are together, compromise is difficult because of their respective experiences as relationship managers.

Whether our field attracts narcissistically oriented individuals or trains us to be that way, is open to debate. The fact remains that few professions offer an individual so much personal power to influence others. The danger lies in taking ourselves so seriously that we start to believe in our own omnipotence.

Overcontrolling

It is our job as therapists to control relationships, to manage their directions. Much of our work involves establishing and enforcing boundaries, structuring time with others, and moving discussions along in a timely and efficient manner, and in spite of the appearance of much freedom in therapeutic relationships, we actually exert quite a bit of control over what takes place. We offer no apologies for this; that is what we are paid to do. The problem may emerge when we leave our offices and then try to adapt to a different set of norms where we are no longer the ones in control. During one conversation with a friend, a well-meaning therapist was heard to say, "Actually, I think it would be best if we moved on to something else." Rather than getting the compliance she was used to receiving from her clients, she heard her friend respond angrily, "So who the hell are you to tell me what I am ready to do?"

Interpretive Stance

It is part of the therapist's role to remain detached and objective to a degree—at the least reasonably neutral and, in extreme cases, even wooden, apart from others. Such an interpretive stance allows us to focus more clearly on what is taking place, to extricate ourselves from the clients' attempts to distract or mislead us and themselves. Yet sometimes this "shrink" mask does not come off easily. We do not check it at the office door as we leave. Especially during times of perceived threat, or when we wish to enjoy an interpersonal edge, we easily lapse into an interpretive role that can be infuriating for those close to us, so that when we say, "How interesting that you would bring that up," friends and relatives complain, "Will you please stop acting like a therapist and remember you are a person? I hate it when you do that!"

Overanalyzing

Therapists are good thinkers and talkers and can thus take unfair advantage of others. We are used to attending to metacommunications, deep as well as surface structures of messages, and underlying and disguised motives of actions. We are trained well to try to explain why certain behaviors occur, why people act the way they do ("The reason you are so angry with me is because you are really upset with yourself. It is a simple case of projected identification").

If solid relationships are built upon a degree of spontaneity and playfulness, there is no doubt that being overly analytical can get in the way. We become mistrustful of others, always searching for their hidden agendas. Seeing people as we do, when they are at their worst, when their defenses are down, when they are falling apart at the seams, we tend to carry around these images, much as a trauma surgeon has nightmares of discarded limbs.

Dogmatism

Therapists are often portrayed as smart alecks. We think we know what is right. Yet, since we are prohibited from telling clients directly what we think they should do with their lives, we may indulge in this luxury with family and friends ("I wouldn't do that if I were you"). Moreover, put a group of therapists in a room together, and there will be considerable debate about the best way to do the therapeutic job. Undoubtedly the same could be said for physicians, attorneys, or most any other profession, but we are even less in agreement than most others about the best way to proceed with clients. In spite of the relatively low reliability of our methods and the lack of consensus as to what to do with particular cases, there sure are a lot of opinionated professionals who believe they know what is best.

Assume, for example, that a new client walks into your office complaining of mild depression and a lack of direction in her life. You further learn that the symptoms started at about the time her husband graduated from business school and began a job that takes him away from home quite a bit. In addition, you see evidence of poor self-esteem and a mild thought disorder ("It's all my fault and I'll never get any better"), as well as issues of lingering dependency on her parents. It is likely that each person in the group of therapists would have a very strong opinion about the best way to treat this woman and that each of them would be convinced that he or she was right and the others misinformed. Some would treat the case systemically, although they would not at all be in agreement about who should be seen— the woman alone, the woman conjointly with the husband, the woman's parents as the family of origin, or all these people together. Some of the therapists might treat the case as an endogenous depression, others as reactive symptoms, and still others as not a case of depression at all. Some would prefer a cognitive orientation, some would work more behaviorally, and others would insist behavioral change is the legitimate focus of helping efforts. Some would stay in the present, others would concentrate on the past. And amidst all of these debates and discussions, each clinician would feel that his or her approach was better suited to the client than the approaches of the others. There is some carryover of this attitude to other relationships in our lives. Friends and family members feel that we may be overly rigid and opinionated in the ways we express ourselves. And no wonder— we are used to getting our way!

Loss of Identity

It may be difficult for us to shed our roles as helpers and find the person underneath. Many of us define ourselves as therapists. It is not just a job but an outlook on life. We cannot just turn off what we know, what we understand, what we have learned to do. People can pick us out of crowds. They can tell by our manner, the way we carry ourselves, and the ways we express ourselves that therapy is our profession. Whereas our therapeutic skills can enrich our relationships, they can also keep people from getting too close to us ("You ask how I feel about that but what you really want to know is whether I approve of what you are doing").

Unrealistic Expectations

We are used to a high level of intimacy and sharing in our therapeutic relationships. We can become impatient and frustrated when personal relationships are more superficial and less intense than the other relationships we are used to. During our therapeutic encounters, we are permitted to ask most any question, to be as nosy as we like, to probe wherever our curiosity leads us. We ask about fantasies, about secrets, about shame, about things that have never been disclosed before. Whenever conversation becomes too predictable or shallow, we immediately take things to a deeper level. Any resistance we encounter is met with a similar degree of force to counteract it. If the truth be told, this is one of the best parts of the job—in a matter of hours, we learn more about a person than most others have ever known before. In fact, some of the most intimate relationships we have ever had (as one-sided as they might be) are with our clients.

Time Is Money

Private practitioners may adopt a mentality in which time is measured in hourly rates ("Well, if I do meet you for lunch, I not only have to pay for the meal, but I will lose the income from two canceled sessions. I don't think I can afford it"). The cost of a two-week vacation, including not only the expenses but lost income, can be prohibitive. One therapist in private practice relates how this orientation to money rules his life: "I bill my time at roughly two dollars per minute. Wherever I am, I think in those terms. I sit in a boring conversation, and I think to myself this is costing me twenty bucks just to listen to this stuff. I go shopping and figure that anything I save by finding sales costs me more than my time is worth. I calculate how much it costs me to take a Saturday off to go skiing. Even as I sit in my sessions, my mind calculates automatically how much I have earned so far."

A therapeutic relationship is essentially purchased or contracted for. As friendly and responsive as we might feel, we are with the client because we are being paid to be there. Our contractual obligations also have implications for our personal relationships, as the therapist mentioned earlier explains: "In some ways, I feel like a prostitute. I don't mean that derogatorily, merely as a statement of what I do: people pay me to be with them just as others might contract with someone for sexual favors. Given this experience, I have different standards than I used to for the time I spend with others. I become impatient easily if I am not getting what I want. Ironically, the best relationship in my life right now is with my own therapist whom I pay to be with me. Something in me got lost along the way."

Pushed Buttons

Our own unresolved issues may be elicited by the things we hear in sessions, to the point that they block our ability to help clients ("I just can't stand having you depend on me right now. I feel smothered by some of my clients who want to consume me, just like I felt when I was a kid"). Then there are the emergencies that we must deal with, the late-night calls, the cries of panic or outrage, the attempts at self-destruction, all affecting our emotional health, our ability to sleep, and certainly the relationships with those whom we are closest to. In a survey of family therapists practicing in one state, Wetchler and Piercy (1986) found that almost half of the respondents felt that their work left little time and energy for their own marriages and families, and one-third experienced difficulty switching roles from therapist to "civilian," finding it troublesome to listen to the problems of their own family and friends as well. Yet fully 85 percent of the therapists surveyed believed that they were able to apply a greater level of empathy, appreciation, problem solving, and communication skills to their personal relationships than they would have been able to without their training. This is certainly consistent with an earlier study by Cogan (1977) in which well over half of the therapists surveyed reported a significant improvement in their friendships, in terms of openness, depth, and intensity, as a result of their therapeutic training.

It should be noted, however, that whether the effects of therapeutic practice have positive or negative influences on a clinician's relationships depends on a number of variables. Guy and Liaboe (1986), for example, note that those who practice individual therapy in private settings are more likely to experience negative effects, because of the isolation they frequently encounter. The recurrent cycle of intimacy, separation, individuation, and termination may often leave the therapist feeling abandoned and lonely. When this process is coupled with the kind of one-way intimacy that exists in therapeutic relationships in which the clients reveal themselves while the therapist is careful to exercise restraint, a similar cycle can emerge in the therapist's other relationships as well.

From Personal to Cultural Concerns

There are, thus, a host of personal issues and filters that therapists bring to their relationships with clients. This personal thread, however significant in accounting for the distinctly human process that takes place in therapy, is accompanied by another that also has quite an influence: the cultural context for both the client's and the therapist's behaviors. If the focus of the personal thread has been on some of the micro-level factors that are involved in the therapeutic relationship, the next thread operates on the macro level as the final chapter of this section delves into the nature of healing relationships as they operate in various parts of the world.

Chapter Four

Diversity and Multiculturalism

One of the major impediments to the task of unraveling the mysteries of therapeutic relationships has been the fairly narrow, parochial lines of investigation taken by scholars and practitioners. Although we may be fairly literate in the history of our own profession and the values of our own culture, we are mostly shielded from what healers have been doing in other cultures and in other helping professions, such as nursing, physical and occupational therapy, medicine, law, and folk healing. Western professionals' limited exposure to the diverse settings in which healers practice, throughout both history and the present-day world, has led to flawed models of therapeutic relationships. Educators of therapists in Southeast Asia complain, for example, that Western theories do not work very well for them, since these theories embrace values that are incompatible with cultural standards imbedded in Asian values. A similar phenomenon is operative on the North American continent, which has become a melting pot quite different from the one our foreparents imagined. Any day in the life of a contemporary therapist, whether he or she is based in a mental health center, school, hospital, agency, or private practice, resembles the experience disclosed by one practitioner in these words:

> I was simply never prepared for the incredible diversity I would have to deal with. When I learned to do this stuff, we were taught to pick a theory we liked (preferably one our professors and supervisors approved of) and aim for consistency in its application. Help the clients learn the language and concepts. Teach them to be the ways we need them to be in order to help them.

Nowadays, there are so many exceptions I can't figure out the rules. This Tongan client I see (hell, I didn't know where Tonga was until she showed me on a map) was sent into "the great white world" by her family to "make good." She doesn't answer to herself but to her whole village, which has its hopes riding on her efforts. I see a Mexican-American couple whom I also thought would be kind of similar to a Cuban family I work with. I was dreaming. Then I had to get educated about the intricacies of LDS [the Latter Day Saints] to work in this town, not to mention a hundred other distinct "cultures" I never thought of as cultures. With each one of these clients, I have different relationships that are based not only on who they are and what they want but where they came from.

The sense of weariness, if not panic, reflected in this therapist's perceptions is a consequence of training that is now obsolete because it does not fit the increasing diversity of the world. Further, most healers may have been exposed to the history of their own professions (social work, psychology, counseling, nursing, family therapy, or psychiatry) but know considerably less about what has been going on in other eras, in different parts of the world, among diverse healers. The fact is that therapeutic relationships have existed for thousands of years, and with remarkably universal properties. If we can come to grips with what has worked consistently through time with different groups of people in very diverse professional settings, then we will be well on our way to understanding the underlying dimensions of the powerful forces of these relationships.

Cultural Influences

Ethnocentrism is an anthropological term for the belief that one's own race, nation, or culture is superior to all others. There are indications that many therapists tend to see Western culture as the most sophisticated and exemplary model in the world. This is not an unusual attitude since most individuals view the world in terms of the culture in which they were raised, creating a filter by which they perceive and interpret information. But this attitude does mean that judgments about what is right or wrong, good or bad, helpful or destructive are made from an ethnocentric valuation.

The culture in which a therapist or healer operates strongly shapes the kind of professional relationships that will develop. In our society, which values formal communication, scientific verification, problem solving, and intellectual inquiry, psychotherapy has become the model for psychological helping. In regions of the world that give greater priority to supernatural and natural phenomena; unity between people and spirits, and mind and body; and analogical and symbolic thinking rather than rational discourse, the relationship between client and healer is going to have a somewhat different tenor (Neki, Joinet, Hogan, Hauli, & Kilonzo, 1985). As Legrand (1989) facetiously states, you cannot exorcise a Parisian intellectual nor can you psychoanalyze an African Pygmy.

In his study of healing practices among Nigerian tribal villages, Bourdillon (1982) reminds us that the beliefs of a particular culture are not a coherent and homogeneous body of knowledge but a collection of independent thought systems, which are usually consistent with the values of that culture but not necessarily consistent with one another. The same could certainly be said by an anthropologist from Efik-Ibibio, a rural community near the Nigerian capital, if he visited our culture and observed our healers at work. As an example, if this African anthropologist came to our culture to study our treatment of headaches, he might be utterly bewildered by the number of ways that a client suffering from headaches might be treated in our culture. Some of our healers would simply talk to the client and offer encouragement; others would explore what is going on in his family; still others would teach meditative exercises. In other settings, the anthropologist would note that the healing relationship seemed virtually nonexistent; the so-called healer would not speak much to the client at all but instead hook him up to machinery, cut open his head, fool around inside, and close him back up. Other healing relationships in our culture would look even more distinctly different, such as relationships with practitioners who would put the client into a trance, order him to complete nonsensical tasks, ask him to lie on a couch and talk about dreams, or even bring the client's whole family in and talk to them.

Yet all these methods of healing and the belief systems behind them are linked, are threads in a value system, consistent with our culture, that states that headaches are caused not by supernatural forces but by biological events that can be exacerbated by emotional stress; that the relationship between healer and client is primarily a means by which to collect relevant information, offer encouragement, and ensure compliance to a treatment plan; and that certain core conditions such as trust and confidentiality are important variables in the relationship.

Most of us work with clients from cultures that differ from our own, and this trend is likely to increase as North America continues to become so culturally diversified that in many regions English is the minority language that is spoken. It is therefore extremely important that we take into consideration the indigenous healing practices of any given client's culture, even if it is not our intent to imitate these procedures. For example, Jilek and Todd (1974) report a number of cases among the Salish Indians of British Columbia in which traditional medicine and conventional therapy proved ineffective in instances of school phobia, suicidal depression, drug abuse, anorexia, and psychosomatic complaints, yet shamanistic healing rites produced immediate relief. In the case of a twenty-one-year-old woman suffering from depression, emotional abuse from her alcoholic husband, suicidal ideation, and prolonged grief reactions to the crib deaths of her two infants, psychiatric hospitalization made no dent in her symptoms. She was subsequently referred to a medicine man of her own tribe. He diagnosed her problem as a "lost soul," resulting from the death of her children. He promised he could find her soul and replace it. *She believed him*. He then conducted a ceremony consisting of singing healing songs and drinking "purified" water. He gave her a pep talk and said he would check up on her. One day later, her symptoms were gone. She appeared relaxed, happy, and smiling. The interesting question in this example, of course, is, what really happened? Was it the woman's belief in the healer that promoted this miraculous cure? Perhaps the incantations and purified water reclaimed her soul as they both believed. Maybe it was a spontaneous remission, or even a delayed reaction to the medications she was given in the hospital. Whatever the cause, this case nevertheless illustrates a principle of therapeutic relationships that is central to any positive effects they can produce: the importance of cultural relativism cannot be overstated.

Cultural Relativism in Emotional Problems

The Safwa are a people of Tanzania who believe that both emotional problems and physical illnesses are a form of punishment by the spirits for deviant behavior, which usually is conceptualized as family disputes or social disregard. This conception asks members of the tribe to try to avoid conflict with one another at all costs, since the consequence is illness or possibly death. Thus, relationships between family, friends, and neighbors are viewed not only as healing but also as potentially toxic, while the emotional and physical health of individuals is measured in terms of the quality of their transactions with others (Harwood, 1970). The sorcerer of the tribe, not unlike a family therapist, sees his main role as settling interpersonal disputes. Although his methods are somewhat different from ours, favoring ceremonial dances and animal sacrifices over hierarchical realignments of family structure, the results are often the same in terms of smoothing interpersonal cooperation. He also holds a magic trump card to enforce compliance to his treatment regimens: the threat that, unless the client cooperates, further degeneration is likely. The Safwa healing relationship thus contains a strong element of fear. In other cultures, such as those of the aboriginal tribes of Australia, the propensity to develop emotional disorders or mental illnesses is also not ascribed to empirically verifiable causes but to supernatural forces beyond human comprehension. The stuff of dreams and the spirit world, subjects that nobody really understands very well, can only be the result of divine intervention.

In all cultures, therapeutic relationships are constructed according to the practitioner's theories of what causes illness (Murdock, Wilson, & Frederick, 1978). In the theory of "natural causation," for example, perhaps the etiological theory most familiar to us, it is believed that physiological events inside the body create illness. These events include everything from infection and aging to stress, trauma, and human conflict. A healing relationship based on natural causation is one in which a working alliance is established in order to harness the natural recuperative forces of the body, solve interpersonal problems through dialogues, and offer advice regarding healthy options.

In the other three models of causation described by Murdock and his coauthors—"mystical," "animalistic," and "magical"—it is believed that fate, a supernatural agent, or malicious energy, respectively, are responsible for emotional suffering. Thus, faith healers and sorcerers construct relationships with their clientele designed to capitalize on forces of the spirit world. In folk or faith healing, the *curandero* or church elder seeks to create a relationship with the afflicted in which the healer is an intermediary with the spirits, whether defined as God, fate, or ghosts.

Even in our culture, there are times when, although we might believe that a therapeutic relationship is taking place between just ourselves and the client, the client secretly harbors the belief that there is quite another force involved. That is, by cooperating with us in therapy and doing what we ask of them, some clients believe that the gods will be appeased, retribution will have been served as a result of this torturous trial they must undergo, or fate or bad luck will loosen its grip on their lives as a result of this "gunslinger" they have hired for extra protection. However, rarely will these beliefs be shared aloud; often clients will not even articulate them to the therapist. One depressed person who did explain such feelings, saw them this way:

> I know that there was nothing I could do to avoid that child riding out in front of my car. I didn't mean to hit her. I have replayed that scene a thousand times trying to think of some way the accident could have been averted, but there was nothing I could do. She came out of nowhere. I also know that my depression and guilt are a result of my own self-punishment. You have explained all that. I am an educated person and I know this sounds ludicrous, but I can't help but think that I am being punished because I have angered the gods or fate or Karma. I sort of thought that by coming in to see you, maybe these forces would understand that I am trying so hard; maybe you could help me make amends with whatever I have done.

The implication of this client belief is that therapeutic relationships rarely take place only between the participants in the therapist's office. Whereas we have known for some time that systemic forces of the family play a crucial role in what happens in therapy, we now also have to consider the other relationships the client brings into the session—those with God, fate, or the realm of the spiritual.

Cultural Assumptions About Therapeutic Relationships

Culture influences the practice of all activities, and therefore, cultural values dictate people's view of what constitutes a therapeutic relationship. In our culture, there are some general expectations concerning the type of relationship a professional will develop with a client. Being ethnocentric, we tend to view these expectations as the correct and only manner in which a therapeutic relationship can be established. However, if we contrast the assumptions about therapeutic relationships in Native American, Eastern, and African cultures to our own assumptions, a number of differences emerge, summarized in the following list. These differences illustrate the crucial role that culture plays in people's perceptions of therapy.

Western Relationships	Non-Western Relationships
Impose role on client	Accept role expected by client
Possess a clearly defined structure	Possess flexible boundaries
Search for etiology and scientific causes of disorder	Acknowledge supernatural forces at work
Use interpretation and explanation	Use explicit rituals
Communicate verbally	Communicate with body contact, songs, chants, dances
Avoid dependency at all costs	Do not consider dependency an issue
Set relationship in therapist's domain	Set relationship in client's home; sometimes in healer's home
Harness principles of logic, problem solving, catharsis	Harness forces of nature
Emphasize cognitive and affective functioning	Emphasize spiritual aspects of life
Plan treatment by deduction	Plan treatment by divination

As an example, Eastern approaches to psychotherapy are decidedly different from Western ones in their emphases, eschewing intrusive methods in favor of those that are more introspective.

Bankart, Koshikawa, and Haruki (1992) describe several other distinctions between Eastern and Western approaches to psychological healing, and hence, different purposes for therapeutic relationships.

No artificial dichotomies are made between mind and body. Eastern healers treat the whole breadth of human experience—mind, body, soul, consciousness, Karma, spirit, social behavior—as inexorably linked.

Contemplation is emphasized over analysis. Applying the philosophies of Confucianism, Shintoism, Taoism, or Buddhism, the Eastern healer helps clients to reflect on their total experience rather than to dissect, analyze, or compartmentalize some aspect of it, whether that aspect is affect, cognition, or behavior.

Self-control is valued over autonomy as the primary goal. Health and optimal functioning are defined in terms of a person's ability to exercise control over physical and mental states.

The Eastern therapeutic relationship thus serves the purpose of helping clients achieve unity with their different selves (a gestalt idea), with their families and culture (a systemic idea), and with cosmic consciousness (a Jungian idea). The "talking cure," which so dominates Western forms of healing, plays a relatively small part in Eastern therapeutic approaches as the therapist functions more in the role of a teacher than a listener, instructing disciples to master techniques of meditation, yoga, fasting, martial arts, and communal living and to use other strategies designed to foster self-discipline.

Morita therapy is one example of an Eastern approach that demonstrates how differences in cultural values are embodied in the process of psychotherapy (LeVine, 1993; Reynolds, 1976). Since the Eastern view conceptualizes that people who are depressed, anxious, obsessive, narcissistic, or otherwise emotionally disturbed are already overly focused on their inner states of minds, it is thought to do little good to encourage even more of this self-absorbed behavior. Therefore, whereas the Western therapist would use the therapeutic relationship to encourage clients to talk about themselves, to share what is bothering them, to monitor carefully their inner experiences and disclose them fully, the Eastern therapist might do the exact opposite—the goal, after all, being to help clients stop being so self-obsessed and to get outside themselves. Thus, the Eastern client might be completely isolated in a room with an adjoining garden, where he is visited daily by the therapist for a brief fifteen-minute session. During this time, he is absolutely forbidden to talk about himself and, instead, must speak only about the garden that has been assigned to him to tend. The therapist becomes a conduit between the client's self-encapsulated ruminations and the larger world of nature. In their investigations of permutations of healing relationships in Africa, Neki, Joinet, Hogan, Hauli, and Kilonzo (1985) conclude that empathic understanding and cultural sensitivity are the most important ingredients of these relationships. Client populations in Tanzania, for example, are helped to understand the unity of life, the continuity of dreams and reality, and the connections between the world of spirits and the world of people.

Look more closely at the ways the cultures of many Native American tribes produce values that influence healing relationships and compare these values to your own and you will see a number of polarities. Whereas Anglo Americans value sexual equality, individual achievement, competition, youth, science, and the future, Native Americans prize the opposite: specific sex roles, group accomplishments, humility, respect for elders, mysticism, and traditions of the past (Richardson, 1981). Even cultural concepts of time may influence how relationships are constructed: Native Americans respond better to longer sessions rather than more frequent meetings (Baruth & Manning, 1991). These Native American values have a number of other implications for therapeutic relationships. Among Native American medicine men, the healing relationship is seen as but one of many facets of the medicine wheel, which has the form of a circle—the universal symbol of health and perfection. Black Elk, a great Oglala Sioux healer of the nineteenth century, explained that everything of consequence forms a circle: the earth, sun, and moon; the seasons; even the cycle of people's lives—however much these things change, they return full circle back to where they were (Neihardt, 1961). Black Elk explained that once his people were relocated from the circles that dominated their lives—from tepees to government lodgings in square reservations—they lost their power. The healing relationship, too, according to Native American healers, forms a circle, not a square. It helps a person to become realigned with the forces of nature, to be part of the earth, not separate from it.

The ways therapists may work with clients, whether in the inner cities of North America, the rural plains of Africa, or the congested communities of India, reveal differences that need to be taken into account. Whereas the next chapter will examine conceptual features that are common to effective therapeutic relationships, it is vital to emphasize, at this juncture, the importance of our being culturally literate about differences that might affect relationships that we develop. One of the themes this book will visit again and again is that different kinds of relationships are necessary for different kinds of clients, depending on their values, interests, and cultural backgrounds. To some readers, this may sound like the old rhetoric about being politically correct, but the following example of the influence of culture on individuals' views of dependence and independence illustrates how difficult it sometimes is for therapists to avoid being ethnocentric.

Encouraging Independence: Laudable or Ethnocentric?

Palmandra and Emma came to marital therapy on the advice of Palmandra's mother, who was concerned about their relationship. The couple's marriage had been arranged. After completing medical school in the United States, Palmandra had sent to India for his mother and her choice for his wife, whom he never met until she arrived with his mother. (The therapist was aghast at this "courtship.") The mother also called to make the original appointment, a situation the therapist neither understood nor tolerated. He asked to speak to the couple and thereby alienated the mother before the treatment ever began. When Palmandra and Emma showed up for their first appointment, they presented themselves as timid and deferential; Palmandra did all the talking for both of them (the therapist was concerned about this "codependency" and so sought to dilute it by asking questions directly of Emma, thereby humiliating Palmandra, who had to listen passively).

Among all the strategic mistakes the therapist made, his most fatal error was failing to take cultural differences into account in the way he structured the therapeutic relationship. He fully expected that, like most enmeshed couples, Palmandra and Emma would follow his encouragement to differentiate, to not speak for one another, nor to wait for the therapist to do all the work. Yet in this case, the couple virtually threw themselves into his lap, implying, "Tell us what to do, and we will do it." Palmandra even carried a clipboard to take notes on what the therapist wished them to do. Palmandra was a physician, after all, so he had great respect for specialists who could prescribe treatments. Because the therapist was ignorant of the relative meaning dependence had for this couple, he was unable to connect with them satisfactorily. They did not return after that first encounter, and when the therapist called to find out why, he was politely informed by the mother that they had gone to see an *Indian* doctor.

In the case of Palmandra and Emma, the relationship quickly deteriorated because of the therapist's failure to adapt his approach to fit his clients' cultural norms, especially with respect to their view of dependency. From our Western cultural perspective, the matter is quite simple: dependency in relationship, *any* relationship but especially a therapeutic one, is a very bad thing; it demoralizes individuals, diminishing their belief in their own power to find answers.

We value above all else qualities of autonomy, independence, and self-sufficiency. It is even stated as part of our ethical codes that we must avoid creating or perpetuating dependency in clients, since that long-term dependency meets only the professional's needs, creating a form of annuity or guaranteed income. How many times have you heard yourself say to clients, in one form or another, "If I give you advice as you request, one of two things can happen, both pretty awful. First, if what I tell you to do doesn't work out, you will blame me for screwing up your life. Second, and probably even worse, what if the advice I give you does work out? Then you have learned to come back to me, or some other authority in your life, next time you have a problem."

Dependence thus is seen by many Western therapists as the culprit that blocks an individual's growth, that keeps people stuck in dysfunctional relationships and prevents them from meeting their own needs. There are a number of reasons commonly offered for this position: dependence reflects the strongest human needs, which are for protection and security; it represents an overcompensation for care that was missing in childhood; it is a form of learned helplessness resulting from parental overprotection; it implies an inability to make one's own decisions; and/or it represents bonds with parents that have yet to have been severed. The consensus of all these perspectives, as well as more modern views, is that dependence is the source of much human suffering. Bowlby (1969) speaks for many contemporary practitioners when he prefers to substitute the word "attachment" for the best part of human connectedness and "dependence" for the worst part. A person who is dependent is weak, has no choices, and does not stand as a whole person. Independence, by contrast, is our most sacred value, the very spirit of North American initiative and resourcefulness.

It is clear, then, that working on issues of dependence and independence in the healing relationship is often significant for Western therapists. One practitioner explains: "When a client becomes dependent on me, it feels like a leech draining out all my life energy. The late calls at night, the deference, the shuck and jive reluctance to accept responsibility for his or her own life drive me nuts!" And our attitude about dependency becomes part of the very fabric of the helping relationships we construct. When a client asks us what to do, we ask him right back. When a client attempts to give us credit for her progress, we carefully point out that she was the one who did most of the work. When a client claims that he cannot make it without us, we vigorously work to counteract that dependent belief.

Yet Neki (1976) points out that dependence is culturally relative and not universally viewed as something to be avoided. In New Guinea and other South Pacific cultures, for example, children are encouraged to grow up as slowly as possible. They are not weaned from the breast until age four or five, nor are they pushed off to school at age seven. In Latin or Oriental cultures, as well, interdependence among members of an extended family or social organization is greatly valued and encouraged. Speaking principally about attitudes in India, Neki explains that dependence in relationships is the ideal. Parenting is indulgent; clinging is not only permitted but encouraged. Conversely, in our culture, infants are weaned as quickly as possible. They sleep in separate cribs and are encouraged to crawl, walk, get a driver's license, and leave home as soon as possible. This is in startling contrast to India, where infants can stay attached to their mothers' breasts as long as they wish and children sleep in the same bed as their mother throughout childhood. As adults, they are most interested in creating traits of dependability rather than independence. These same relationship ideals operate in Indian healing encounters; whereas we abhor client dependence, the therapist in Indian culture encourages it and utilizes it to direct the course of treatment.

Table 4.1 sums up the ways in which independence and dependence are culturally guided attributes of therapeutic relationships.

Neki's contrasting model of dependence highlights how all

Table 4.1. Divergent Views of Dependence in Relationships.

	Western Ideal of Differentiation	Indian Ideal of Affiliation
Developmental ideal	Independence	Dependence
Social mechanism	Individuation	Belongingness
Motivation	Achievement-oriented	Approval-seeking
Family attachment	Dependent only during childhood & only with nuclear family	Dependent on extended family throughout life span
Verbal interaction patterns	Self-oriented, assertive talkative, & dominant	Other-oriented; emphasis on listening & deference
Fears	Fear of disappointing others by being too dependent	Fear of forsaking others by being too independent
Therapeutic relationships	Rely on therapist only as an aid to self-help	Rely entirely on therapist to direct treatment

Adapted from Neki, 1976.

healing relationships must be examined within a cultural context. An Indian couple considers family bonds sacrosanct. They fully expect that the therapist will direct the course of action and tell them what to do. Pedder (1991) has therefore expressed concern about Western therapists' reluctance to permit dependence in relationships with members of diverse cultures. He believes that independence is a myth based on an idealized dream. For Pedder, the problem in dependency lies not in relying on others but in not feeling internally secure during encounters with others. Our job as therapists, then, is to spend as much time investigating a client's cultural perceptions and expectations for a therapeutic relationship as we do exploring the background of that client's presenting complaints.

Consequences of Cultural Unawareness

Sue Whiston relates another example of a situation in which cultural awareness was essential.

When I first began my career, I was asked to work with a group of adolescents on the Wind River Indian Reservation in Wyoming. I was working at the time with a federal program designed to keep minority adolescents from dropping out of school. With all of the best intentions, I began a group with those Native American students who were believed to be at risk of dropping out. Naïvely, I jumped right in with some structured exercises to build trust, just as my instructors had told me to do. The group members simply looked down and did not participate, a situation I had anticipated with my limited knowledge of their culture and customs. As the day proceeded, the participants eventually loosened up a bit, and I seemed to gain some credibility in their eyes (I think they felt sorry for me).

At one point, when I began to administer an interest inventory, a couple of the boys explained that there was no sense giving any test to Native American kids, especially one created by whites, because they would all flunk it anyway. Even though I explained that this test could not be flunked, that the information would help them find out what was of interest to them in school, they continued to think it was a waste of their time. To my surprise, they agreed to flunk this test for me because I was older and should be respected.

I sent off the inventories to Minnesota and received the results before my next visit to the reservation. The inventory contained a validity scale for inconsistent responses, and the majority of the children had such high scores that no interests appeared on the profiles (they had, in fact, flunked an interest inventory!). Whatever credibility or trust I had gained in that first encounter was now permanently lost because of my stubborn refusal to abandon "generic" techniques in favor of those that might have been more responsive to the needs and values of those children.

It has long been one of the major criticisms of our profession that we have failed to reach the people who need our services the most. Whereas wealthy, professional, or privileged classes have no trouble finding excellent mental health care, it is the disadvantaged in minority groups, such as Hispanics, African Americans, Native Americans, and Asian Americans, who receive inadequate therapeutic services (Sue, Fujino, Hu, & Takeuchi, 1991). Those who are culturally different from the majority in our society rarely take advantage of mental health services (Snowden & Cheung, 1990), and when they do, they often end treatment prematurely because of problems in the therapeutic relationship. Yet the more culturally sensitive and responsive therapists are to clients' ethnic values, the more likely therapeutic efforts are to be successful (O'Sullivan, Peterson, Cox, & Kirkeby, 1989). That conclusion is certainly no surprise. Any relationship, therapeutic relationships most of all, is going to work more effectively if clients feel they are respected, their needs and interests are understood, and their preferences for communication are acknowledged and responded to.

Feeling Understood in Any Language

Betty was embittered and resentful toward all whites. As a full-blooded Cherokee Indian, she had known her share of abuse at the hands of numerous white men, since she had been raped at age eight and, subsequently, dozens of times by men of all colors and creeds. She had reason to be distrustful of all whites, but men most of all. When numerous complaints from her fellow workers regarding her obvious hostility toward whites reached her supervisor, she was threatened with dismissal unless she sought psychological help. Once again, she found herself in the company of a white man (her assigned therapist) who held the power to destroy her life, just as her ancestors had been subjected to systematic genocide. For some reason that she could not explain—perhaps feelings of surrender or indifference or even assertiveness—she voiced these very thoughts to her therapist. Much to her surprise, he did not react defensively, nor did he threaten retaliation. In fact, he became visibly angry toward her tormentors as he heard her story. Betty shared with him that this was the first time in her life that she had ever felt understood by anyone, much less a man, and a white man at that.

Apart from any specific interventions and therapeutic techniques, what made the treatment work most of all, and what kept Betty around long enough to listen to what the therapist had to say, was a relationship that worked between them and was responsive to her needs. This was a very different kind of encounter than any the therapist had experienced before, but the relationship is what made it work. He let go of his preconceptions and relinquished his expectations for what would and should take place. He demanded nothing of her. He begged her to teach him about her ways; he learned some of her words and customs. Most of all, he did not try to change her or manipulate her as white people had tried so many times before. Building a bridge of trust between them became their joint mission. The relationship was successful because the clinician was culturally responsive to her needs.

All therapeutic relationships exist in a social and cultural context. It is thus difficult to do justice to the one without considering the other. The act of healing is one in which the relationship between client and helper attempts to mediate an understanding of what is taking place and its particular meaning within the individual, family, community, and professional systems. Clinicians who are culturally literate are those who have certain awarenesses, understandings, knowledge, and skills that allow them to construct relationships that are ideally suited to the needs and preferences of their clientele (Arredondo, Dowd, & Gonsalves, 1980). They are aware of their own cultural values and how those values tend to shape their perceptions of others (Baruth & Manning, 1991). Specifically, they have specialized knowledge about each culture to which their clients belong. This background allows them to construct individualized relationships that emphasize family functioning with Hispanic clients, expert roles with African Americans, and a directive therapist stance with Asian Americans.

In short, the implication of multicultural research is that in order to construct relationships with clients from different backgrounds, it is necessary for us to adapt our working styles to client needs. While maintaining appropriate boundaries and universal standards of care, it is possible for us to become more flexible in the kinds of alliances that we create, especially with regard to how roles are negotiated, how active we are, the types of interventions we rely on, and the degree and kind of intimacy that we develop.

Are We Really All That Different?

In spite of the many cultural differences between helpers in different societies, there are central similarities. For example, Torrey (1986) has identified a number of similarities between what therapists do in our society and what helpers do among the Iban, a tribe of Borneo headhunters. One particular "therapist," or *Manang*, was scrutinized and was observed to be quite careful in establishing the right kind of connection to his patients—one in which he was viewed as a technical expert to be consulted. Since his principal therapeutic technique consisted of suggestion, he was especially concerned with capitalizing on his capability for influencing patients.

Sue and Zane (1987) contend that the key to developing healing encounters is credibility and giving. We need to examine the individual and determine how to become a credible source with that individual and then determine how to give to that individual. In the process of becoming credible sources, we may be able to learn a great deal from healers' activities in other cultures. For example, Harmer's description (1980) of a shaman's activities sounds remarkably similar to descriptions of therapist roles by Frank (1961) and Kottler (1993). In his study of healers in the Amazon, this cultural anthropologist depicts the expert shaman as one who has not only mastered basic knowledge and healing rituals but who has also been able to create special relationships with clients and their families. The shaman makes a tremendous emotional commitment to the well-being of a client, with an investment of time and energy that goes far beyond a fifty-minute therapy session. He "may work all night, or several nights, for the recovery of a single patient, involving himself and the patient in a dyadic alliance that intertwines the unconscious of both in a heroic partnership against disease and death. But the alliance is more, for it is an alliance with the hidden powers of Nature, unseen in daylight where the material impingements of daily life clutter consciousness" (p. 136). The client thus relates to the shaman as a guide who can see in the dark, who has traveled this arduous journey before, who knows the easiest routes and can interpret signs along the way, and who can offer assistance in the form of neutralizing obstacles and suggesting means by which to attain desired goals.

The healing rituals of shamans (a.k.a. witch doctors, healers, *curanderos*, and soothsayers) are remarkably universal around the world. Harmer (1980) suggests that, through trial and error, professional helpers in all times and cultures have discovered the same healing principles, including the use of a state that transcends normal reality and is initiated through psychotropic drugs or altered states of consciousness. Most of all, however, healers everywhere have discovered the magically curative powers of the human relationship, to help people feel cared for, nurtured, and understood.

The relationship between shaman and client is characterized by the following components:

Emotional commitment to positive outcomes. Not only does the healer care deeply about the client's welfare but his or her own reputation hinges on the balance of what transpires. If the client worsens, or even dies, the shaman can be out of business.

Infusion of mysterious powers. The shaman is seen as possessing extraordinary powers that allow him or her to see deep inside a person's soul, communicate with the spirit world, and initiate healing rituals that will cancel out evil energy.

A triangular alliance. The shaman not only seeks to forge a rela-tionship with the client, but also attempts to create a partnership with the forces of nature.

Status as an expert. The client must trust that the shaman knows what he or she is doing. Then this unwavering confidence in the healer's curative powers facilitates complete compliance with the treatment plan. Whatever the client is asked to do, he or she will do it with the full expectation that it will work. If for some rea-son, the symptoms persist, the client is the one who must accept responsibility for spiritual impurities, laziness, or other faults that are blocking progress. The healer's reputation is thus afforded some measure of protection.

The shaman tells stories and explains things. He or she is a benevo-lent parent figure with a special pipeline to "truth." Parables, stories, chants, and dances are seen as containing symbolic representations of what needs to be done in order to restore mental and physical health.

The shaman combines holistic treatment of mind and body. Part psy-chotherapist in the use of interpretation and catharsis; part psy-chiatrist in prescribing psychoactive medicines; part chiropractor, physical therapist, and osteopath in manipulating the body; and part movement therapist in prescribing dances and chants, the shaman creates a relationship that is more like our conception of a relationship with a doctor or wizard than with a friend.

Cultural Awareness

Taken together, all these characteristics create an image of a ther-apeutic relationship that is both familiar to us and different from what we are used to. Thus, this chapter's summary of some strands in the cultural thread that should influence the way we construct our therapeutic encounters should give us pause for thought, encouraging us to consider what we are doing in our work and why we are functioning in that particular way in our interactions with clients.

Part Two of this book introduces a conceptual overview—a map of sorts—that highlights the universal factors that operate during therapeutic relationships in a variety of settings and contexts. With such a template, we can trace several of the most prominent conceptual models that are of use to those of us who wish to strengthen the power of our relationships with clients.

Part Two

Conceptual Puzzles

Chapter Five

Maps of Relationships

In the hundred or so years that psychotherapy has been part of Western culture, we have been engaged in a quest to find the perfect model that could explain the mysteries of the process that we participate in every day. If physicists are capable of discovering such a definitive conception about the nature of matter or time, why should we not be able to discover much the same thing about human change? If researchers can figure out the complex workings of DNA, if physicians can find cures for so many diseases, if experts can invent such wonderful things as Velcro and frozen yogurt, why, oh why, can't we figure out the workings of therapeutic relationships?

Truth Comes in Many Different Packages

What we therapists have gathered along the way is an amazingly diverse array of theoretical and scientific "truths." Today, we are confronted every month with announcements from publishers and workshop presenters proclaiming the latest revolutionary techniques that we absolutely must learn if we are not to be left behind. Yet we have long memories. Primal scream therapy urged us to create a special kind of relationship with our clients. So too did rational emotive therapy (RET), transactional analysis (TA), neurolinguistic programming (NLP), and now eye movement desensitization and reprocessing (EMDR). We have been told over the years that the best relationships to create are those that are primarily authentic or businesslike or that fit a dozen other models that all seem to conflict with one another.

Those who fled to science for the answers, frustrated with the unsubstantiated claims of clinicians marketing their favored methods, encountered just as much confusion. Although empirical methods are supposed to offer a relatively unbiased approach to the challenge of discovering the best models, the results of experimental studies are oftentimes inconsequential, producing irrelevant morsels of information in which the big picture is lost. It is also not uncommon to find one study that reports a "truth" that is directly opposed to "truths" found in others. While many academicians and researchers may thrive in the terrain of an ever-changing conceptual landscape, practitioners must struggle to find some useful model to guide the ways they operate. For the last several decades, many of us have been trying to sort through the noise—the conflicting data, the grandiose claims, the divergent theories—to find some reasonably universal model for our professional relationships. It is the clinicians who have discovered that we ought to be looking at what is common to these different models instead of always highlighting their differences.

Conceptual, Empirical, and Personal Threads

If each of us were to look beyond the theoretical labels and across the multitude of "scientific" findings, we would find that a set of common dimensions runs through *all* successful therapeutic relationships. Yes, it certainly *appears* that strategic therapists create quite different kinds of relationships with their clients than do existentialists, and there is no doubt that a gestalt therapist does things a bit differently from a cognitive therapist. However, many of these differences in philosophy and technique do not necessarily lead to significant divergences in the therapeutic relationships that are created. Almost any clinician, regardless of theoretical allegiances, is going to begin with a relationship that is designed to build trust and credibility, whether he or she is dealing with a single client, family, or group. Likewise, at stages in the process at which a client may begin acting out, most of us would structure quite a different sort of relationship, one in which stricter boundaries were maintained. It is thus, from the best that diverse theories and research have to offer, that each of us has tried to create some universal principles to guide our thinking and behavior. This is our conceptual thread, which binds together all that we know and understand, regardless of whether that wisdom is pirated from other theories, garnered from empirical studies, or distilled from personal experience.

Maps to Make Sense of Relationships

If we look at the interactions that take place between one thera-pist and her client, there are an almost infinite number of concep-tual maps that may be employed to make sense of what is taking place, who is doing what, and where treatment should go next. As you read this case description, your own cultural/conceptual/per-sonal filters will map the features you consider most critical.

Jody complains about chronic feelings of emptiness. [*What does that mean to you?*] She has attained a degree of security in her life, but not without a certain number of sacrifices. [*What associations do you have with that image?*] Most notably, she feels estranged from her hus-band, whom she rarely spends much quality time with, and at odds with her two adolescent children, who have made it known in no uncertain terms that they would prefer her to stay out of their lives. [*How are you feeling about that?*]

As Jody tells her story, her therapist, Maxine, cannot help but personalize, to some degree, the issues of balancing a career with family life. [*How have you personalized this so far?*] At the very moment this session is taking place, at 5:30 in the evening, Max-ine reflects she would much rather be at home with her own spouse and children. [*Ring a bell?*] Before Maxine can indulge herself too long in this reverie, Jody muses aloud about her dilemma—if she were to decide to make it a priority to spend more time at home, it would cost her dearly in her professional position. [*How do you interpret that?*] Besides, she wonders, maybe she does not even want to spend time with those who are leading their own separate lives. [*What diagnostic impression have you formed so far?*]

Maxine points out to Jody that it would certainly be important to find that out (and also resolves to do a similar self-assessment). [*What would you have done instead?*] They part ways, Jody determined to confront her husband on the status of their relationship, Maxine a little uneasy about where her reactions to Jody might lead in her own life. [*What part of this story do you feel uneasy about?*].

There are now several other people who are being influenced by Jody and Maxine's initial interaction. Jody, her husband, and children, and even her mother and best friend, become involved in the dialogue she has begun as she sorts out where she is headed in her life and what her priorities really are. [*What predictions would you make?*] Maxine, as well, cannot help but bring these issues up at her first opportunity when she and her husband are alone. Yet her husband is not the only person affected by the issues sparked by the interaction during the session: several colleagues at work become sounding boards for Maxine in her struggle to make sense of what is taking place; they, in turn, conduct their own self-exploration. What began as a dialogue between a client and her therapist soon spreads, like mutant cells out of control. Before long, the ripple effects were felt by dozens of other people.

It will be interesting for you to compare your reactions, impressions, feelings, and clinical judgments about this relationship to those of therapists who subscribe to other cultural/conceptual/personal filters. A humanist therapist might suggest that it was immediate, authentic, and mutual understanding that promoted the experiences of both Jody and Maxine. By providing unconditional caring and closeness for Jody, Maxine was able to help her to express herself fully, finding meaning in their interchange. As therapy progressed, according to this humanistic conceptual filter, the conditions of positive regard would facilitate Jody's further growth and personal development. A psychoanalytically oriented therapist would contend that Maxine was providing a neutral and detached relationship, so that Jody could transfer or project her pervious experiences and conflicted relationships onto the therapist. Much of what occurred in their relationship would have little to do with the present and more to do with Jody's past. The act of working through these past conflicts in the confines of the relationship with the therapist would manifest the healing nature of therapeutic interaction.

The theoretical arena is not limited to these rather traditional schools of therapy; there are also quite a number of contemporary views to be considered, which are introduced in the remainder of this chapter. In addition, it is likely that your own impressions about this case were influenced not only by your theoretical preferences but by a host of other factors, many of which you may hardly be aware of.

Overview of Some Contemporary Concepts

Sometimes, we all wonder if there are any new ideas; if what is supposedly on the cutting edge this year is not simply a repackaging of what has been said many times before. In fact, amidst the current myriad of theoretical ideas, there are a number of contemporary models that offer unique pieces for the complex conceptual puzzle that is therapy. These approaches are special because they offer a perspective that stretches the more familiar theoretical maps. However, the intent is not to dazzle you with ideas that are unfamiliar to you, but rather to introduce (or in some cases, re-introduce) you to ideas that will help you to think differently about the kinds of relationships you construct with your clients. The ultimate goal is to present a conceptual map that integrates ideas that often seem at odds. It is first necessary, however, to make sure that we are all speaking roughly the same language.

The Working Alliance

Like so many of the basics of our profession, the whole concept of therapeutic relationship has its roots in psychoanalytic traditions. In more contemporary views of this relationship, it is called a *working alliance* (Bordin, 1979; Greenson, 1967; Luborsky, 1984), a term that has come to imply that there is an emotional bond that develops between client and therapist, a closeness that is felt by both parties; that the partners in this relationship come to a consensus as to what they will do and how they will do it; and that the extent of their agreement will influence the success of their mission. Maxine and Jody's interaction can continue to serve as an example. In terms of the working alliance model, Maxine and Jody have negotiated a working alliance and appear to be in basic agreement about the direction they are heading and how they propose to get there. Each of them appears to feel some emotional connection to the other, a bond of mutual trust that permits them to proceed further.

It is consistent with the original ideas suggested by Freud to say that any use of technique is important only to the extent that it enhances or enacts this alliance between client and therapist (Stiles, Shapiro, & Elliott, 1986). Thus, it is perhaps encouraging to know that there is significant empirical support for the importance of this perspective, since several studies have found that it may account for up to 40 percent of the variance in successful outcomes (Horvath & Symonds, 1991).

Social Influence

Functioning from a different perspective, the social influence model is based on the vast work generated by social psychologists' attempts to explain interactions between individuals. It is only recently that this unique perspective has been specifically applied to the therapeutic relationship (Strong & Claiborn, 1982). At its most elementary level, the social influence model posits that the client is in need of something that the therapist is perceived to have. In order for the therapist to have an impact on the client, he must be credible. Being credible is defined as being trustworthy, attractive, and expert (Strong, 1968). Thus, the important issues in therapy revolve around the enhancement of therapist credibility in the eyes of the client.

There seems little doubt that Jody perceived Maxine as a credible source of social influence. She is open to listening to her therapist, even following through on their plans together, because she trusts her, not only as a human being with integrity but as a professional with specialized skills and knowledge.

The Interactional View

The interactional perspective takes a unique, microanalytical approach to understanding the therapist-client relationship. In this approach, change does not arise from internal processes that take place within the client, whether these processes are cognitive or affective, as other clinical models posit. Rather, change results from forces generated by the interpersonal engagement. Accordingly, interpersonal behavior is control oriented in that each person actively, though not necessarily consciously, invites others to act in ways that complement and augment desired relationship roles. In this view, Maxine sets the initial tone for her relationship with Jody by inducting Jody into an ideal client role. Or then again, perhaps Jody is the one who starts things off by the way she presents herself during their first interactions. In either case, each of them affects the other through complex and covert negotiations about how they should be with one another. Both client and therapist are working their hardest to get each other to comply with the other's expectations.

Unlike therapeutic models that emphasize congruence and stability in relationships, the interactional approach values compatible discordance (within limits) as a stimulation for change. It is the mismatch and the discrepancy of views between helper and client that are most healing and change producing. In fact, in order to be optimally effective, stability must be avoided at all costs!

Different Paths to the Same Place

Whether we look at traditional or contemporary views, it is the diversity of these conceptual approaches that is at first most obvious. Even though each model may go about its business in different ways, the purpose of each one is identical: to explain the events that take place in therapy, to provide a framework within which therapists can understand the information and events they encounter, and to suggest a systematic plan for intervention. The value of a theoretical model is that it ties these elements together in such a way that practitioners and clients can understand and choose their way through the process as they live it.

Table 5.1 is a way of summarizing the schools of thought that have been competing for our allegiance, before their salient features are tied together into a conceptual map that integrates each significant thread.

The Empirical Thread

If there is one thing that many practitioners resent more than abstract theories that contradict one another, it is empirical research that they perceive as irrelevant, incomprehensible, compartmentalized, and virtually useless as a guide for clinical behavior. Yet the conceptual and empirical threads of healing are hardly separate entities; they have long been intertwined, as empirical study has led to theoretical innovation and as theoretical leaps have spawned empirical investigations to test their assumptions. For example, when Eysenck (1952) challenged our profession to prove we really make a difference, he sparked a dramatic increase in empirical studies to validate our claims. This was the period in our recent history when research efforts began to focus on the structure of the therapeutic relationship, the ways it is important, and the factors that contribute to its optimal form. Research groups and centers such as the Menninger Foundation, Jerome Frank and his colleagues at Johns Hopkins University, and Lester Luborsky at the University of Pennsylvania contributed to the growing empirical knowledge base. In addition, the research designs and methodologies became more sophisticated and precise, which added to the scientific respectability of the research that was conducted.

Although scholars have been quite excited about these advancements, some clinicians have asked, "So what? What does this have to do with helping me with my clients? I already knew that therapy works, and I already had some idea of the best kind of relationship to promote changes most efficiently." As these questioners would also, no doubt, be quick to point out, there are a number of problems with empirical methodologies when they are employed with complex human phenomena. The scientific method is supposed to be nonbiased, discover unanticipated results, specify cause-and-effect relationships between variables, accumulate knowledge systematically, and replicate previous results. Yet it is limited by the degree of accuracy of its measurement tools, its linear thinking, its aura of "truth," and the way that the essence and context of a problem may be lost in the empirical process. For example, a research article's abstract boasts of consequential findings, yet the sample is with college freshmen and although the correlation is statistically significant, the shared variance is so small that is has no practical meaning.

By sorting through the thousands of empirical studies that have been completed in the last few decades on the intricacies of the therapeutic relationship, the authors of this book identified six common strands in the empirical thread that runs throughout many of these studies. Many of these strands are things that you already "know," in the sense that you have observed/sensed/felt/reasoned similar ideas; others may run counter to what you deeply believe. (Citations to the principal studies are provided for those who wish to consult the studies themselves and test the conclusions drawn here.)

Table 5.1. Conceptual Models of Healing Relationships.

Theory	Primary Processes	Therapist Roles	Client Roles
Psychoanalytic	identification, transference, unconscious wishes	neutrality, interpretation of dynamics	free expression of unconscious desires
Object relations	parent-child bonds, ego relatedness, attachment	providing a holding environment, therapeutic parenting	full experience of rage, love, hate; acknowledgment of self-destructiveness
Humanist/ Existential	immediacy, authentic engagement, mutual understanding	unconditional caring, reflection of feelings, building trust	expression of feelings, encountering self and other, search for personal meaning
Behavioral	social exchange, reinforcement	problem solving, training of social skills; ensure client receptivity	compliance to plan, complete assignments, shared responsibility for outcome
Cognitive	rationality and objectivity, controlled partnership	challenge of thinking, disputing beliefs, engaging interaction	respond logically, cooperation with premises, application of self-talk

Social influence	influence is used for behavior & attitude changes	being an attractive and credible expert, use of influence	accept self-responsibility, abandon dysfunctional patterns, influence related to perception
Working alliance	emotional bonds, mutual interaction & agreement on goals	join forces, assign responsibilities, create mutual contract	follow contract, interact honestly, develop personal attachment
Interaction	co-constructed reality, rules and sequential patterns, interactive effects, complementarity	define relationship, find position of influence, lead and direct process, control own style	negotiate from good faith, develop flexible reactions
Social constructivism	meaning of behavior, reciprocal influence, social context, co-constructed reality	interested inquiry, influence cognitive perceptions, change narrative	join partner in process, collaborative synthesis of meaning and perception

The client-therapist relationship is an essential ingredient in success-ful therapy. There is virtual unanimity in the empirical studies that the therapist-client relationship is critical in psychotherapy. This may not be all that surprising to you, but it has taken quite a lot of time and effort to validate this belief empirically. According to Luborsky, Crits-Christoph, Mintz, and Auerbach (1988), 88 per-cent of the studies they reviewed found the therapeutic relation-ship was related to positive client outcome. Orlinsky and Howard (1986) similarly reported that there was a significant relationship between the therapeutic relationship and client outcome in up to 80 percent of the studies they reviewed. In addition, some studies have shown that failure to form a therapeutic relationship is strongly associated with client noncompliance with treatment plans (Eisenthal, Emery, Lazare, & Udin, 1979) and premature termina-tion (Tracey, 1977; Saltzman, Luetgert, Roth, Creaser, & Howard, 1976), as well as poor outcome (Alexander & Luborsky, 1986).

The assorted theoretical approaches are generally about equal in their success. This is a conclusion we might "know" but not in a way that affects our behavior to a great extent. Leaders in our field are still fighting with one another over which model of the relationship is superior to all others. We flock to their workshops and read their books with a fervor that rivals religious conversion, as we search for the true path to therapeutic heaven. However, Garfield and Bergin (1994) have concluded, after interpreting a number of stud-ies, that therapeutic effectiveness can best be explained by several common or nonspecific factors that are shared by many approaches and exhibited by a variety of skilled clinicians, regardless of their espoused theories. But, since therapy research is often designed to investigate the effects that are incremental to the common factors, it has been difficult to ferret out these elusive, general variables (Lambert, Shapiro, & Bergin, 1986). Most writers in the field, even many behaviorists, also consider the therapeutic relationship to be a nonspecific factor that operates regardless of the circumstances and interventions employed (Patterson, 1985). Finally, to the best of the present authors' knowledge, there is little evidence to indicate that any theory works much better than others (Orlinsky, Grawe, & Parks, 1994), although there are clear indications that the quality of the relationship between client and therapist is a critical ingredient (Beutler, Machado, & Neufeldt, 1994).

Most effective therapeutic relationships have elements in common. Watch any skilled clinician, regardless of what he calls himself, and you are likely to see several features in the relationships that he creates that you would consider to be universal features. At least three of these universal features have been identified (Orlinsky & Howard, 1986): role investment, empathic resonance, and mutual affirmation. *Role investment* occurs when the client is encouraged to develop some attachment to the therapist, usually in the form of sharing something personal. A commitment to the process, as well as to completing necessary tasks, occurs when the therapist has been successful in getting the client to invest time and energy on an ongoing basis. *Empathic resonance* is the good personal contact that is made by the participants with one another. It occurs when rapport exists, when both participants feel trusting and comfortable, and willing to take risks with one another. Finally, *mutual affirmation* is an expansive good will mobilized between the participants.

Effective relationships involve more than therapist-offered "facilitative conditions." This conclusion may be news to those practitioners who still operate exclusively in a client-centered mode of accurate empathy, nonpossessive warmth, congruence, and unconditional positive regard (Rogers, 1957). Once there was believed to be general empirical support for these conditions that had such an impact on training a generation of practitioners (Mitchell, Bozarth, & Kraft, 1977; Gurman, 1977; Patterson, 1984). However, although these conditions, which dominated our thinking for decades, are certainly important, they may not be enough. Recent comprehensive reviews have not found support for the importance of all aspects of Rogers' conditions, especially when they are compared to other aspects of the therapeutic relationship. For example, Beutler, Crago, and Arizmendi (1986) found that the facilitative conditions were inconsistently and only modestly related to successful outcome.

There does appear to be a strong relationship between empathy and successful therapeutic outcomes. In addition, positive regard and warmth on the part of the therapist toward the client also seem to be related to desirable results, but not at a high level. In other words, these factors may be more important to the therapist than to the client (and that finding may also be important). On the other hand, therapist genuineness, or congruence, which we ordinarily think of as being so critical, has not been empirically shown to be related to successful outcomes (Whiston & Sexton, 1993). This could mean, of course, that the studies have just not been designed properly to measure qualities that are so elusive. Or, it may be that although being congruent sounds important it is not really a major ingredient. We may have been overstating the importance of these conditions as compared to other factors that exert even more influence.

Clients make an important contribution to effective therapeutic relationships. Although it is not much of a surprise to suggest that client involvement in the process is a critical factor, client contributions have been ignored by empiricists until recent times. It seemed that if the therapists did their jobs of providing the right ingredients and employing the correct interventions everything should fall into place. Yet we are well aware that clients have much say in whether the relationship is helpful or not. How open the client is to the relationship is certainly a critical variable (Kolb, Beutler, Davis, Crago, & Shanfeld, 1985; Lorr & McNair, 1964). Also, although we know that therapist understanding and acceptance are important, it also seems that these same qualities are important in clients and that clients who are understanding and accepting profit the most (Bent, Putnam, Kiesler, & Nowicki, 1976).

Therapeutic relationships are dynamic and change according to the stage of the process. One challenge in making sense of relationships in therapy is that they are hardly static entities, and as a relationship evolves, so too do the therapeutic forces that provoke change. Take empathy, for example, an ingredient that seems to be less important in the early stages of the relationship than later in the process (Barkham & Shapiro, 1986). Many therapists, however, believe empathy is more important in the early stage, even though clients themselves indicate quite the opposite. In addition, Klee, Abeles, and Muller (1990) found that the working alliance was not consistent throughout treatment and that clients who benefited most showed an increase in collaborative involvement as the process moved from beginning to end.

These six conclusions hardly exhaust what is known from research about relationships in therapy. They are but a sampling of how the empirical thread intersects with attempts to create a conceptual framework that can guide clinical decision making and action.

A Multidimensional Model
of Therapeutic Relationships

If we are to use theoretical and empirical findings about psychotherapy more effectively, we need to integrate them with the realities of clinical practice and form a unified model of the therapeutic relationship. Perhaps the most prominent of previous efforts to construct such a model was Frank's work (1961, 1973), which sought to identify the active ingredients shared by all approaches. He proposed that all good clinicians are powerfully persuasive. They genuinely care about their clients, and they are skilled at communicating this regard. In addition, they are perceived as being powerful enough to intervene on the client's behalf, whether with the spirit world or the larger society.

Other attempts to follow the path blazed by Frank were initiated by Bordin (1979) and, later, further elaborated on by Gelso and Carter (1985). Gelso and Carter described three aspects of therapeutic relationships. The *real relationship* is an aspect intended to capture those factors in the client-therapist interaction that are reality based, undistorted, and appropriate. In contrast, the *unreal relationship* describes that part of an interaction based on distorted perceptions, in which the client treats the therapist as someone else (transference) and/or the therapist does the same (countertransference). The *working alliance* is that aspect of the relationship in which both partners function in a collaborative way to conduct their desired business.

These models have offered initial glimpses into a multidimensional model that includes sufficient freedom for practitioners to adapt their style, interventions, and structures according to what the client is most likely to respond best to at any moment in time. And they are not unlike ideas others (such as Lazarus, 1981; Thorne, 1967; and Truax & Carkhuff, 1967) have attempted to implement in their efforts to develop an integrative model of the therapy process.

The multidimensional model proposed here builds on the work of these predecessors, as well as on the five threads of healing in relationships. It can be employed regardless of the theoretical orientation, cultural background, or clinical setting of the practitioner. Its four dimensions act as independent yet mutually interactive levels that operate throughout the relationship. The impact of each dimension will change, however, depending on the participants (therapist and client), the cultural context, and the stage of the relationship. The four dimensions, based on solid research findings, are authentic engagement, projected images, interactional patterns, and healing alliances, and it is proposed that these dimensions primarily represent what is healing in therapeutic relationships. These four dimensions originate from the empirical threads. Figure 5.1 illustrates the interrelationship among these dimensions.

Authentic Engagement

It is during authentic engagement between client and therapist that the attributes and experiences of both client and therapist merge. Who they are as human beings, their mannerisms, their interper-

Figure 5.1. A Multidimensional Model
of Therapeutic Relationships.

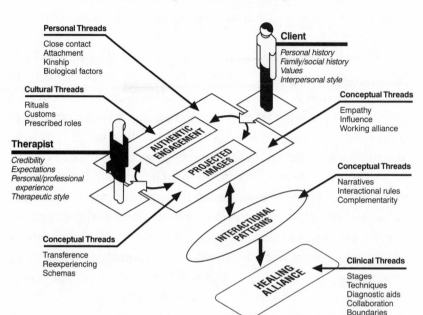

sonal styles, their very essences, come into play as they relate to one another. This is the most tangible and "real" part of the therapeutic exchange, when two people are making contact, when empathy and understanding are flowing.

Authentic engagement captures many of the principal relationship characteristics traditionally viewed as humanistic. They include the facilitative conditions we know as warmth, positive regard, congruence, genuineness, and empathy, but also much more. This dimension also encompasses the biological factors mentioned previously, the kinship bonds and attachment instincts that lead people in need to reach out to others for comfort. In addition, social influence and social psychological factors create a complex interactive pattern that is part of authentic engagement.

Page and Berkow (1994) juxtapose the existential concepts of freedom and responsibility as the essence of what is most healing in therapeutic relationships. Furthermore, they borrow Tillich's (1952) elements of love, power, and justice to demonstrate how relative harmony or disharmony is maintained during authentic encounters.

When therapists are able to establish a sense of fairness and caring in their connections to clients, their power helps to create an atmosphere that is both permissive and restrictive. The client is invited to act in ways that are authentic, but within a context of accepting responsibility for this behavior. The therapist, as well, acts in an authentic manner to encourage such behavior in clients.

Although Page and Berkow are speaking about relationships in unstructured group settings, similar dynamics operate in most any influential encounter. Perceptions of both client and therapist are altered as a result of sharing different views about the nature of what it means to be free and responsible. According to the authors, "Because awareness not only registers but also makes experience, freedom is not merely passively perceived; it too is actively created" (p. 137). It is in this act of pursuing freedom in the therapeutic relationship that clients learn to respect the rights of others as they become more responsible for their choices.

This authentic relationship becomes the training ground for initiating several types of changes: the discovery of new meanings in the ways experiences are interpreted, the acceptance of greater responsibility for experiences/feelings/reactions/ that have been denied or disowned, and the movement toward greater intimacy and satisfaction in other relationships. It is through the sharing of self—one's ideas, feelings, compelling thoughts, and unique perceptions—with an attentive listener that personal transformation begins. If there is one thing that therapists do well, or at least have been so trained, it is to listen carefully and respond compassionately to what is offered.

Jeffrey Kottler describes what a therapist might feel and think in this dimension of the therapeutic relationship.

I am with a client just now, *with* him in the best sense of what that means. I know that he is a client, that I am here to serve him, but I blink my eyes, for just a moment or two, and I see a person sitting there, a man I care very much for.

He is smiling at me now. I can feel the gratitude, even the love that he feels for me. Part of this, of course, is the result of my professional role. Another part, however, is the very real connection that we feel toward one another. I am aware of his quirks and moods just as he senses mine. We feel close to one another; there is a bond of trust that helps each of us to feel comfortable in one another's presence. It is from this very real affection and respect that we have both built a collaboration that has worked quite well. This is hardly the only part of our relationship; it might not even be the most significant part in terms of provoking changes in his life. But it is where we started together. Now, it is where we are ending.

I am restraining myself from reaching out to hug him. Not just yet. Maybe a little later. I feel sad that he is leaving. I will miss him, just as he is telling me how he will miss me now that our collaboration is over.

The mutual feelings, in this case very positive ones, that client and therapist have toward one another are the essence of their authentic engagement. This is the unique dimension of their relationship that is real, as opposed to the projected dimension.

Projected Images

This dimension is composed of those concealed or unseen forces that influence the relationship. The "ghosts" that inhabit a therapeutic relationship cannot be observed, touched, or easily identified, yet their influence powerfully affects what takes place. Look more closely at the case of Maxine and Jody, for example, and it becomes apparent that there were a number of ways in which therapist and client brought both their personal histories and present life circumstances into their relationship. Although these activities have traditionally been called transference processes, quite a bit more is going on. A framework of cognitive schemas, for example, functions in this dimension, shaping the particular ways that individuals are predisposed to view and react to others, based on previous encounters.

For Maxine, the conversation with her client Jody was very personal. It was as if Jody were telling Maxine's life story. Like her client, Maxine could not balance her life and career; she felt inadequate in her relationship with her husband, her children, and her job. She honestly believed that she must try harder, that if she only worked at it, she could be all things to all people. In her most professional way, Maxine confronted Jody with her lack of effort. She pointed out to Jody that while she wanted change, she only talked and did not act. She challenged Jody's desire to be a career woman. Jody looked confused and was disheartened. That session ended quietly. On her drive home, Maxine wondered, if only to herself, if she had pushed too hard. She even wondered whom she might have been speaking to.

Projected images are very real. They influence therapist and client alike to both filter certain information and act in particular ways. To some degree, these ghosts seem present. Yet this is the part of the relationship that is not real, that is distorted, that is a perceptual mistake. (Chapter Eight considers the vast conceptual maps of this dimension.)

Interactional Patterns

The nature of the authentic engagement and the nature of the projected images that are present in the therapeutic relationship result in a unique set of co-constructed interactional patterns that develop between therapist and client. These patterns emerge as a *product* of the mutual influence between the authentic and projected dimensions. The patterns are important because they can either hinder or facilitate the healing nature of the relationship. And what is unique about this perspective on the dimensions of the relationship is that it offers a mechanism for systematically understanding the mysterious interactional glue that seems to bind us in both helpful and harmful patterns.

For example, in the early stages of their relationship, both John and his therapist have engaged in a curious interactional dance. John has a history of failed relationships in which he usually steps into the role of being the dependent one. He prides himself on being totally honest in his relationships and on showing the real person that he is from the very beginning, yet the usual result is that he ends up feeling abandoned. The accumulated pain from these losses has become increasingly difficult for him to tolerate. He begins this new relationship with the hopeful yet hidden expectation that this therapist will be the first person to support him without leaving in the end.

From an interactional perspective, the development of a therapeutic relationship is a process of covert negotiation. The client and therapist each offer a proposal for what the relationship is to be. John's expectation is that his therapist will be that all-supportive and caring individual for whom he has been searching. John's therapist, however, has a somewhat different agenda, one that is in direct conflict with what John prefers, since its ultimate goal is to foster John's greater independence and self-responsibility.

It is through a process of predominately covert negotiations over these goals that their relationship forms. While John and his therapist each discuss what they want, they also behave in ways they believe are most helpful to the relationship. Eventually, the two of them settle on a compromise they can both live with, a relationship stabilized into a set of roles for each to play. As they continue to spend time together, further refinements are made in the rules for their exchanges, negotiations that hopefully lead to the kind of structure that is going to help John function more effectively.

Healing Alliance

As Figure 5.1 illustrates, the end result of the authentic, projected, and interactional dimensions of a successful therapeutic relationship is a healing alliance. This dimension distinguishes therapeutic relationships from other close personal affiliations. It is the immediate outcome of a set of interactional patterns in which the therapist and client have agreed to pursue stated goals. This alliance thus sets the stage for any techniques or interventions attempted by the therapist. While these therapeutic rituals become the focus of change, it is the healing alliance that is the source of that change.

Tom Sexton tells of his experience in reaching a healing alliance with a particular client.

> I worked with Molly for three years. The first of those years was a struggle. I had a very clear picture of where we should go to help ease her depression. She seemed vested in maintaining the long-term (eleven-year) relationship she had with a married man. Despite our mutual frustration, she continued to show up each week, and each time we would struggle—I was promoting one path, she another. My supervisor believed that we were spinning our wheels, that therapy was going nowhere. He suggested that I confront what he saw as her resistance to change. In our conversations, I did not have the sense that the difficulty was resistance. It just seemed that we had different agendas, different directions, each making sense to us.
>
> It was not any specific event that seemed to turn the tide. Instead, it seemed that slowly we began to forge a common direction. I became aware of the change when, one day, for what seemed like the tenth time, I suggested exercise as a stress reduction plan. This idea, which she had countless times rejected, she suddenly believed to be a great idea. I was initially shocked and somewhat suspicious. But in the end, we had forged a common direction, built on an emotional bond.

It is the healing alliance that is the foundation for the clinical work that we do. The stages of therapy, methods of intervention, and collaborative problem solving (among other elements) come into play only after the emergence of this healing alliance. It is the existence of such an alliance that gives each of us the feeling of "things" working. It is the absence of the alliance that is the source of our concern when we know that "things" are not going well, when we are missing the mark, when we are struggling for some missing element.

Isn't There More?

The essence of the conceptual thread in therapeutic relationships is that it helps us understand the dimensions as they run across *all* approaches. Thus, a multidimensional model based on common dimensions has the advantage of being flexible and adaptable in various therapeutic settings and with a wide variety of clients. Regardless of the setting in which you practice, the client population you serve, the mission of your organization, the conceptual models you prefer, the personal filters with which you view the world, the interventions you rely on most, a multidimensional map can guide clinical decisions and plans related to where you have been and where you are headed.

The model illustrated here, while empirically, clinically, theoretically, culturally, and personally based, is necessarily a simplification, a very basic map of the main highways rather than all the secondary roads. At this juncture, there are still probably as many questions as answers. What about therapeutic factors unrelated to the relationship? Which interactional patterns promote healing more than others? How is a healing alliance best constructed? How do I identify the projected images that are influencing the relationship? What does all of this have to do with the client I am currently stuck with?

The remaining chapters of this section elaborate on the four dimensions introduced here, and each chapter describes more completely the conceptual threads that make up the fabric of the therapeutic relationship model. After that exploration of the authentic, social psychological, projected, and interactional approaches to the relationship, the multidimensional model will be examined further as a means to help us to operate more effectively with our clients.

Chapter Six

Being Authentic

There is nobody in the world who knows me as well as my therapist. We have spent dozens of hours together talking about stuff that I have never really talked about before—to anyone. I have several other very intimate relationships in my life, with my sister, my dad, a few of my close friends, and certainly my husband, but nobody has ever really known me the way I have felt understood in this relationship with my therapist.

We have discussed that there are aspects of my feelings for her in which I idealize her, ascribe to her things that are not really part of her as much as they are parts of other relationships that I have had. I do understand that, and to a certain extent, I agree. However, our relationship is also based on some genuine feelings that we both have for one another. I am not deluding myself that I am somehow special, that she likes me more than others or anything like that. I am just saying that some of what I feel towards her, and what I sense she feels toward me, is based on real affection and respect.

I don't think therapists realize the extent to which we, their clients, come to know them almost as well as they know us. I mean, I can tell when my therapist is having a tough day or when she is in an especially good mood. She has told me very little about her life directly, yet I still know many things about her, the way she thinks, what she considers important or insignificant. In my mind, this just makes our work together even more satisfying and more exciting.

I do not think of my therapist as a friend exactly, but neither do I defer to her the way I would towards my doctor. She always maintains a professional air, making sure we stick with the agenda at hand, yet there is something between us that really clicks; at times, it is almost as if we can read each other's minds. I genuinely like her as a person, not just as my therapist. I know she likes me too. I know her caring for me goes beyond professional interest. Perhaps more than anything else she has done for me, this personal, authentic part of our relationship is what has given me such confidence to do what I have needed to do.

Regardless of how professional, clinical, or theoretical we might remain as practitioners, the perspective shared by this client highlights a common experience: at some level, both client and therapist are touched in a personal way as a result of the authentic engagement. This dimension seems tangible because it is experienced on a visceral level. Both therapist and client can feel the connection between them; both can sense the closeness and mutual understanding. For the client whose impressions opened this chapter, it was not special techniques or interventions that made the most difference, but the fact the client liked the therapist, thought the therapist cared about her, and was moved by this expressed concern.

It is hardly new to suggest that it is important for us to develop personal and authentic connections between ourselves and our clients. In fact, it would probably be difficult to find anyone who would not agree that mutual understanding and respect contribute to successful therapeutic efforts. It is curious, however, that there has been so little conceptual attention given to understanding what goes on in this therapeutic dimension that is so strongly felt and so widely accepted. The investigations underlying this book suggest that it may be conceptually helpful for us to think of the authentic dimension as both multifaceted and unique, distinct from other dimensions of the therapeutic relationship (see Figure 5.1). If we are to understand the authentic side of the therapeutic relationship adequately, we must consider it as a *mutual* experience.

The therapist of the client quoted earlier also had strong feelings about her therapeutic relationship with this client.

I feel sad that she is moving on. I mean, I am also proud of her, and proud of the work we have done together. But I have grown quite attached to her, to our talks together. Every Wednesday afternoon, three o'clock, every week going on a year and a half, she has been a part of my life.

I struggle with letting her go. I know I could find reasons to encourage her to continue a bit longer, but the time has come. I know that. I almost feel guilty feeling the way that I do, that I'm some kind of unprofessional wimp or something because I feel a loss. I know if I told my supervisor this stuff he would go nuts over countertransference stuff. My feelings are more than that, though. Apart from any of my fantasies about her and our relationship, how could I not love someone with whom I spent so many hours talking about her most intimate life?

Indeed, with many (but certainly not all) of our clients, we walk away from the encounter feeling a deep personal connection. As will be explored in Chapter Eight, some of these feelings that clients and therapist have for one another are not "real" but represent distortions, fantasies, and projections. Yet, another part of the working alliance consists of a genuine bond between human beings. Whether the language favored talks about mutual empathy, authentic involvement, or compassion and love, the therapeutic relationship consists of a very real involvement between two human beings.

Are Core Conditions Real?

Long before Carl Rogers's classic essay (1957) became a rallying cry for the therapeutic application of authentic engagement in relationships, religious leaders such as Jesus Christ and Siddhartha Gautama, the Buddha, preached the power of love as a healing force. Since contributions from the world of spiritualism were deemed completely unacceptable in the scientific bent that the field of therapy took many centuries later, the early humanists, such as Abraham Maslow and Rogers, conceived and packaged love in more digestible forms. "Empathy," "unconditional positive regard," "genuineness," and "authenticity" sound much more professional as core conditions of helping. Nevertheless, as mentioned in the previous chapter, however intuitively compelling and personally appealing these core conditions appear, when empirical researchers attempt to measure them, the results are inconclusive (Beutler, Crago, & Arizmendi, 1986; Sexton & Whiston, 1994). Thus, equivocal empirical support for facilitative conditions is another paradox of our field. Every practitioner knows that authentic feelings and caring make a difference, even if such phenomena cannot be accurately measured. One way to make sense of the discrepancy between research and experience may be to conclude that, while warmth and genuine caring are important dimensions, they are not enough to be helpful unless paired with other therapeutic ingredients. If it were otherwise, then any friend or relative of the client could do what we do, without the benefit of any training or expertise.

Genuineness and Respect

We may also conclude that not all the core conditions are equally important. Perhaps some make more difference than others to particular clients. Maybe others are more important in helping the therapist feel comfortable than in directly benefiting the client.

Genuineness, for example, is the willingness and ability to be authentic, open, and honest, to be "real" in the relationship. Although Rogers (1957) cast genuineness as unconditional positive regard for the person of the client, Patterson (1985) has argued that it actually represents *respect*. While many others have lauded the importance of genuineness, few have sought to describe what it actually means. Tom Sexton describes how the difficulties of understanding the concept were brought home to him.

I had a recent experience that made me wonder about the way in which this notion of respect was understood by a group of trainees. Each of the beginning therapists in the supervision group talked at length about the importance of being genuine in their work with clients. For some of them, genuine meant "to be themselves—to say what they feel." For others, it meant being in touch with their ongoing reactions to the presence of the client. What I found most interesting, however, was that, a few minutes later, each of these students was questioning his or her clients' motives, stories, and willingness to be in therapy. The trainees appeared mistrustful and cynical.

After a long discussion about these issues, one of the quieter students remarked, "It seems to me that these clients are doing the best they can with what they have got. Why can't we just respect that and go from there?" As an observer of this conversation, I was struck by the curious inconsistency between promoting genuineness and yet harboring disrespect.

Compassion and Love

The way authenticity and genuineness are defined is of interest, but it is how these core conditions are practiced that makes the difference. We are uncomfortable talking about concepts that are ambiguous, ethereal, abstract, or intangible. However strongly we may *feel* something, if we cannot see it, hear it, or touch it, we think it must be our imagination. That is why training institutions offer courses to therapists on research but none on intuition and why we speak so much about assessments, diagnoses, data, and test results but so little about felt experiences. Jeffrey Kottler suggests what a course in felt experiences might look like.

I once taught the course Intuition, Power, and Enchantment, designed to help beginning therapists develop their internal capacities for awareness, observation, and sensing. We visited art museums to study thematic symbolism. We went cross-country skiing in the woods to observe the spirit of nature. We experimented with music, poetry, meditation, Tai Chi, yoga, and a dozen other modalities to explore these phenomena, not one of which involved a direct discussion of therapy.

After the sequence of these activities, the learners were challenged to articulate how their experiences made a difference to them as clinicians. They talked a lot about some breakthroughs with their clients, about impasses that were worked through in some particularly difficult relationships. They spoke of feeling more comfortable in their roles as helpers, trusting their instincts tempered by the caution of their training. Most of all, they talked about love and compassion.

When we speak in the language of scientists, we are concerned with measuring outcomes. When we delve into the realm of intuition, that elusive dimension that invisibly guides our behavior, concepts of compassion and love are infinitely more descriptive. All the books that have been written on the subject of relationships in healing sort themselves into basically two categories—the syrupy, feel-good kind that appeal to those with a spiritual orientation (for example, the works of Scott Peck, Leo Buscaglia, or Thomas Moore), and those that are designed more for conventional professionals, valuing documentation of ideas and rational inquiry. In other words, we are given a choice between poetry or science, as if both were not a crucial part of the human experience.

Love is a factor that is often overlooked in what is most healing about relationships. As professionals, we are uncomfortable talking about this concept ordinarily reserved for intimacy between family members or partners. It is a sentimental idea—a romantic one as well.

Yet in the broadest definition of the term, that is, a deep, affectionate regard for another, what is often felt by both client and therapist toward one another certainly qualifies. Clients so often feel impoverished in the love they have received and offered throughout their lives. They have felt frustrated and stymied. Finally, they feel the consistent, soothing care of someone who, although she is paid for her efforts, brings the heart of healing through a transcendent state of affection and regard.

Unlike romantic love, or "limerance," as this passionate feeling has been called, "the other, an act . . . is chosen, not something merely endured" (Tennov, 1979, p. 15). In this sense, love is the choice to feel caring for clients, inviting them to reciprocate. The very image of this book's title, a heart, implies not only that relationship is the essence of what we do, but that our helping efforts emanate from our hearts. We can speak as euphemistically as we like, using such terms as *positive regard* or *caring*, distancing ourselves through clinical language, but it is indeed a kind of love that we are sending and receiving. This is not to say that this is nearly enough to promote healing by itself, nor is it always necessary in high doses in order to accomplish our work, but the act of loving clients is what helps to teach them, just as it does our children, friends, and spouses, that they are worthy of reaching their personal goals. In the following account, Jeffrey Kottler offers another personal example of love in a healing relationship.

> Every several months, I get a letter from a client I have not actually seen for a few years, telling me how he is doing, catching me up on his life, checking in to keep the connection going. Each time I see his handwriting, I feel tears well up in my eyes, a circumstance I feel a little embarrassed about because I wonder if that is not evidence that I care a little too much. We spent a couple of years together, and just like the therapist and client described at the beginning of this chapter, we struck up quite a relationship. It was as if we could read each other's minds. We could finish each other's sentences and express things quite clearly without saying very much at all.
>
> There is no doubt in my mind that I loved (love) this guy, in the absolutely perfect way that is possible without erotic feelings (that I am aware of anyway) and with the boundaries in place characteristic of therapy. I care for him deeply, as I knew he felt the same way toward me. Typically for two men, we did not talk much about these feelings. In retrospect, I am not certain whether it was important that we discuss them, whether they were relevant to why he was in my office in the first place.
>
> Yet because we felt this connection to one another, marked by

affection, respect, and genuine caring, the therapy proceeded as smoothly as I could have dreamed possible. The authentic part of our relationship was not the only ingredient that made a difference. I cannot say, with any assurance, whether it was even the most important one. I do know, however—I know it as surely as I recognize my own face in the mirror—that the "therapeutic love" (or whatever it is called) that existed was quite real. There is a part of me that is embarrassed about revealing this. This is evidence that I am out of control. After all, I love many of my clients. Why don't I get a life, and then I will not need to act out these feelings with unsuspecting people.

It also seems to me that the language associated with love is limiting. I simply do not know of another word that describes as well what happens when we truly connect with someone in any relationship, much less a therapeutic one.

Empathy Revisited

Our word *empathy* goes back to an ancient Greek word that implies an active appreciation of another's felt experience. In therapy, empathy is intended to promote client self-expression, and in some conceptualizations, even healing. Even researchers are comfortable with this concept, since it is the one facilitative condition that is most clearly related to positive therapy outcomes (Luborsky, Crits-Christoph, Mintz, & Auerbach, 1988). Many practitioners, however, are sick of hearing about empathy. We had it drummed into our brains in graduate school, drilled into our helping skills during beginning courses, and are still reminded constantly that whatever this phenomenon really means, it is extremely important. Unfortunately, empathy is often cast in a relatively narrow theoretical mold and taught to beginners as a set of skills designed to communicate understanding to the client. It is as if the theory is that once we learn active listening, reflecting feeling and content, empathy will inevitably result. Developing empathy, however, is a much more complex and interactional process.

Therapist empathy is typically described as the practitioner's understanding of the client as well as of what is being expressed. It is primarily viewed as an affective event. From the broader perspective, empathy involves two distinct dimensions: affective and cognitive. The affective component, with which therapists are usually most familiar, is the therapist's ability to share and experience the client's feelings. This side of empathy has been described as merging with and sharing the inner psychological state of another. We have all had the experience of listening to a client only to find ourselves drawn to her, to feel a tug at our hearts, an understanding that cannot be put into words. The cognitive component is usually defined as the process of accurately perceiving the client's experiential state (Truax & Carkhuff, 1967). This is the part of the therapeutic relationship that is often analyzed rather than simply felt. We ask, What is this client saying to me right now? Which feelings is he expressing? When we stop to make sense of what is going on, our empathy takes on a cognitive as well as affective texture.

In addition to understanding these traditional views, we can also consider empathy as an interactive process between two people. In a unique model, Barrett-Lennard (1981) describes three types of empathy that are part of a sequential interaction between therapist and client. *Empathic resonance* describes the internal responses, both cognitive and affective, that we have to what the client is communicating (*This guy seems to be telling me with his eyes that he is frightened, but his words are saying he has everything under control. I feel his fear. It is as if I am him. My chest feels tight, my breathing constricted. I can feel tremors in my hands as he speaks. I see his hands, as well, shaking a bit. I wonder why he is unwilling to express how he really feels, if this is what he feels. I've got to check it out. Is he ready to hear this yet?*).

During such internal dialogues of empathic resonance, the therapist alternates between affective attunement based on intuition and cognitive processes through which she attempts to make sense of what is occurring. Both affective and cognitive components come together as she makes clinical decisions as to how to proceed next, perhaps by answering the questions, What is this all about? (cognitive) and, Do I sense he can handle this right now? (affective).

The next stage in the cycle, *expressed empathy*, is the therapist's action that results from what was felt, experienced, observed, and analyzed. Both verbal and nonverbal communication express to the client what the therapist understood (after a thoughtful pause and with a warm smile, she says, "I hear you telling me that everything is under control, that you have no worries in the world, but I sense something else as well. I can see your hands clench, the muscles tighten in your neck. You have a sickly smile on your face, as if you were caught doing something you should not have been. But I feel your fear").

Of course, we are off target some of the time, no matter how positive we are about the validity of our perceptions. We may have misread certain cues, projected our own feelings onto the client, or distorted what was going on because of our own needs or personal issues. That is why the third part in the cycle, *received empathy*, which is the client's empathetic reaction, is so critical. The client who appears to be fearful might be thinking, *What? Is this woman deaf or something? I just told her everything was fine and now she is insisting I am afraid. That's a bunch of crap!*

The empathy cycle is an ongoing process rather than a static event. For example, the interaction with the apparently fearful client might proceed in this way:

CLIENT (*Expressed empathy*): Uh. I am not sure that is so. It is not that I feel afraid, as much as I am uncertain about how to continue. I don't know where to go next.

THERAPIST (*Empathic resonance*): [*Oops. Did I miss it that far? He is angry at me now for misunderstanding him. I can see it in those eyes. But I thought I saw fear before. Yes, he is uncertain, but I still feel the fear. Perhaps I should try to be a little more cautious.*] (*Expressed empathy.*) You seem a bit perturbed at

me for misunderstanding you. We may be just quibbling
with words. I had said I could feel some fear and you said it
felt more like uncertainty. Whatever we call it, you do seem
hesitant to go on to the next step.

CLIENT (*Received empathy*): [*Well, that is a little better. I can see
that she is just trying to help me, not hurt me. Maybe I do feel
a little fear. I wonder if it is safe to tell her that?*]

It is clear that empathy is not a simple process of understanding. We might understand very well what the client is feeling but
still not be able to communicate this in such a way that the client
feels understood by us. That is why the perception of empathy is
often more important than its actual enactment. Unless we can
look and appear as if we understand, all the resonance, love, and
compassion in the world are useless.

Since being able to communicate effectively what we understand is such a crucial component of the therapeutic relationship,
it is helpful to be able to adapt the way we operate to the client's
preferred style of received empathy. In the methods proposed a
decade ago by Ericksonian, strategic, and neurolinguistic practitioners, we have all noted how important it is that therapists match
their language to clients' language. There is nothing more frustrating than trying to tell a client how you understand her experience
and observing that she doesn't seem to hear you.

To construct one empathic framework, Bachelor (1988) identified four distinct styles in which clients receive the empathic communication of their therapist: cognitive, affective, shared, and
nurturant. Using this framework, we can adapt the way we express
ourselves in order to accord with the client style we perceive to be
dominant and increase our likelihood of being favorably received.

For those clients who receive primarily *cognitive empathy*, the
therapist shows understanding by employing language that matches
the clients' internal experiences. One client who has experienced
this process, reports:

> I was never very good at expressing myself. It just seems as if my words can't capture what I mean—it is just so frustrating. When I went for my first therapy session, I wasn't sure why, [but] I knew I would just make a fool of myself. The therapist was incredible! How could he know what I was thinking? It just seemed as if he asked the perfect questions that helped me find the right words. He used words that I never thought of that were just what I wanted to say. What he would say would also make me think—think about what else there was inside me. I walked away knowing that I was understood.

With clients who prefer the cognitive style, reflections of content work better than reflections of feeling. Interpretation, rephrasing, and questioning also help them to express what they are thinking and to feel that they are being understood accurately.

Clients who prefer *affective empathy* are also those who are comfortable accessing and expressing feelings. They, too, may find it difficult to express verbally what they are experiencing, but they rely on their intuition to tell them what is going on. They respond well (initially, anyway) to a therapist who matches their style with comparable feeling-based language. Rather than responding to interpretative or questioning interventions, they feel understood when they can stay in the affective domain.

Joan, for example, had been seeing her therapist for three weeks. During that time, the therapist had asked what seemed to be the right questions, but even though Joan knew the therapist was working hard to be helpful, she felt there was something missing. She just did not feel the close connection she had been hoping for. Then, in what she had intended to be her final session, Joan had a feeling that was very different: "It wasn't even anything in particular that she said, but I felt this great sense of intimacy. As I was talking, I even noticed that she seemed to understand what I was trying to say. In fact, it was more than understanding, she seemed to feel what I did. I felt an enormous sense of unloading and relief—then I felt embarrassed, but somehow I knew it was okay."

A more egalitarian style, *shared empathy* is preferred by some clients who are feeling isolated and alone. They are hungry to make an authentic connection with someone, and until they can feel some reciprocal bond with the therapist, trust is not likely to develop. These clients respond especially well to the judicious use of self-disclosure, in which opinions, ideas, thoughts, and feelings flow in both directions, and in which there is a natural and spontaneous exchange. They are after a shared, authentic experience in which they can relate to someone who has experiences in common. One such client noted, "The time I felt most understood by my therapist was one day when I was talking about my parents. Almost without hesitation, she began to tell me about her family life and her struggles with her parents. It was the perfect example, just what I had been saying to her all along. I knew it wasn't one of those times when she was just trying to make me feel comfortable—it was real."

The client who prefers *nurturant empathy* has a strong desire for a sustained caring presence rather than any particular response mode that might be offered by the therapist. This is the client who wants to feel love and compassion rather than empathic resonance, who might say, "I am not sure what specific things my therapist has ever said to me. What has been most important to me is that I have known that she was always there, she was always on my side, always supportive of me. It really didn't ever matter what I was feeling. If I was sad, I knew she would be there. If I was mad, I knew she would listen and not hold it against me. She just knew me, she just knew how to be there."

These examples highlight that empathy can contribute to the authentic dimension only when it is therapist felt (resonated), therapist communicated (expressed), and client perceived (received). Our therapeutic flexibility will depend on our developing a range of ways to understand and communicate our understanding rather than our relying on any one standard response. Since we must match our responses to the client's perceptual styles in order to be maximally productive, it is up to us to assess the style of each client and tailor our responses to a mode that allows us to communicate what we feel and how we understand the client's situation. What makes this challenge especially difficult is that these different types of empathy may also vary in their effectiveness depending on the stage of the therapeutic process, the goals of treatment, and the personality of the client. For example, affective empathy may be crucial in the initial stages of therapy but of less importance during termination. Also, some clients may respond to cognitive empathy at some points along the way, but later in the same session want to be responded to on another level.

In one other variation of empathy that emphasizes gender differences, Nevels and Coché (1993) studied the practices of distinguished women therapists. Offering a feminist perspective on the subject, these prominent clinicians spoke about how their femaleness allowed them to combine empathy with power. It was in their personal relationships that they learned as much about listening and loving as in their professional training: "What makes therapy work is what makes relationships work: a trust in the process, the give and take of a mutual effort to move through the hard times to get to the better times, a respect for the person's own uniqueness" (p. 66). The respondents to their survey also articulated, in a way that men rarely speak about, how their experiences as parents and children influenced the ways they understand and relate to their clients.

In whatever form empathy is delivered, this strong thread of healing is a foundation for everything else that we do. Sometimes we believe, and even tell clients, that the things they are doing—abusing drugs, flirting with disaster, committing crimes, abusing others' rights, running away from troubles, or sabotaging relationships—are downright stupid, if not evidence of lunacy. Yet we are clear, consistent, and passionate about how thoroughly and completely we are in the clients' corner ("I could not disagree more strongly with what you are doing, but you know that whatever you decide, and however you choose to act, I will be here for you to deal with the consequences. I care about you so much that I am willing to tell you how inappropriately I think you are acting, even though I know that you will not like what I have to say. That, after all, is what a healthy relationship is like between people: we are able to tell one another what we think and feel while we still communicate a deep caring and commitment to work things through").

Sharing the Therapist's Self

Mutual self-disclosure is one of the most common ways that empathy and authenticity develop in the therapeutic relationship. When the therapist is revealed not only as a competent professional but as a genuine human being, there is a greater likelihood an authentic connection will evolve. While most of us would agree that self-disclosure can be helpful in this regard, certain questions remain: What types of disclosure are most helpful? How can disclosure make the therapeutic difference we intend?

A useful approach to the ways therapists reveal themselves distinguishes those revelations that are *self-involving* from those that are *self-disclosing*. Typically, self-involving statements require the therapist to express his current feelings toward the client, as they occur in the session ("I feel so much closer to you since you shared that"). Whereas self-involving statements reveal feelings the therapist has in the immediate present, self-disclosing statements focus on the past ("I recall a similar time in my life in which I couldn't deal with a situation, and like you, I just shut down for awhile, kept my distance from everyone"). Statements such as this, however, although ordinarily encompassing what we think of as typical self-disclosure to build trust and credibility in a relationship, may not be as valuable as the self-involving variety (Watkins, 1990). Both types of self-disclosure represent pivotal interventions on the part of the therapist, for better or worse. If therapist self-revelations are among the best things we can do to promote closeness in the relationship, especially when they are timely, concise, and appropriate, they can also be among the most abused interventions. As long as we are talking about ourselves, even with the best of intentions, the focus has been taken away from the client, who may already feel unimportant. It is for this reason that self-disclosures may not be as effective as self-involving statements and, when they are used, should be as concise as possible, used only when other interventions will not work as well; relied on only when it is certain the therapist is not meeting her own needs in the process; clear in what they are intended to accomplish, so the client does not wonder why the revelation is taking place; and followed up with efforts to help the client personalize what was said (Kottler, 1993).

Like all other factors in the relationship, disclosures take place in a cultural context, and ethnicity and cultural norms certainly appear to have a major impact on whether clients prefer a therapist who discloses personal information or one who does not. For example, with many native American clients, it would be just as rude and inappropriate to reveal personal details of our lives as it would be to intrude into their life circumstances. With clients of many other cultures, as well, talking about ourselves, revealing intimate feelings or stories of our lives without explicit permission to do so, might be viewed as insensitivity or arrogance.

Authenticity Within the Working Alliance

Jeffrey Kottler recalls meeting a new client who, during the intake interview, resisted quite strongly the idea that client and therapist would work together within an intimate, authentic kind of relationship:

> At that time, I virtually insisted that all my relationships with clients be warm, engaging, intimate encounters in which the conditions of genuineness, authenticity, transparency, and empathy prevailed. Yet this client seemed not to care whether I liked or

respected him. Furthermore, he had very little interest in getting to know me. His attitude was, "Look, Doc, can't we dispense with this foreplay stuff and get right down to business? I am not really all that interested in letting you get close to me; I have friends and family for that. What I am asking you for is some specific help sorting through this problem. If you can't do that in a straightforward, businesslike way, maybe I should see somebody else."

Of course, I said to myself (and later complained to my colleagues), this guy had some serious unresolved intimacy issues, but if I am really honest with myself, I have to acknowledge that working the way he requested did prove to be helpful to him. Although I prefer to do relatively long-term relationship-oriented therapy, he seemed to respond best to a very short-term consultation based on a relationship that had very few of the characteristics that I was used to.

As is evident from cases such as this, authenticity may be desirable in therapeutic relationships but not necessarily needed in strong doses. It has already been mentioned how many other professionals—doctors, attorneys, hairdressers, teachers, supervisors—also employ a kind of working alliance. In each cases, one person acts as a guide for the other in reaching desired goals. The working alliance may thus be seen as a central component of any situation in which one person wishes to change something about him- or herself and seeks the services of another person who is viewed as a change agent (Bordin, 1979).

The term *working alliance* represents the collaboration between client and therapist that is "real," as opposed to the transference neurosis favored by the psychoanalyst, with its projection of fantasy. This collaboration, with assigned roles and responsibilities, is seen as the basis for working together toward treatment goals that have been mutually negotiated. It is viewed as a joining of forces between client and therapist, a mutual, interactive collaboration that, while crucial to any therapeutic progress that is made, is hardly the single key to successful change. Rather, what is primarily healing in this alliance is that it makes it possible for the client to accept and follow through on whatever treatment program has been mutually agreed upon (Bordin, 1980).

From this perspective, the authentic engagement in therapeutic relationships is helpful because it lends credence to other active elements (Horvath & Greenberg, 1989). Practically every mode of psychological helping now acknowledges that a universal therapeutic ingredient, operating as a primary or secondary process, as a sufficient or insufficient condition, is certainly the alliance that is developed between client and therapist (Kottler, 1991). The strength of this relationship, the relative emphasis placed on it as a significant factor, will vary depending on the orientation of the therapist and the needs of the client. Nevertheless, the working alliance has some universal factors that are operative in all therapeutic work.

Components of the Therapeutic Alliance

The working alliance is quite a different model of "realness" in relationships than the authenticity described earlier. If the latter emphasizes empathy and compassion, the former connotes a businesslike arrangement in which the emphasis is on completing tasks designed to reach stated goals. The working alliance is viewed as being composed of these aspects: agreement on goals, agreement on tasks, and development of an emotional bond. Any emotional bond that develops during this process is considered the by-product of two people working together under such intimate conditions. Both participants in healing relationships enter the alliance with preconceptions about what they would like to see happen.

The client, for example, may be thinking along the following lines: "I will tell him what is bothering me. He will listen carefully and then tell me what the problem is, probably something in my unconscious. Then he will tell me what to do to make my life better." In contrast, the therapist will have quite a different agenda, one that involves self-determination and personal responsibility. He will see his role as that of a consultant more than that of an advice giver and expert problem solver. Whereas the client imagines the relationship will be similar to her experiences with her family doctor, the therapist expects an alliance that is more egalitarian. These divergent expectations can be negotiated into a consensual agreement that is satisfactory to both participants and that forms the basis for both emotional attachment and goal attainment.

The implications of this premise are profound: it suggests that effectiveness depends less on what the goals of therapy are than on both (or all) participants' being in agreement about what they will do together. The importance of consensus in the working alliance is illustrated by the case of a graduate student who was feeling frustrated in her relationship with her advisor. She felt devalued by him, treated as if she were "only a student" and not really important compared to priorities like preparing for class and doing research. It was her expectation that an advisor would be more than someone who would just tell her what classes to take and sign her registration forms. However, the advisor had on other occasions attempted to engage some of his students in personal discussions about how their classes were going and how they were feeling about their training. Most of them indicated quite clearly that they found these inquiries to be intrusive ("Just sign my form so I can go register"). He was thus operating under a different set of assumptions, seeing the working alliance between instructor and student as an administrative rather than intimate relationship.

The advisor and the student eventually addressed their different expectations for their relationship, principally because they were both willing to engage one another in a more authentic manner. The advisor was willing to make some adjustments in which he made himself more accessible to deal with personal concerns as they related to professional development. The student, as well, realized that her advisor could not, and should not, serve in a counseling capacity. They were able to reach agreement on what they would and would not work on and, together, created a collaborative relationship that proved to be quite satisfying.

Critical to the structure of any working alliance, whether between advisor and student or therapist and client, are the defined tasks that each participant engages in during the exchange. This is essentially the substance, the "magic" of the therapeutic process: the actions that are requested by the therapist and acted upon by the client in order to accomplish the specified goals. Although the three aspects of the working alliance are not restricted to therapeutic relationships, since they are evident in educational and other healing encounters, there are two characteristics that are unique to this model of the therapeutic relationship. First, no other professional helping relationship has emphasized *mutual* interdependence so explicitly. Second, the working alliance is not viewed as a mechanism for change but as a *vehicle* that facilitates the success of various therapeutic actions.

The Authentic Dimension

This chapter has outlined several ways that therapeutic relationships represent very real, authentic engagements between people. The stronger the personal connection between therapist and client, the more solid the therapeutic alliance. Similarly, the more realistic the perceptions of the therapist and client, the stronger the alliance. As this connection strengthens, the authentic nature of the encounter deepens.

From the client's viewpoint, the authentic and personal dimensions of the relationship are often those that are most memorable. For many therapists, as well, the realness of therapeutic encounters is related to their own perceived satisfaction with the way things are proceeding. The perspective in this chapter, however, composes only part of the picture. There are additional significant forces at work in the authentic and personal dimensions, among them the dynamics of social interaction. It is through this lens that we peer next to further explore the authentic dimension.

Chapter Seven

Impress Me, Influence Me

Each of us has the opportunity to develop an infinite number of interpersonal relationships. At a party we gravitate to certain people, while ignoring others. We jump at the chance to talk to some people on the phone but conveniently forget to return the calls of others. It is indeed perplexing why we become involved with certain individuals and not others, why some relationships lose their appeal while others flourish, and why, in some relationships, both partners remain committed even when faced with adverse situations.

Throughout, this book takes the position that therapeutic relationships are a special kind of universally occurring close personal relationship and, therefore, are governed by some of the same principles as other close relationships. The last chapter examined helping relationships through the lens of authenticity. This chapter looks through quite a different lens to shed further light on the mechanisms by which individuals are affected and influenced in relationships. Also, whereas previous chapters relied on the language and concepts of phenomenology to describe the essence of relationship experiences, this chapter adopts a social psychological orientation. Consistent with this perspective is the more scientific approach that this chapter takes while examining the dynamics and processes of social interaction.

The social psychological viewpoint has been all but ignored by those of us operating in the clinical realm. It is difficult enough to keep up with literature in our specific area of interest, much less branch out into the vast land of social psychology. When we do venture that far, many of the laboratory studies do not appear relevant to us as practitioners, and as we wade through the research, we may wonder if the conclusions are anything but common sense.

Nevertheless, there is great benefit in expanding our understanding of the authentic dimensions of the therapeutic relationship by including the perspective offered by social psychology. Healing relationships are far too complex for us to think that we can restrict ourselves to concepts grown in our own backyard. We must peer over a few fences to see what our neighbors are doing and then adapt some of these ideas to the special challenges that we confront on our own turf.

I Like You, So You Can Help Me

We have all had the experience in which what we do in the first few minutes with a client sets the stage for the rest of therapy. Although we usually do not label it attraction, this event plays a critical role in therapeutic as well as other close personal relationships. A therapist is attractive when the client perceives that the therapist is approachable, friendly, and compatible, and holds values similar to client values. This feature was discussed in the previous chapter in the context of being authentic. Therapist self-disclosure that is designed specifically to enhance perceived similarity is only one way that attractiveness is developed ("Yeah. I know what you mean. I had run-ins with a few teachers myself"). The bottom line is, quite simply, that unless a person feels attracted (sexually, intellectually, interpersonally, or emotionally) to someone, he or she will not invest much time or energy into developing that relationship. No matter how professional we may attempt to remain in a relationship, we must also recognize that our techniques and interventions will rarely be effective without the initial attraction that pulls the client in.

Attractiveness is somewhat of a paradox. On the one hand, there is the stereotype that attractive people get everything they want. On the other hand, many of us believe that it should not be the physical nature of people that is the major element in attraction. Numerous studies have found a strong relationship between physical attractiveness and relationship interest (Brislin & Lewis, 1968; Curran & Lippold, 1975), yet the construct of attraction is not as simple as looking pretty. In fact, in the context of what therapists do, interpersonal similarity is probably more important. Research not only supports the idea that those similar in personality and attitude are initially attracted to each other (Barry, 1970; Boyden, Carrol, & Maier, 1984) but also the view that both personality and attitude play a role in the development of long-term close personal relationships (Schullo & Alperson, 1984; Thelen, Fishbein, & Tatten, 1985). It is also the case that similarity in attitude influences both the development and maintenance of relationships. It was Neimeyer (1984; Neimeyer & Neimeyer, 1983) who extended the role of similarity by suggesting that people tend to be attracted to those who are similar to them in terms of the complexity with which personal perceptions and thoughts are organized.

One of Sue Whiston's cases illustrates some of the importance of attraction.

Wooson came in for therapy because his Caucasian wife had given him an ultimatum that she would leave him if he did not. He explained to me that he really did not desire to be there, but he did not wish to lose his wife. Furthermore, he wanted me to tell him what he could do to keep her from leaving. Wooson's title was Assistant Director of Computer Services, at a large university in the Midwest. He had been born in China, but had moved to the United States when he was three. His parents never learned very much English, and he was the conduit between his parents and the American culture. He explained that he was raised to work hard and that he did that. In fact, he had persuaded his wife recently to have an abortion. He did not wish to start a family at this time because he needed to concentrate on his job. He now just wanted to know the correct way to keep his wife.

As the therapist in this case, I conveniently forgot much of my training in client-centered therapy. I had the sense that if I did not appear "attractive" to Wooson in the first fifteen minutes, if I could not help him to like and respect me, he would be one of those many minority clients who only attend a single session. I said in a direct, simple, and quiet way, "I am a woman, like your wife, and I would want flowers from my husband if that had happened to me. Go buy your wife flowers and come back and tell me how it went next week." Violating everything I had ever learned, I chose to conform to his vision of what was most helpful: I told him exactly what to do. Wooson returned for eight more sessions continuing to seek my "advice."

The Battle for Best Impression

As appears to have been the case with Wooson, when a therapist impresses a client as an attractive (that is, competent, credible, and so forth) professional, the client is open to what the therapist has to offer. And, indeed, one of the critical concepts from social psychology applicable to therapeutic relationships is the notion of *impression management*. The degree to which we are able to establish and maintain favorable impressions with our clients is directly related to their willingness to stay involved with us. Of course, this phenomenon works in both directions in that clients are working just as hard to impress us. In Wooson's case, it was critical for him to maintain his image. If he had lost too much dignity he would not have been able to continue working with the therapist.

The process of maintaining appropriate client and therapist images continued in Wooson's sessions.

As therapy progressed, I learned how to interact with Wooson; he taught me how to be with him. I realized that I had to be careful in how I spoke to him.

By coming to me in the first place, Wooson was in a cultural bind. On the one hand, he was interested in seeking and taking my advice. On the other hand, he needed to "save face" by not compromising his own self-image. He was relentless in his pursuit of having me believe that he was competent, aware, and capable of running his life and working with his wife. I had to cast my suggestions as though I were an expert giving guidance, but these directions also had to be offered as if they were his ideas. It was like a dance, a theater of impressions.

What makes the battle of impression management so important is that the presentations of therapist and client influence the future course of their relationship. Therapeutic relationships are essentially object lessons in power. The struggle for control over the agenda, the content and style of interactions, and the very momentum of where things go and at what velocity are the primary tasks of the early stages of treatment. The challenge is that we must be careful to demonstrate what the client most expects from us, while still remaining true to our professional standards. During the early stages of therapy, especially during the first minutes of an initial encounter, clients are sizing us up as intently as we are forming diagnostic impressions of them. They are looking to see if we match their expectations, as well as determining if we will allow them to preserve their own self-images. The paradox is that in order to help them, we must act as if we will respect their current conceptions of themselves, knowing that at some point, we may very well have to challenge those self-images in favor of others that we believe would be more self-enhancing.

It is not enough for either client or therapist to create just a favorable impression; it must also be one that conforms to what the one person intends and the other expects (Friedlander & Schwartz, 1985). If, for example, the therapist wishes to appear as a friendly confidante but the client prefers a parental figure, there will not be a successful match. Similarly, if the therapist is trying to convey an impression that she is a wise sage but the client is looking for a nurturer, there are likely to be problems in the relationship. That is why some experienced practitioners have learned to ask clients what they are looking for before the practitioner adopts too strong a position.

To illustrate the importance of this battle of impressions, consider the following internal dialogue that might take place during an initial session.

THERAPIST: *I notice that he says "you" a lot but does not talk about himself as "I."*

CLIENT: *She seems awful young to be doing this kind of work. I wonder how old she is?*

THERAPIST: *There seems to be a lot of evidence of passivity and dependence. I wonder what his relationship is like with his wife?*

CLIENT: *She does not seem to like me very much. She keeps nodding a lot but she doesn't say a lot.*

THERAPIST: *Definitely passive-aggressive tendencies. He probably has trouble being direct, so I will have to be careful to check his reactions to what I say to him.*

CLIENT: *I'm just not sure if this lady can help me. She seems nice and all, but I wonder what she is really like. What does she really think of me?*

To some extent, all therapists are in the business of theater. We construct a stage from which to act out our dramas, complete with props that create the perfect atmosphere. Books, diplomas, muted lighting, comfortable chairs—all convey a perfect balance, a professional setting that resembles a study where profound thought takes place. We dress the part as well, using our wardrobe to convey the image we wish to project. Clients are looking for evidence the therapist is knowledgeable, can understand, and can bring relief. It is as if at least part of becoming involved in the relationship is based on the early impressions each participant gathers of the other and the "grades," or evaluations, given to those impressions.

Some therapists may claim that all impression management is really just a form of manipulation, but that is not what is happening here. It is not that the clients are lying about themselves or that we are manipulating appearances to make particular impressions. If we look through the social psychological lens, we can see that the battle of impression management is probably a natural and inevitable process within relationship development. We must realize that both client and therapist are doing their best to present themselves as they wish to be seen. For the client, it is a struggle to be viewed as valuable and worthy. For the therapist it is a challenge to become important enough to the client to make a difference. Inevitable conflicts arise when the client desires approval and validation and the therapist wishes to be respected.

It is our behavior that is most critical in conveying the image that we wish to communicate. To be effective, we sometimes radiate confidence that we hardly feel. We speak like authorities about things that we are actually uncertain about. We show patience that we hardly feel, sometimes bursting inside to take the client by the scruff of his neck and shake him into sensibility. On the other side of the relationship, clients spend a lot of their internal activity asking themselves such questions as, Am I appearing too crazy? Can this professional help me? Does he really like me? Both clients and therapists are chameleons, doing their best to be what the other needs them to be in order to establish trust and credibility or to gain help.

You Seem to Know What You Are Doing

For Wooson, the therapist became someone in whom he could trust, and therefore he could be influenced by the therapist. Despite the great differences between him and his therapist, Wooson was willing to follow through with her suggestions and continue in their relationship. Without the initial attraction to the therapist and the belief that this relationship would help, Wooson would never have returned. What is even more curious is that the suggestions of the therapist were the very same ones that Wooson's wife had been making! But something in the therapeutic relationship made a difference so that he was willing to listen to the suggestions when they came from the therapist.

We have all had this experience of clients who believed in us so much they were willing to do most anything we asked of them. The lenses of other schools of thought might illuminate this behavior as dependent, or lacking in personal boundaries. The social psychological lens proposes that these experiences illustrate the therapeutic power attractiveness can wield. Strong (1968) was among the first to apply the principles of social psychology to clinical applications. He suggested that psychological change was an interpersonal influence process that depended on the client's perceiving the therapist as a credible resource to which he could turn. In order to be credible, therapists must be perceived by their clients as not only interpersonally attractive (as discussed earlier) but also professionally expert and personally trustworthy.

The therapist is an *expert*, in this context, to the degree to which the client views him as a competent resource for help in the presenting concerns. All cultures grant helpers some degree of expert status. In many cultures, the shaman occupies a sanctioned role that brings with it the assumption of great knowledge and skill. In our culture as well, our reputations in our communities, objective evidence of training (diplomas, titles, office surroundings), and behavioral evidence (delivery of speech, method of questioning, confidence in presentation) all contribute to clients' perceptions of our expertness. This, however, will only take us so far.

None of us would be naïve enough to suggest that the perception of expertness arises only from external trappings. It is during the initial sessions that clients find additional cues about whether we can be considered expert. Often, it is our more indirect actions—thought-provoking questions, accurate interpretations and reflections, sincere and valuable offerings—that contribute to our clients' perceptions that we know what we are doing. Tom calls this happening among his clients.

Bob, for example, was very reluctant to come to therapy. He strongly believed that no one outside his family could ever understand what went on between him and his wife. He also believed, even more adamantly, that simply talking about the matter was a waste of time. At home, when he and his wife tried to talk about their difficulties, it only ended in fights.

When I first met with Bob, it was clear that he was uncomfortable. The usual means by which I try to establish some credibility with clients did not make a dent. In fact, it seemed clear that my diplomas and professional demeanor were actually intimidating him. The more we talked, the more aware I became how different we were. He was from a blue-collar background and had lived a very difficult childhood with parents who did not care much for him. He had been left on his own from a very early age.

What has always been curious to me is that, for two people who were so different, we worked together quite well for a long time. I later discovered that nothing else I could have done with Bob would have worked as well as the efforts I made to challenge many of his assumptions. It was my direct confrontations that established my expertise in his eyes, far more than any credentials.

The therapist is *trustworthy* to the degree that the client believes the therapist will work in the client's best interests. While all of us intend to be trustworthy, the client's perception of this dimension is based primarily on our reputation, as well as on more indirect aspects of sincerity and openness and a lack of motivation for personal gain.

What is most important about these three dimensions of attractiveness, expertness, and trustworthiness is that they give us a perspective on how to set the stage for a therapeutic relationship. In Chapter Six discussed genuineness and empathy appear as critica components of the authentic dimension. The social psychologic; perspective suggests that perceived credibility, based on initi attraction and impression management, is yet another operati principle.

For many of us, the concept of managing attraction and impressions runs against our professional and personal beliefs about the genuineness of the therapeutic relationship, and indeed, framing authenticity in terms of impressing and then influencing the client is a startling contrast. There is evidence, however, that these concepts are valid. For example, LaCrosse (1980) found that initial client perceptions of a therapist's expertness accounted for 31 percent of the variance in favorable therapeutic outcome (p. 324). Confirming these results, McNeill, May, and Lee (1987) found that premature terminators viewed their therapists as less expert, attractive, and trustworthy than did clients who completed therapy successfully (for additional sources that summarize studies on the power of these three therapist qualities, see Cormier & Cormier, 1991; Heppner & Claiborn, 1989). Of course, the terms expert, attractive, and trustworthy are not necessarily descriptions of the way therapists actually *are*, but rather represent how therapists need to be *perceived* by clients. This point explains, in part, how some practitioners who function ineffectively in their own lives can be skilled at making good impressions when the meter is running. As abhorrent as the idea may seem, it does not appear all that crucial that we be authentic, just that we act that way, convincingly. Nevertheless, since we are dealing primarily with what the client believes about us, and the client's beliefs will be influenced by what we believe (think of the placebo effect or the Hawthorne effect for example), we probably have the potential to be a *lot* more persuasive when we genuinely believe we are competent professionals (even when this belief certainly could be based on distortion).

Another aspect of the phenomenon of making impressions worth emphasizing involves the cultural thread of healing. The factors that affect clients' perception of trustworthiness will be different in an African-American adolescent and a middle-aged woman. To find the key to establishing credibility, we must know what each client considers impressive, a finding that will depend on clients' historical backgrounds. Thus, the single most useful question we can ask a new client is, "What have been your previous experiences with being helped with concerns like this in the past?" From the client's answers, we can then trace a blueprint of those expectations that are most likely to be valued. For example, a client might respond, "Hey, I don't know. I once saw this guy before, but he didn't say much. Just looked at me and took notes. I thought that was pretty weird. Another time, I was sent to see this lady, a social worker or something, and she was pretty straight with me [authentic dimension]. She reminded me of what my aunt use to say to me [projected dimension]. In my family, in my culture, it is common to talk this way [cultural credibility]. Anybody with any authority whatsoever is respected because she is direct and straightforward." With many clients, we are often able to discover, just this precisely, what we need to do in order to establish ourselves as credible, attractive, and trustworthy experts who are likely to be influential.

What Does It Compare To?

The concepts of attraction and impression management describe how and why people initiate a relationship but do not explain the process by which relationships move to a deeper level. However, another social psychological concept, *social exchange theory*, explains why some relationships work while others do not. This theory of relationship development is based on a utilitarian economic model that suggests behavior is motivated by individuals' maximizing profits and minimizing losses (Blau, 1964; Thibaut & Kelley, 1959).

It is only through a degree of satisfaction and commitment that any relationship can continue to prosper. *Satisfaction* is a form of profit. When people receive some reward as a result of their interaction with a person, they continue to seek out the same person in the future. When the costs they must expend to maintain the relationship exceed the potential gain, the relationship ends. *Commitment* (motivation) is based not only on the success of the current relationship but also the client's assessment of what other options are available.

For example, a client is feeling apprehensive about therapy. She has attended the first session and found it a mildly unpleasant experience. It felt good to unburden herself (satisfaction), but this was a perfect stranger she talked to. It felt humiliating to tell him about the intimate details of her life (cost, or loss). Moreover, she does not really have the time or the money to devote to this enterprise (further losses). Using social psychological arithmetic, we could predict that her ongoing commitment to this relationship, in terms of investing time, money, energy, and risk, would be directly related to what other people in her life she might go to as an alternative. In this case, because she had already exhausted her supply of perceived options (her minister, older sister, and roommate), she was willing to stay with the therapeutic relationship in the hope that, ultimately, the pain, discomfort, and inconvenience costs would be compensated by gains.

In other words, clients feel satisfied in their therapeutic relationships as long as they continue to get "good value" for the time and money that they spend. Some of their rewards come in the form of feeling supported, accepted, and understood. Certainly, these rewards can feel good in and of themselves, even when the client does not reach stated treatment objectives. This effect explains why some clients will continue in therapy indefinitely, never reaching their desired goals but enjoying the process in much the same way that other people enjoy weekly massages.

Along with these rewards comes a cost, not only in terms of time and money expended but also in terms of effort. After all, we do ask clients to face their demons, to get off their backsides and do that which they fear the most. Finally, as the client in the previous example found, therapy is expensive in terms of the humiliation that may be suffered: it is embarrassing to ask a stranger for help and to do so when one feels most vulnerable. It is for these reasons that the risk of the client's dropping out of the relationship is so great during the initial meetings, when the costs seem to outweigh the benefits.

In the economic model, the guide an individual uses to make decisions about whether to continue relationships is called the comparison level (CL). The CL is any personal standard against which a person measures a current relationship to assess its degree of satisfaction. People are constantly making comparisons in their minds between present relationships and those of the past (*How is this similar to other relationships I have had? This person is kind of like a friend I once had, but that was not nearly this intense. She also kind of reminds me of my mother, only more tolerant and less judgmental. She is also much nicer than the school counselor I once saw but not as warm as my minister*).

Clients, like anyone else, enter a relationship with certain expectations, which they then use in judging their level of satisfaction with the current interaction. Note, for example, how two clients approach their therapy with the same practitioner quite differently. In each of the following cases, the therapist is doing similar things, but the client comments reveal that the results are quite different. The first client reports, "This is frustrating for me. I mean, there are plenty of other people whom I can talk to if I want. I resent having to tell him a bunch of stuff that *I* already know. When I saw a therapist once before, we went through all this stuff. I wish that we could get on with things already." However, the second client says, "I don't really have anyone else in my life whom I can trust. I have never had an experience quite like this before. I think it is wonderful that I can talk about whatever I want and that I have someone in my corner who supports me. He lets me go at my own pace, which I greatly appreciate."

Satisfaction alone is not enough. Participants must also be committed if the relationship is to be maintained. Commitment is based on the comparison level of available alternatives. That is, people compare to outcomes of the current relationship the outcomes they think they might receive in another relationship if they invested the same degree of energy.

Investment as a Road to Satisfaction

It appears that there is also an important relationship between relationship commitment and investment. *Investment* is the output required to remain in the relationship. It can include effort, time, energy, or other costs. Furthermore, these commodities could not be recovered if the relationship were to end. Therefore, as the amount of investment grows, the level of commitment correspondingly expands and increases.

Commitment that develops by way of investment can result in both positive and negative outcomes. On the one hand, if the relationship is satisfying, the client will feel as if his investments had paid off and will continue to feel committed to the relationship. On the other hand, if the client invests a great deal and the relationship remains unsatisfying, a dilemma results that is similar to the one faced by those who invest the stock market ("Should I cut my losses and invest elsewhere, or is it better to wait things out and hope the situation improves? After all, there is already so much time and energy involved; it would be a shame to walk away now"). So goes the reasoning of those who realize that they are putting a heck of a lot more into a relationship than they are receiving in return. Thus, paradoxically, bad investments may actually strengthen rather than weaken attachment and commitment to a relationship (Brehm, 1992). That is why clients will sometimes stay in therapy (or a marriage) for years, reporting that they have received relatively little for their effort yet unwilling to leave.

Commitment also describes the strength of a person's intentions to continue a relationship. The following factors are related to increasing the degree of commitment in a relationship:

Explicitness of behavior. Publicly expressed commitment to a relationship increases commitment more than privately expressed commitment.

Importance of the behavior. Expression of a positive attitude toward the relationship to someone known contributes more to commitment than expression of positive views to a stranger.

Number of actions. Consistently positive actions in regard to the relationship produce more commitment than infrequent actions.

Degree of volition. Commitment is greater when a person expresses positive reactions toward a relationship freely rather than under coercion.

Degree of effort. Commitment is increased when a person goes to the trouble to act positively toward the relationship.

Once we understand the factors that enhance commitment, we can use them to enhance the therapeutic relationship. We may, for example, encourage the client to act cooperatively in a way that requires some degree of effort to comply ("I want you not only to think about what just took place but also to talk to those you are close to about how they perceive you"). We should also understand that commitment fluctuates naturally during the therapeutic process—sometimes to the point where the client has one foot out the door—and during other times of excessive dependency. For example, clients can become so invested in a therapeutic relationship that the cost of working with someone else is considered too high ("It is too much trouble to develop intimacy with someone else now that you already know me"). Hence, they may remain in a long-term therapeutic relationship purely for the feeling of belonging.

It is also interesting to apply this same model to the commitment that therapists feel to their relationships, as Jeffrey Kottler has done.

Particularly with some of my more challenging cases, my moods change from session to session, and sometimes from minute to minute. Sometimes, I think there is no amount of money in the world to compensate for the abuse I feel I am suffering. Here this client is, playing games with my head, trying to get underneath my skin. (Yeah. Yeah. I know he is only doing the best he can.) And I am putting up with it because it is my job.

Then, there is a glimmer of hope. The guy seems to be understanding something that, previously, seemed out of reach. *Wow!* I think. *Maybe it is worth all this work and aggravation. In fact, this is downright wonderful!*

And then: *Damn! He was only faking. Yanking my chain. He knows just how to get to me. Maybe I can get him to take a break from therapy for awhile, give ourselves a vacation from one another. Well, that's a lie. I just don't feel like investing anymore of myself in a relationship that doesn't seem to be meeting my needs. Since he isn't paying much for my time, isn't committing himself enough to this relationship . . . actually, that is not strictly true. On the one hand, he is investing himself, just not as much as I prefer. On the other hand . . .*

And so continues the inner dialogue we often go through, in which we question, just as our clients do, whether the amount of commitment we are making to the relationship is reaping sufficient benefits for the relationship to continue. Of course, being paid professionals, we are not supposed to admit publicly that our needs are a major factor. The reality, however, is that we each have our own style of chasing away those clients we do not really wish to work with (Kottler, 1992a). A number of these ploys follow:

"Gee, I'm sorry. The only appointment time I have available next week is at 7:00 A.M."

"You seem to be awfully defensive about this. Maybe you just can't handle the heat."

"Let's take a break for awhile. Therapy often works better with greater time in between sessions, to give you the chance to practice what you are learning."

"Hey, if you don't like the way things are going, perhaps it
would be better for you to see someone else."

The Cognitive Aspect of Close Relationships

None of us would argue the existence of a cognitive component in
the development of relationships. However, it is surprising that the
available information regarding how people perceive, organize, and
cognitively process relationship experiences has had so little impact
on our field and our client interventions (Lopez, 1993). An area
that could be especially fertile for us is the process of attributing
and creating meaning in the relationship.

It may very well be that each participant's interpretations of
the other person's behaviors are even more significant than the
behaviors themselves (Bradbury & Fincham, 1990), a view consistent with the principles of cognitive therapy many of us already
employ. For example, an individual may be irritated when she finds
towels left on the bathroom floor. Now she could attribute these to
her husband's running late that morning and assume that he simply forgot the towels on the floor. But she could also attribute the
towels to her husband's not really caring about her, since she has
asked him previously not to leave the towels on the floor.

People are most likely to engage in such attributional activity
when they are faced with novel stimuli (such as a new therapeutic
relationship) or when disruptive events occur (such as those that
lead clients to seek help in the first place). In the presence of either
circumstance, people are motivated to search for causes that
explain things, in order to reduce their anxiety over uncertainty
and the unknown (Heider, 1958). Their goal is to figure out what is
happening so that equilibrium can be reestablished (Lopez, 1993).
However, the research on attributional activity has suggested that,
while attempting to explain the world, people are not particularly
accurate observers of others' behavior, especially in those situations
in which they are emotionally involved (Elwood & Jacobson,

1982). Two types of attributional bias influence misperception. The first is the manner in which the perceiver believes the problematic behavior is controllable. The perceiver may see the causes of an event or behaviors as dispositional (internal) or situational (external) and will view a relationship partner's behavior negatively if it is seen to be dispositional, since this attribution fosters the belief that the partner is the perpetrator of sinister deeds. By contrast, if the perceiver attributes the partner's behavior to situational causes, then the belief will be that the partner made an unfortunate reaction to a "bad" situation. For example, if a therapist is five minutes late for a session, the client may attribute this circumstance to causes that are unintentional (traffic congestion or a crisis with another client), or the client may attribute it to the therapist's careless nature or lack of concern.

The second type of attributional bias is the perceiver's view of whether behaviors are global or situationally specific. Negative behavior attributed to internal causes might also be perceived to happen globally, that is, across a variety of situations. Those same behaviors attributed to situationally specific events will have a less pervasive effect on the relationship. The wife who finds the towels on the bathroom floor, might well attribute that behavior to her husband's not caring for her feelings and his lack of commitment to the relationship if he has also left dirty dishes in the sink (another sign that he does not care!).

Many of the studies regarding the nature of attributions have focused on married couples. Jacobson, McDonald, Follette, and Berley (1985) found that distressed spouses were more likely to attribute positive partner behavior to situations and negative partner behavior to dispositions. Similarly, Fincham and O'Leary (1983) found that nondistressed married couples attributed the positive acts of their partner to volitional intent, while distressed couples attributed their partners negative acts to volitional intent. Clearly, attributions have self-fulfilling qualities, creating those confirmatory biases which encourage the members of relationships to see what they already believe to be true.

Cognitive attributions influence whether a relationship founders or develops into a close and intimate connection. If our intention is to increase the likelihood that our clients perceive their relationships with us as positive, then much of our efforts should be (and are) directed towards shaping clients' cognitive activity in such a way that they are not unduly alarmed by the unpredictable aspects of therapeutic work. Furthermore, we systematically emphasize our preference for their making attributions that are internally and situationally based, and we increase the client's tolerance for conflict by using cognitive activity as a means to avoid overreacting.

Conversely, we must also look at the attributions we make about our clients. This is especially true when we work with so-called difficult clients, who do not meet our expectations or needs. Under such conditions, we are often predisposed to call them derogatory names, such as "borderline," "noncompliant," "resistant," or "stubborn," as if they were doing something to us rather than simply trying to cope as best they can (Kottler, 1992a).

Therapeutic Influence

It has already been mentioned that once therapist credibility has been established, the cognitive aspects of social relationships can be used to influence the client. This strategy is based on the notion that individuals, when confronted with various life circumstances, usually search to explain those events in terms of cause and effect. Often it seems that the clients who enter therapy tend to attribute their difficulties to factors that they believe are out of their control. For example, some clients contend that their lives would be just fine if only someone else (spouse, boss, daughter) would change. The therapist then influences the client to promote greater client self-awareness and self-understanding. Furthermore, the therapist encourages the client to reattribute her difficulties to factors over which she has some control. The following example, shows this exchange in its simplest form:

CLIENT: My mom just pushes me to the point where I just have to explode. I can't help it. If she would just get off my back, then I wouldn't get into trouble so much.

THERAPIST: So what you are saying is that your mother is the one who is making you get in trouble. She is the one pushing you to get into fights, not turning in your homework, stealing from friends.

CLIENT: No, that's not what I'm saying! It's just that she drives me crazy, she gets on my case to the point where I don't have a choice.

THERAPIST: Again you are saying that you are not in control of yourself, that what your mother says or does, that determines how you must act. I understand that living with your mother is tough for you, that she can be a real struggle to be around, but how does that dictate what you do?

CLIENT: Yeah. Yeah. I know what you mean. It's just that . . .

And so goes the dialogue in which the therapist attempts to convince the child to abandon a perspective that attributes causes of difficulty to external sources in favor of one that emphasizes, in this case, internal responsibility. The therapist uses everything within her power to influence the client to focus on that which the client may control, rather than forces that are beyond the client's reach.

Research on the social influence process has supported utilization of the therapeutic technique of interpretation for encouraging clients to reattribute their circumstances (Dorn, 1986). In this model, therapists can expect to generate some discomfort, due to the dissonance between their interpretations and clients' perceptions. As we well know, dissonance is an internal condition that motivates people to do a variety of things to reinstate a degree of balance and stability. The relationship between client and therapist is thus marked by a degree of activity in which the client attempts to reduce the psychological discomfort associated with cognitive and affective dissonance. As Dorn (1984) and others have observed, this process can occur in any of the following ways.

The client may accept the therapist's reattribution of the situation and drop his own view ("Okay. I can see how I have been blaming my wife for keeping me stuck in a no-win situation when actually *I* have been the one who structured things in this way").

The client may seek out items of information or opinions that invalidate those of the therapist ("It is not just that I disagree with what you are telling me, but several books I have read on how to have a loving relationship indicate I should do what I have been doing rather than trying what you are suggesting").

The client may dismiss the therapist's reattribution by implying that it is based on inadequate or insufficient information ("Well, I can see how you might think that, based on what I've told you so far. But there are a whole lot more things involved. If you could see the big picture from where I am sitting, I am certain you would change your mind").

The client, after an alternative interpretation, may elect to deny that the presenting problem is any longer a bothersome issue ("I appreciate all that you are trying to do to help and all, but frankly, it is really not such a big deal anymore. Maybe we could move on to something else that has been concerning me").

The client may try to influence the therapist directly to change her perspective to bring it into line with his own point of view ("Why must you always be right and I wrong? I don't think you are giving me the benefit of the doubt. You assume that it must be all my fault, that my wife is a perfect angel, but let me tell you, she *is* the source of my trouble. That's why I think you should get her in here and straighten her out. Wait! Before you disagree, why don't you at least give that idea a chance?").

Relationship Stages: A Mediating Factor

Earlier it was suggested that a critical dimension of the therapeutic relationship was its changing, dynamic nature. One of the primary contributions of social psychology to the therapeutic field is the recognition of the fluid nature of human relationships. Different effects result from the same activities occurring at different stages of a developing relationship. This finding suggests that particular therapist behaviors and interventions are effective at different times. Techniques that we might employ early in the relationship (questioning, interpreting) might not be especially helpful toward the end, when other strategies (summarizing, supporting) are more appropriate. Looking at the various stages of the relationship process, Levinger (1980) observed four distinct transitions that apply to all relationships. The first stage, *zero contact*, begins before two people even meet and refers to what they bring to the relationship. It is during the second stage, *unilateral awareness*, that initial impressions are created and determinations made as to the extent of investment each person is willing to make. While there is no actual interaction at this point, the decision to affiliate may be related to the degree of interpersonal attractiveness, the expectation of interpersonal rewards, and the other alternatives available.

The third level of relatedness is *surface contact*, when the initial interaction begins. This stage is distinguished by role expectations that govern the appropriate behavior between the individuals. Surface contact is characterized by each partner's adopting the roles considered appropriate for the particular situation in which the interaction occurs. There is little concern at this point whether the relationship will, or should, continue (Levinger & Snoek, 1972). Instead, the relationship is based largely on such self-centered criteria as rewards, costs, and impression management (Winstead, Derlega, Lewis, & Margulis, 1988). Factors of interpersonal attraction can become extremely important at this stage as the decision regarding potential outcomes is made.

The final stage, *mutuality*, is one in which the relationship partners have shared something about themselves with one another and have assumed some responsibility for the outcome of the relationship. Responsiveness becomes critical as the partners develop a sense of reciprocal exchange and interdependence. Consequently, the partners coordinate their efforts in order to maximize the outcomes.

Therapeutic relationships can be described along similar lines, although we usually begin our descriptions at the stage of unilateral awareness. Clients frequently come to therapists knowing little about them except what the clients may have learned from a referral contact ("He is a really nice guy"; "She is very smart"). At the surface level of contact, the therapist concentrates on modeling dimensions of attractiveness, attempting to create a favorable impression by appearing nurturing, wise, or supportive. The client makes a decision as to whether the match seems right, based on assessment of personal costs and rewards.

As mentioned previously, the mutuality stage may create the greatest difficulty because of the nature of our work. Whereas in close personal relationships, this stage is marked by reciprocity and a sense of "we-ness," in our therapeutic relationships, we do not necessarily come across as "real" people in the sense of being spontaneous and self-indulgent. Conflict may very well result when the client's expectations for reciprocal sharing do not match the therapist's intentions.

Multiple Views of Being Authentic

As members of the therapeutic community, we have become accustomed to thinking of healing relationships as compassionate, genuine, and empathy-based phenomena. However, as discussed here, in addition to this prevalent conception of authenticity, there are also ways of viewing this same relationship as the result of attempts to, first, impress clients with our attractiveness and expertise, and then influence them through this same power.

In the end, our flexibility and adaptability depends on our adopting multiple views of the same events. That, after all, is what we teach our clients: when a particular way that you do something or think about your predicament is not working for you, then try something else. The intent here is not to suggest that one approach is better than another but rather that empathy alone, without client perceptions of therapist attractiveness, expertness, and trustworthiness, may not be enough. We must heed all the perspectives described here (and others to follow) if we are to understand and capitalize on the authentic/real dimensions of what goes on during therapeutic engagement. And there is much going on in addition to authentic interactions, including "ghosts" in the room, remnants of the past that continue to haunt the way individuals relate to one another in the present. It is these projections, transferences of templates, that are addressed in the next chapter.

Chapter Eight

Ghosts in the Room

Neil is listening to Saul whine on about how everyone he meets takes advantage of him, how he can't make any friends because people just use him. Neil is paying little attention because he has heard this same "sniveling story" for the past five weeks. Saul's tone has even changed from their first meeting; its pitch is higher and closer to the whine of a child. Neil brought up "Saul the Sniveler" in staffing last week. His colleagues jumped on him for being so critical of this client. Where was his compassion? They were a little puzzled by this relationship, since Neil and Saul had a number of similarities (both are Jewish, male, in their late thirties). After sufficient encouragement, as well as some good-natured heckling, Neil resolved to be more understanding with Saul in the future. Surely this man deserved to be treated with more respect than Neil has been showing so far.

It was only seven minutes into the next session before Neil was already entertaining elaborate fantasies about covering Saul's mouth with rags and tape, anything just to get him to shut up and quit the whining.

If we were to make some sense of what was happening in Neil's session, we would see in Saul a client who is feeling quite lonely and isolated. He is frustrated by his lack of close friends. Yet he seems to be really trying to open up with Neil, to trust him in a way unprecedented for him. On the surface, it appears as if Neil is responding warmly to his client. He is showing appropriate levels of empathy, nodding his head in all the right places, offering reactions at regular intervals. Yet there is also a dynamic to their relationship that is not quite right. There is some underlying tension that both of them can feel, even if they are not consciously acknowledging these impressions.

Most of us have had this eerie experience when a routine discussion with a client, family member, or friend takes an abrupt left turn, and we cannot understand what happened nor why the person is reacting so strangely. When clients base their responses to patterns and cues on invisible factors, it is essential for the therapist to understand how these ghosts from the past have entered the room and are influencing the healing interaction. *Transference* is the label often used to describe this phenomenon, but unfortunately, transference is often viewed solely as an extension of psychoanalytic thinking and not of much use to those who do not subscribe to the basic psychoanalytic tenets. Therefore, the term *projected dimension* is used to describe all those complex undercurrents in our ways of understanding that influence the ways we react to other people but that have little to do with people's present actions. The projected dimension encompasses not only transference but also countertransference and all projective undercurrents that affect every therapeutic relationship.

Configuration of the Projected Dimension

Sigmund Freud is credited with discovering the projected dimension and the process known as transference, although psychologically sophisticated writers from Shakespeare to Dostoyevsky had been describing the phenomenon for some time. Specifically, transference refers to "inappropriate behavior that reflects the unconscious reenactment of pathogenic and conflictual relations with significant others" (Kernberg, 1984, p. 9). It is the influence of the past on the immediacy of the present.

Therapists are more than a little familiar with Freud's thinking on this matter. In a remarkably succinct description of his discovery, Freud (1912/1958) wrote:

> In the psycho-analytic treatment of a neurotic patient the strange phenomenon that is known as "transference" makes its appearance. The patient, that is to say, directs towards the physician a degree of affectionate feeling (mingled, often enough, with hostility) which is based on *no real relations* between them and which—as is shown by every detail of its emergence—can only be traced back to old wishful phantasies of the patient's which have become unconscious. Thus the part of the patient's emotional life which he can no longer recall to memory is re-experienced by him in his relations to the physician [p. 51, emphasis added].

In the same lecture in which he made this statement, Freud argued persuasively that transference arises spontaneously in all human relations. He further contended that transference is the true vehicle of therapeutic influence, and the less its presence is suspected, the more powerfully it operates.

Two ideas are particularly important if we are to understand this view of the projected side of the therapeutic encounter. The first suggests that, in our earliest relationships, each of us establishes templates into which we fit all future relationships. These relationship patterns become the foundation upon which we come to expect others to act, and the basis upon which we choose to respond to others' behavior. The second important premise is that people feel a compulsion to repeat or replay the patterns of early relationships. These relationships may have been difficult or painful experiences, but they may also have been quite pleasant and satisfying. It is as if people's first relationships create themes that come to dominate their later interpersonal lives. Quite often, these templates are based on perceptual distortions. Furthermore, Freud believed that this compulsion to repeat patterns provides material from the past that is accessible and can be worked through in the present (Freud, 1912/1958).

Freud would not have been pleased with Neil's initial sessions with Saul. Neil was initially blind to Saul's transference of his relationship with his mother to other relationships (including the relationship with Neil). Neil was also blind to the fact that he found Saul's whining extremely irritating because of his own ghosts, whom he projected onto the situation. Therefore, he stayed primarily within an active (non)listening mode so as to avoid telling Saul what a "schmuck" he thought Saul was. Then, with the help of a supervisor, Neil came to see that his relationship with his client was, in fact, distorted by projections taking place on both their parts. Saul, a thirty-eight-year-old accountant, was raised by parents who had managed to escape the Holocaust in Germany by immigrating to the United States in the late 1930s. It was certainly easy to see how Saul could believe that people were untrustworthy given the losses that his parents were forced to endure. However, the transference that occurred between Saul and Neil was somewhat more complex. Saul's mother would probably have been diagnosed as depressed if she had ever sought treatment. Saul's father was a bitter man, who came home to their small apartment continually complaining about his work, the children's behavior, the neighbors, the government, or anything else he could think of. Saul soon learned that the manner in which to interact with his mother was to whine and complain and, therefore, was inadvertently using this method of interacting with Neil.

From a classical psychoanalytical view, the relationship between therapist and client represents a microcosm of the client's larger problems. Freud believed that therapy was helpful because the client remembered early material and realized how it affected his or her present life. Therefore, in this view, Neil's focus should have been on identifying Saul's feelings of neglect from childhood and working through how the whining for attention affected Saul's interactions in current relationships.

Reexperiencing as the Foundation of Projection

Gill (1982) is representative of a number of contemporary analysts who now believe that clients' recalling and understanding early childhood experiences is not necessarily enough to promote desired changes in those clients. As in so many parts of our field, the impact of ideas from other disciplines and philosophies (such as humanism) has led to a cross-fertilization of thinking in the area of the projected dimension, creating some hybrid conceptions about the nature of transference. In this new view, transferential behaviors are not so much distortions as they are clients' best efforts to make inferences and decisions based on limited information. Faced with a novel, ambiguous situation (such as therapy), clients act on the basis of past actions. That is, in the absence of clear guidance and cues, they use old patterns to attempt to construct their own understanding of what is going on. If we could hear a client's unconscious reasoning process, it might sound something like this: *She is staring at me. What does this woman want from me? She is waiting for me to do something but I don't know what that is. Can I ask her? No, then she would know how stupid I am. Well, what I have done before in these situations is to try and create some sort of conflict so that things stay interesting. Otherwise, she is just going to get bored with me. Better that we should fight together than sit here like a couple of slugs.*

Although Freud believed that the value of transference lay in its power to help patients recall the past, there is evidence that remembering is not enough. Gill argues that, because the individual's difficulties are acquired experientially, they must be transformed experientially. In this view, the primary value of the therapeutic relationship is that it is a new experience in which the client has the opportunity to learn to react differently, since the therapist will (it is hoped) refuse to engage in previously dysfunctional patterns:

> You seem to want to fight with me. If I back off, you say you will not respect me and think of me as 'weak,' the way your father labeled you when you tried to stay out of his way. Yet, if I respond to your provocation defensively, you will withdraw, feeling hurt. That leaves me only one choice, to do what I am doing with you right now, to talk about what is being played out so we can each react differently from what has ever occurred before.
>
> Now, what I would like you to try is quite a different way of responding to me. Let's continue our dialogue where we left off, but this time I want *you* to be the one to stop at some point, rechanneling us in a more constructive direction.

This conception of transference differs from the traditional view in that both participants have a shared role. We hardly present a blank screen, nor can we ever be completely neutral. Clients' reactions to us are based not only on their prior experiences in similar circumstances but also on their observation of the most subtle nuances of our behavior. A stifled yawn, a glance at the clock, a wry smile, a stiffened posture, or an impatient foot all spark some reaction in the client. This means that therapists not only have to help clients recognize the baggage that they bring into the sessions but also have to be exquisitely sensitive to the most minute impact of everything that they do and say ("I notice that you are becoming increasingly angry toward me because I won't respond to you the way you prefer. In fact, your reaction seems way out of proportion to what took place. I wonder who else you are speaking to besides me?").

Dialogues Between Ghosts

One of the most challenging (and exciting) aspects of dealing with the projected dimension is identifying not only the source of the client's projected reactions but also the triggers that provoked them during the therapy session. Although sometimes we are able to make both these complementary identifications during the session, so that we too can learn from the experience ("So what was it that I said or did that got you going?"), it is more common for us to explore our own role in the struggle after the client leaves the room. Either through supervision, processing with colleagues, reviewing tapes or notes, or self-reflection, we replay the sequence of interactions in such a way that the transference becomes more clear.

What is so helpful about this expanded thinking on the projected dimension of relationships is that the client (or her past) is no longer seen as a solitary culprit in creating therapeutic impasses, because the therapist is also a partner in this exchange and he too brings ghosts and interpersonal styles into the room. In this view, so much more than the discrete, simple entities of transference and countertransference results from the unresolved issues of the past. Instead, there is a shared responsibility for those interactions that spin out of control.

In the case of Neil and Saul, although the client certainly had propensities toward whining behavior when faced with ambiguous circumstances, the therapist as well played a role in the struggle. Neil had lost his compassion for his client because of his own low threshold for dependency. He became a therapist in the first place because he absolutely despised feeling out of control in his life. Armed with therapeutic skills, Neil vowed he would always find a way to preserve his autonomy, unlike his father whom he had perceived as a passive weakling. In spite of Neil's best efforts to remain neutral, to stay within a fairly benign framework of reflecting Saul's underlying feelings of helplessness, there was no doubt that his frustration and disapproval were leaking through. It is utter arrogance on our part to assume that our clients are not as sensitive to our moods and feelings as we are to their internal reactions. Saul could feel his therapist's critical judgment of him. Although this awareness was not clear enough for him to articulate, even to himself, its presence was powerful enough to have a significant impact. For example, Neil's and Saul's probable thoughts the first time that Saul had complained are instructive.

SAUL (*Complaining*): Couldn't I have an earlier appointment?

NEIL (*Frowning as he gently chides Saul to be patient*): This is the best I can do for now.

SAUL: Gee, I'm sorry. I don't mean to be an imposition. [*That is just how I felt when my mother would not address my concerns. This guy doesn't seem to like me. Maybe if I try a little harder to be cooperative.*]

NEIL (*Impatiently*): No. No. It's no bother. [*What a wimp! This guy backs down so easily. No wonder he has problems.*]

SAUL: [*I can tell I already disappointed him. He is looking at me as if I were a specimen in a bottle.*] This time is fine. I don't know what I was saying. [*He doesn't believe me.*]

Kohut (1984), who is often credited with bringing together the psychoanalytic and humanistic traditions, stresses the importance of empathy when dealing with projection. If it is accepted that both therapist and client are continually projecting and distorting what is taking place in their interactions, feeding off their respective perceptions of the other's behavior, then misunderstandings are inevitable unless both participants are willing to assume responsibility for the interaction. More often than we would like to admit, a dialogue ends up sounding something like this:

CLIENT: It seems to me that you are not understanding the point I am trying to make about the difficulty I am having with my daughter's current attitude. In fact, it doesn't feel like you have really been listening to me at all.

THERAPIST (*Pleased with herself at realizing that this is the perfect transition to discuss transference*): Could it be that your perception of my disinterest is really related to the neglect you felt from your mother?

CLIENT (*With considerable irritation*): Excuse me?

THERAPIST: It seems to me that you're transferring your feelings about your mother into our relationship. [*There is a lot of resistance here.*]

CLIENT: Huh? [*She isn't hearing a word I say.*]

THERAPIST: I was just wondering if those old wounds that we talked about last week, your mother not really being involved and loving toward you, are not manifesting themselves in our relationship. [*She is not hearing me.*]

CLIENT: Maybe this would be a good time for us to stop. [*And good riddance!*]

THERAPIST: [*That's what I'm supposed to say!*]

This, of course, shows a lousy way to interpret transference in a session. Psychodynamic practitioners with greater sensitivity and skill are likely to be considerably more deft at working through this kind of impasse in a relationship. The point, however, is that, even when we interpret the transference perfectly, we may still be leaving out of the picture some of the interactional dynamics that transcend both the client's individual transference feelings and the projected reactions of the clinician. The idea is not to question the value of working with transference dynamics in the relationship but to find greater value by expanding the conception of transference to include features from other schools of thought, in such a way that almost any practitioner, regardless of theoretical preferences, can make use of the projected dimensions of a therapeutic relationship.

Schemas as the Basis of Projection

One such alternative model, proposed by Jerome Singer and his colleagues (Singer, 1985; Singer & Kolligian, 1987; Singer, Sincoff, & Kolligian, 1989), introduces a unique view of transference by employing an information-processing perspective. Basing their thinking on the research indicating that cognitive functioning is intimately linked with personality, they have applied the concept of schemas to understand how clients process their experiences in therapy.

Schemas, the most basic of all cognitive structures, are frameworks for regulating attention and organizing the encoding, storage, and retrieval of information in a domain. They allow a perceiver to identify stimuli quickly, cluster them into manageable units, and select a strategy for obtaining further information. For example, when we see the acronym "ANOVA" in a research article, we go to what might be called our statistic schema in order to retrieve relevant information and understand the acronym. When clients enter a therapeutic relationship, they go to what might be called their relationship schemas in order to understand the dynamics of the interaction.

From this perspective, the projected dimension is viewed as a process in which the client constantly organizes the current relationship with the therapist into an existing cognitive structure that is based on past relationship experiences. This is, naturally, quite a challenge, since the therapeutic relationship is quite unlike any other experience that the client has experienced before. Does it fit in the schema reserved for parents, authority figures, or confidant/friends, or perhaps the one for coaches, teachers, tutors and the like? Saul's sniveling, that Neil found so annoying, was the outcome of his schema that people were not interested in him and that the only way to get them to react was to whine, while Neil entered his own schema, which prescribed an irritated attitude toward dependent, weak males.

Moreover, the idea that schemas constitute a cognitive organizing principle that influences relationships does not preclude more traditional views of transference as distorted projections, for when the two concepts are combined, they greatly enrich the therapist's potential ability to expand the meaning of what is going on in the relationship, in relation not only to the present but also to the ghosts from the past.

An examination of how schemas develop provides insight into the ways these information-processing structures may be distorted and biased, adversely affecting clients' and therapists' perceptions of what is happening in the relationship. There are four principal influences on the development of individual schemas: cultural influences; differential socialization practices within a particular culture; unique childhood experiences; and experiences and current concerns in adulthood.

Throughout, this book stresses the importance of considering the influence of *culture* on the therapeutic relationship, and nowhere is this consideration more crucial than when therapists are exploring the projected dimension. For example, it has been well documented that cultures that encourage verbal behaviors produce more verbal children than those that emphasize perceptual-motor skills. Similar cultural influences can be seen in the development of the schemas that govern transference and countertransference reactions. Thus, if a therapist's schema about gender roles is decidedly different from that of the client, conflicts are likely, as this example from Tom Sexton reveals.

> I was working with a Saudi woman in a university counseling center. She lived in a world in which her father controlled every facet of her life, told her what to do and when to do it. I was working to counteract what I perceived to be "poisonous" influence, based primarily on what I thought of as more appropriate assertive autonomous behavior for a woman. Once this student began to enact our plan to stand up for herself, her father yanked her out of college and made her stay at home until he could find her a suitable mate. As appalled as I was by this circumstance, I regret that my own personal reactions sabotaged any chance we might have had to help her within her own cultural values.

Since the variations between individuals in any given culture are even greater than those between individuals from different cultures, *socialization practices* also play a significant role in the development of schemas. Again, gender differences provide the most obvious example of this phenomenon. Much has been written about transference problems from the perspective of the female client and the male therapist, yet the field of therapy is occupied primarily by female practitioners (though certainly not in the positions of greatest power). Gornick (1986), among others, has stressed the need for additional therapeutic methods formulated for relationships between female therapists and male clients. Sue Whiston describes how a socialization schema might make gender an issue in a therapeutic relationship.

> I have had an experience that I believe has been shared by quite a number of other female therapists. When I think about socialization practices in our culture, a couple I once worked with comes to mind as a blatant example of therapist expectations based on gender. I was gathering some background information with this couple, and I thought it was progressing fairly well. I then went into my canned speech about appointments, fees, expectations, and so on, asking if they had any questions, since both of them were looking a little bewildered. The wife finally spoke up and said, with a slight Southern drawl, "Why yes, I was just wondering when we saw the doctor."
>
> When I explained to them that I *was* their doctor, they both looked at one other with unmistakable disappointment, which clearly reflected that they had gotten an inferior product. Even though I tried my best to appear as a credible expert, my efforts were to no avail since the schema they had was of a male professional and a woman as his aide. They were happy to provide information to me, as they would to a nurse before they saw a physician, but they did not return for another appointment.

Childhood experiences are the third influence on the development of cognitive schemas. Given that schemas are generalizations based on actual experiences, the joys, traumas, and daily interactions of childhood cannot help but shape the way current relationships are perceived. The *experiences of adulthood* then continue to shape, modify, and maintain schemas.

Rather than viewing transference and countertransference phenomena as anomalies to be vanquished, the schematic viewpoint looks at projected images as normal consequences of processing information. Every moment that we spend with a client involves continual cognitive activity as well as intense emotional reactions. Some of the ways we respond, both internally and interpersonally, are overreactions that are immediately evident in the dramatic client responses they elicit. Yet the great bulk of this mental and emotional activity is simply the routine way that we make sense of what transpires in our relationships. The following example of the internal dialogue that might go on in a session between a client and a therapist illustrates people's routine use of schemas.

> THERAPIST: *I wonder what this means that this client isn't saying anything? Sort of reminds me of when my teachers would look at me blankly as if I wasn't clear in what I said. I suppose I should try to clarify things.*
>
> CLIENT: *This guy is talking to me as if I were a child. I understood him the first time. Why does he feel the need to humiliate me by repeating himself? People like him are always trying to put me in my place.*
>
> THERAPIST: *She seems so angry. I didn't do anything to spark this. I hate it when people are angry at me like this. It is as if I screwed up. I feel defensive and want to protect myself.*
>
> CLIENT: *This relationship is going nowhere, just like all the other times I have tried to let a man get close to me. He doesn't even care.*
>
> THERAPIST: *This relationship is going nowhere, just like all the other times I have tried to let someone get close to me. She doesn't even care.*

The relationship schemas of each participant in this encounter led each to distort the motives of the other. Such cognitive structures exist to help individuals simplify the complexity of the world in such a way that they can retrieve information efficiently and interpret what is going on within a reasonable period of time. However, when these projections go unrecognized, they do far more harm than good to individuals' ability to synchronize communication for understanding.

When the Therapist Is Haunted

Our pretending to be neutral during the therapeutic encounter is perhaps one of the great lies of our time. We act as if our acceptance of the client is truly unconditional and our regard universally positive, as if we really do not care what the client decides or does as long as it is not obviously destructive. Further, we pretend that we are clear headed, fully functioning, and objective enough to dispassionately separate fantasy from reality, that the interpretations we offer are on target and the observations we make are accurate. When there is a tie between what the client believes is going on and what we think, our vision usually prevails because of the shared assumption of client and therapist that the therapist knows better. Through our training, experience, supervision, and heightened awareness, we are supposed to know things that others do not.

The reality of the situation is that we are, first and foremost, human beings. We are blind, deaf, and impaired just like every other mortal being, although, we hope, a little less so. Each of us is haunted by our own ghosts—unfinished business from the past, unresolved conflicts that invade our sleep, soft spots, areas of vulnerability, unfulfilled needs, distortions, distractions, troubles that do not seem ever to go away completely. In spite of our best efforts to work on these issues through therapy and supervision, in journals, and with colleagues, friends, and family, we are always in a state of *becoming* more effective. We are not yet fully effective, and probably never will be. We are a work in progress.

About everything a client does or says, we have a strong opinion, whether we voice it aloud or not—whether to quit a job, get a divorce, confront a boss, reach out to a friend, go back to school, or stop talking about one matter and begin another. Some of these preferences are based on what we think is generally and ideally best for others; other preferences are more honestly the result of thinking about what we would do if we were in that specific client's place. Still other opinions result from our own projected fantasies, from what we deceive ourselves is really happening. If we believe that the experiences of a client's past impact that client's present behavior, then we must also acknowledge that the same is true for the therapist. In spite of our claims that we have already been in therapy ourselves and so worked through our countertransference problems, we know that we are still haunted by ghosts.

One of the most intriguing aspects of projected images is that, because they often take place beyond our immediate awareness, it is easy to pretend that distortions are not taking place at all. It may readily be apparent to us that Neil has some problems he needs to take care of if he hopes to be helpful to Saul, but Neil may be quite forceful that such is not the case. Scoff if you will, but the question remains: Which ghosts haunt you to the extent that you do not see, hear, and/or sense clearly? It is certainly evident that Saul's projection had a major influence on the relationship with his therapist. But Neil had his own problems as well. One of the reasons that Saul had originally been assigned to Neil was their cultural similarity, both of them were Jewish. But they also had differences. Neil grew up in the context of a very large extended family, many of whom had had heart-wrenching experiences with anti-Semitism, but Neil was raised primarily by a stepfather who did not have very much to complain about in Neil's estimation. Like Saul's father, Neil's stepfather also continually whined, but these complaints often went to the point of singling out someone responsible for his difficulty—often Neil. As a child, Neil had constantly battled with his stepfather over being cast as the perpetrator of the stepfather's misfortunes. But in working with Saul, Neil did not immediately recognize his countertransference of his core conflict with his stepfather. He did sense the bubbling anger that was occurring, but he focused on being silent so that his anger would not seep through into his interactions with Saul. This excessive reliance on silence was not particularly effective and just resulted in Saul's whining more.

An interesting question to ask ourselves as therapists, as well as human beings, is the identity of the relationship schemas that guide our own perceptions. For instance, when a client first walks through the door, we may automatically shift to the framework we were taught to adopt (eye contact, responsive stance, a little head nodding, a couple of reflections of content). However, if we look deeper, there are already influences at work—cultural and socialization templates, childhood events, as well as current experiences. How we establish relationships with clients is not based solely on the training we received in graduate school, but also on all the other relationships that have shaped our lives. Jeffrey Kottler offers an example that models some self-observation.

> I take a step back and observe the ways I relate to Marjorie as her therapist. I first note the obvious things—I am careful with her, as if she were fragile and might break if I push too hard. I compliment her a lot, most of it genuine, but some of it a stretch to build her confidence. Sometimes I drift off in the same spots during sessions, at times when she is talking about things that seem important to her but irrelevant to me. I am reluctant to bring this to her attention. I do not wish to hurt her and believe that I could if I told her more directly what I see her doing. I am cautious with her, so much so that things are proceeding more slowly than I think they need to. I understand this but still feel reluctant to break the pattern.
>
> Not so obvious is where these reactions on my part come from. I can see some evidence that Marjorie does invite me to feel sorry for her. She is used to a victim role and plays it quite well. Yet there is much in her, and my reactions to her, that feels familiar to me. There is certainly a "mother thing" going on for me. I saw my own

mother as far more helpless than she really was. I protected her, made excuses for her, did everything except tell her how I felt, which could have made a difference in the quality of our relationship. Then she went and died before we got to know one another as adults.

Even more subtle are some similarities of this relationship to the relationships I have had with other clients. After twenty years of practice, I sometimes find it difficult to see a client as a unique entity; I am constantly making comparisons in my head: *I saw someone like this a few times before. . . . This reminds me of the time . . .* Sometimes the faces and names blur together and I can't remember who is who. What I do know is that sometimes I am not seeing Marjorie sitting before me, but others who have occupied her seat.

As this example highlights, countertransference feelings are not rare events that, once identified, become worked through once and for all. In many ways, the intense personal reactions we have to our clients are among our greatest talents.

It is the contention here that all individuals, and hence all of us as therapists, have a relationship schema that is directly influenced by previous relationships. Of course, the value of these perceptions is directly related to how clearly we can distinguish between fantasy and reality (Blanck & Blanck, 1968). Moreover, often when countertransference is brought up in supervision or case staffing meetings, it is with negative connotations. Yet, the ghost within the therapist may be the warm and caring Aunt Marian who helped the therapist learn about compassion and respect for individual differences. It would be erroneous, however, to suggest that all therapist projections are positive. Certainly, this discussion of the projected dimension would be incomplete without an overview of negative countertransference reactions, which can be particularly prevalent among beginning therapists.

Overprotective countertransference describes one cluster of behaviors that has been identified as a destructive pattern (Watkins, 1985).

As in the example just described, in this pattern, the therapist has an oversolicitous attitude toward the client, who is viewed as fragile and weak. As a result, the therapist is predisposed to shield and protect the client from facing things that are quite important. Statements are diluted or so carefully worded that their meaning or impact is often lost. This overprotection can also result in clients' being robbed of the opportunity to grapple with their issues, since the therapist steps in too quickly to alleviate the hurt, anxiety, or guilt ("Let's look at the positive things in your life"; "I know you didn't mean that"; "It is going to be fine"). The therapist may go so far as to assist the client in externalizing his or her problems so that this "fragile child" will not have to suffer any more heartache.

Similar to overprotectiveness is *benign countertransference*. In this instance, the therapist is also guarded and careful with the client; however, the motivation is different. This pattern often results from the therapist's need to be liked by a particular client. Another cause can be the therapist's fear of a client's anger. Therefore, to guard against either rejection or anger, the therapist responds in benign and innocuous ways. Moreover, in this situation, the relationship can come to resemble a peer relationship. Since the goal is to have the client like the therapist, the relationship will resemble a friendship and feature friendly exchanges rather than a therapeutic alliance.

A third form of projection in which therapists may engage is *rejecting countertransference*. As before, the client is viewed as being dependent and needy. However, instead of attempting to protect the client, the therapist responds to this projection by withdrawing from the client and remaining aloof. Hence, the relationship takes on a unilateral tenor and rapport and mutuality cannot develop. The therapist may even distort the dynamics of the relationship to justify her reaction ("I am encouraging this client to be responsible by refusing to buy into this helplessness game"). However, the real result is that the therapist's projection leaves the client out on a limb.

Another behavior pattern is labeled *hostile countertransference*. This variety of harmful countertransference often grows out of two therapist views: first, the therapist may detest some actions or attribute of the client, or second, the therapist may be afraid of being infected by the client's disturbing behavior or pathology (Watkins, 1985). This pattern can manifest itself either overtly (for example, in the therapist's curt or borderline rude responses) or covertly (for example, in the therapist's consistently being late for the client's appointment). This projected and often unidentified hostility on the part of the therapist can lead to mutual resentment in which therapist and client end up being belligerent to each other. However, what may be even more menacing to the therapeutic relationship is an interaction that involves a hostile therapist and a passive client who is a willing recipient of the animosity.

Moving Beyond Authentic Engagements and Projected Images

The ghosts in the room, or the projected images of the therapeutic relationship, cannot be viewed in isolation since they intermingle with the dimension of authentic engagement as well. Sometimes these two dimensions of the relationship take turns; more often they are inseparable parts of most interactions that take place.

From these two dimensions, a *pattern* of interaction emanates in every therapeutic relationship. The following chapter explores the templates that develop in therapeutic alliances, the rules, or norms, that become part of the relationship. These norms cannot be legislated by the therapist. They are part of an intricate series of negotiations that form the basis for much of what we do in the earliest stages of the relationship.

Chapter Nine

Black Holes and the Patterns That Connect

Porter appeared to be the epitome of the highly motivated client. He not only was enthusiastic in his desire for help but he also seemed to have a good grasp of what he believed was troubling him, mostly related to his desire for greater independence and self-reliance. He was also aware that he was always drawn to the same kind of people, whether as lovers or as friends, with equally unsatisfactory results. No matter how hard he tried, or what he did, Porter almost always ended up feeling like a victim. He made it clear that he would do anything to change this pattern.

In the early sessions, Porter was attentive and meticulous in completing all therapeutic tasks that were developed. His therapist, Alice, was also quite proud of the closeness that developed between them; a close, authentic, mutual affection had evolved. She believed that she had established herself as a credible resource for Porter in his search to become more self-reliant and to break the destructive pattern that kept repeating itself in his life. Yet as Alice continued her work with Porter, she began to feel a certain uneasiness that was difficult to articulate. Inexorably, she could feel herself being pulled into a vortex, helplessly watching their relationship deteriorate. Even though she was well aware of how crucial it was to help Peter be more independent, she realized that she had somehow begun to assume more and more responsibility for him. She found herself rescuing him, helping him as if he was a helpless child. In spite of her resolve to alter this pattern that was mutually self-defeating, she felt herself continuing to be pulled in the same direction. She said, "It was as if I was being sucked into a black hole in which I had little control over myself. I just couldn't seem to respond differently. As I tried to change the way I responded to him, it was as if the force became even stronger. Suddenly, I too was rejecting him!" The black hole Alice experienced had engulfed her.

Despite our knowledge, experience, and best of intentions, we have all had the experience of feeing lost in a morass from which there is no escape. Regardless of the closeness in the therapeutic relationship and the stated desires of the participants, something mysterious, something bigger than either the therapist or client, seems to be in control. We attempt to employ our most powerful interventions, our most potent magic, but to no avail. In the end, the same old patterns emerge, and we are slowly sucked into the black hole.

How Interactional Patterns Develop

The unified, multidimensional model (Figure 5.1) suggests that interactional patterns occur as a result of both the authentic and the projected dimensions of the therapeutic relationship. Some of these patterns set the stage for a healing alliance, while others make such a healing alliance impossible. Regardless of whether they facilitate or sabotage constructive changes, interactional patterns have a major impact on the entire course of a relationship. They represent the invisible forces, those apparent black holes, that exert powerful gravitational pulls on the rotation of each individual.

What is unique about the interactional dimension is that it is based on a different set of assumptions than the previously discussed dimension, assumptions that offer new eyes and ears with which to make sense of what is going on between client and therapist. It provides a truly relationship-oriented view of what happens in therapy, since it focuses on the mutuality and interdependence of people's behavior. It supplies principles and a language with which to accurately describe many of the struggles and triumphs individuals experience every day.

Assumptions of the Interactional Dimension

In any therapeutic relationship, the actions of the participants fit together like the pieces of a puzzle, forming patterns that ultimately provide a context from which meaning and definition can be derived. From these patterns, rules are also abstracted. Like the rules in games, which clearly set some behaviors aside as unacceptable (running outside the bases) and encourage others (fielding fly balls), the rules in therapeutic relationships give direction to the efforts of the participants. However, unlike the rules in games, interactional rules are not explicitly set and agreed upon. Instead, like the interpersonal patterns from which they derive, they are co-constructed and evolve covertly through an ongoing social negotiation process. Typically, there are four assumptions that are part of this process.

Relationships can only be understood when the simultaneous and reciprocal actions of all their elements are considered as a unit. Defining the meaning of the relationship according to an interactional model requires a conceptual shift away from intrapersonal phenomena, and even from individual behavior, because the patterns of interaction created between the participants, the *inter*connections among their actions, are now of primary concern. In fact, some have argued that it is impossible to look at the personality or actions of any relationship participant without considering the interpersonal context (Carson, 1969). As most of us who have been schooled in the principles of Gregory Bateson, Murray Bowen, and other systems thinkers well understand, each person's behavior is simultaneously the cause and effect of the other person's actions in an ongoing process. There is a dynamic interchange that transcends the personalities of the participants, creating a whole that is more meaningful than the sum of the two persons' behaviors (Charzonowski, 1982). Tom Sexton supplies a case in point.

I was recently supervising a beginning therapist. The client was pouting, obviously withdrawn and angry about something. Every effort the therapist made to break through the resistance was met with stony silence—pleading, teasing, confronting, interpreting, reflecting, cajoling—all are met with determined resistance. During a break in the session, we all agreed that this was a particularly difficult client.

As I watched the last part of the session, I noticed something I had previously overlooked. There seemed to be a sequence of interactions that led to the impasses being experienced. At one point, the client felt misunderstood and began to defend himself. The therapist misinterpreted the action and pressed harder. The client retaliated by becoming more and more resistant and argumentative. The therapist then backed off, feeling frustrated, while the client then felt censured and chastised for not being a "good" cooperative partner in the relationship. Unfortunately, this pattern was all too familiar to both the therapist and the client, not only in the current therapeutic relationship, but in other relationships each had experienced previously. It was clear, then, that the label of "resistant client" did not fit, since it was the entire sequence of behaviors of both parties that resulted in mutually obstructive behavior.

Relationships are composed of sequences of interaction that repeat themselves over time, eventually becoming rules. The messages and behaviors exchanged in a relationship are hardly random; they form a sequence, a set of regularities, that becomes stable over time. The outcome of these repeated patterns is a set of covert rules that govern how individuals act, encouraging their freedom of movement in some areas while restricting their movement in others. However, relationship rules are not just corrective; they also provide participants with a sense of consistency, predictability, and equilibrium (Ashby, 1956).

The example of Porter and Alice that started this chapter illustrates this notion. In their interaction, neither of them consciously selected the roles that ultimately led to their difficulties. In fact, each had vowed that he or she would not repeat old habits. However, at some covert level, the familiar old patterns did come to define their relationship. It was as if each elicited behaviors in the other that almost demanded a response quite different from the one intended. Despite vows to be different, both Porter and Alice covertly began a relationship pattern familiar to both. Almost without knowing it, each began to operate as if these patterns were the relationship rules. At that point, it was almost as if Alice could do nothing other than be a mother figure while Porter could do nothing other than be a demanding child. When each walked on to the playing field (therapy), they adopted the rules that had been developed. Hence it was as if these rules, rather than their intentions, directed the course of their relationship.

The meaning of any behavior is dependent upon the social context and interactional sequences in which it occurs. Behavior has meaning in a relationship only to the extent that we consider what has taken place previously. In other words, there is no universal meaning to behavior unless we take into consideration its social and cultural threads. The context may be the immediate behavioral sequence (a smile only has meaning when you consider the compliment that preceded it). It may also be the broader set of rules established in the relationship ("We don't yell in our family"). Thus, the primary concerns for the therapist operating according to this schema are *what* is occurring and *how* it is occurring, rather than why it is taking place. Jeffrey Kottler provides an example of operating within this view.

> Muriel and I were stuck. We circled one another like wary adversaries, although each of us believed the other was the predator. Once aware of this pattern that had developed, we spent considerable time trying to figure out why things unfolded as they did. I wanted to understand this as much as she did. There was a point, I am embarrassed to admit it came several months later, when we abandoned our mission to deduce the whys of our relationship and moved on to the hows and whats. Even though I quite like unraveling the mysteries

of why people behave the way they do (that is one of the reasons I became a therapist in the first place), with Muriel this strategy seemed to be exacerbating our already significant problems.

It was Muriel who first suggested (actually she had mentioned it several times previously, but I had ignored her) that we might proceed a different way, saying, "Who cares why your feelings get hurt so easily or I am so stubborn? Let's move on to what we can do differently and how we can get there." I wish I had said that. Once we abandoned looking for reasons and concentrated instead on specifically identifying the triggers that set us off, we were then able to reprogram ourselves to respond differently.

People are proactive agents who purposefully act in ways to meet their needs. People intentionally seek out and construct relationships designed to serve specific purposes, whether companionship, procreation, or the reciprocal exchange of services. In this context, individuals view needs interactionally as they search to find corresponding, complementary parts to their own styles. Finding the complementary part confirms one's self-image and helps maintain stability in one's life. Jeffrey Kottler's experience with Muriel also illustrates this principle.

In theory, Muriel and I had agreed to do things differently in our interactions once we had identified the covert rules and patterns. Actually, we quite enjoyed the sparring. We both seemed to be getting something out of the exchange. While I cannot speak for Muriel, I can say that she used to cackle gloriously once she saw a potential disagreement brewing. While I ordinarily will avoid conflict at all costs, especially when there is the possibility of explosive anger, Muriel seemed to bring out my most stubborn side. When I asked myself what I was getting out of this dysfunctional exchange (okay, somebody else asked me first), I reluctantly admitted that my needs were being met. I felt powerful when our horns were locked together. She was a scary lady to me, and yet I was holding my own with her. Of course, I was with her to serve in a therapeutic role but as is occasionally the case, I was meeting my needs as well.

Communication That Carries Multiple Messages

It is through the medium of communication that the principles of interaction pull together the authentic and projected elements of the relationship. All too often, communication is viewed as a one-dimensional process (we think, for example, of "I messages" or empathic listening). From the interactional perspective, relationship communication is inherently circular and operates on multiple levels simultaneously as well. The messages exchanged by the client and therapist are important not only because of their direct content but because of their impact on the relationship.

In any interaction, messages are communicated on two levels simultaneously (Ruesch & Bateson, 1968). First is the *report* (Watzlawick, Beavin, & Jackson, 1967), the representational (Danzinger, 1976) or denotative (Kiesler, 1972) message, which is the most overt feature of any communication. This is the direct aspect of interpersonal interaction, in which the literal semantic meaning conveys the information. Accompanying these content messages, usually in the background and out of focus, is the command, presentational, connotative, or *relationship* message (Kiesler, 1982; Watzlawick, Weakland, & Fisch, 1974). This is the covert and indirect aspect of interpersonal interaction, which accompanies content in order to provide additional cues concerning the kind of message that is being sent as well as its intended impact (Bateson, 1968; Watzlawick, Beavin, & Jackson, 1967). The function of this relationship message is to place the receiver in a particular position with respect to the sender. It is an indirect comment about the nature of the relationship between sender and receiver. Furthermore, it predisposes the receiver to make certain responses.

The communication between Porter and Alice illustrates the

power of relationship messages. The content message of each person stated a particular position: she would facilitate his self-reliance; he would take control. However, the more powerful relationship message communicated something entirely different. By assuming responsibility for Porter's treatment, Alice communicated her expert status and her superior knowledge in the relationship. It was true that she did know more. However, in order to continue in the relationship, Porter then had to accept the position of being less than, of being dependent. On this covert level, he accepted the message that he was not capable and could not be self-reliant. Thus, the parties' relationship messages defined their interactional roles in such ways that no amount of good intent could overcome the pull of the messages.

Interactional Negotiation

The product of repeated relationship messages is consistent and patterned interactions. Both therapist and client bring a definition of what they believe constitutes a relationship into every new encounter. These definitions detail acceptable or unacceptable relationships in interactional terms: How should I/he/she act? What behaviors are appropriate? What role will I/he/she play? It is from elements of the present encounter (the authentic dimension), as well as remnants of the past (the projected dimension), that these definitions are constructed by both the client and therapist.

The early stages of any relationship are characterized by relationship negotiation. Both therapist and client offer potential relationship definitions to the other ("I think we should act this way. . . . I would like the dominant role"; "I think it should be more equal." Haley (1963) suggested that these implied relationship proposals can be met with three possible responses. They may be accepted, in which case the other party agrees to the conditions, and the relationship goes on developing rules and consequent roles based on that definition. The proposals may be rejected, in which case tension develops and the relationship ends or a modification of the proposals is suggested. Finally, the proposals may be accepted with the meta-communication that, by accepting the definition, one person is really staying in control. In each case, a lengthy process of negotiation takes place.

Some have even cast the negotiation process as a struggle for control. Both client and therapist would prefer to have the relationship on his or her own terms, although therapists are often the ones who get their way because of the "home field" advantages associated with being a sanctioned healer. However, control is hardly absolute or one-sided, since each participant may control the relationship at different times, depending on what is at stake. There are instances when we are more than comfortable deferring to the client on a particular point ("What is of concern to you today?"), yet there are other areas in which we will not give an inch ("I am sorry, I only do marriage counseling with both partners present"). Control in therapeutic relationships is thus reciprocal in that each person seeks to entice the other to be or act a certain way, yet always in response to previous interactions.

Relationship negotiation in therapy is often confusing. Each party has a long list of imperatives that originate from training, as well as life experiences. For example, we may think it appropriate that both parties take turns speaking and that participation be roughly equal, or we may feel strongly that the client should not interrupt us but we may jump in when he is speaking to keep him on track. Clients who have seen more than one therapist are thus often confused, because they have heard such discrepant messages. The context and setting appear quite familiar to them but the rules may be considerably different. The client may find that it is no longer important to talk about the past, only the present, or that she is expected to carry most of the load when, the last time, the therapist directed things.

Complicating matters further, clients come to the encounter with their own sort of rules that they wish us to follow. Clients may imply to a therapist, "You will tell me what to do; you will let me talk about whatever I want, and if I wish to tell a few lies, you will be polite enough to let them go; or, you will fill the silence with insightful truths that will point me in the right direction." Needless to say, conflict in the beginning of our relationships is as inevitable as it is in any series of negotiations where the participants have competing agendas.

The Search for Complementarity

At the heart of the interpersonal negotiation process is the search for complementarity, the glue that binds certain people together, while pushing others apart. It is when the pieces of the behavioral role fit together and complement each other that a relationship gains stability and is maintained. Stable complementing relational roles can be either positive and satisfying or negative and dysfunctional.

Leary (1957), Kiesler (1984), and Benjamin (1987) suggest that at the center of relationship negotiation there are two main themes: *affiliation* (how friendly or hostile each party should be) and *control* (how much control each party should keep or give up). In the affiliation realm, several different behavioral styles are possible, some of which are more dominant (leading) while others are more submissive (cooperative). Hostile behavior can be relatively assertive (self-enhancing or critical) or passive (distrustful or self-effacing). As a person exhibits one of these styles in a relationship, his or her behaviors evoke complementary responses in the other person. The control dimension is characterized by the degree to which one is dominant or passive. According to Kiesler (1984) complementarity occurs when friendly or hostile styles elicit like responses (friendly or hostile) while controlling styles elicit opposite responses. Thus, a therapist who comes across as leading, or dominant, in a friendly way will spark a friendly but passive reaction in the client, unless her behavior is misinterpreted as evidence of hostility ("She is trying to put me in my place"). If the client feels put in his place, his behavior may then take on a hostile complementary response, perhaps reflecting feelings of mistrust.

When complementarity exists on one end of a continuum, symmetry resides at the other extreme (Bateson, 1958; Watzlawick, Weakland, & Fisch, 1974). Complementary interactions occur when the two participants assume unequal status and opposite control positions (as they do in the common one-down configuration in therapeutic relationships). This is a position in which the relationship definition offered by the person with more control is accepted by the one with relatively less power. Since the participants define their roles in relationships differently but agree to those differences, the participants then fit into a complementary pattern. They reach a state of comfort and stability, and cease to struggle.

In contrast, symmetrical interaction is marked by equal status between the participants, with neither one controlling the other. These relationships are characterized by interactions in which both participants compete for control because they cannot agree on a relationship definition. This pattern, commonly seen by marital and family therapists, is marked by conflict and turbulence.

Symmetrical interactions that take place in therapy and escalate conflict that might look like one of the following examples.

Postponement:

CLIENT: I would rather talk about this later.
THERAPIST: Perhaps it would be better if we dealt with it right now.

Denial:

CLIENT: I don't think we have a disagreement at all.
THERAPIST: I'm glad you feel all right about this. Since I still have some lingering doubts, I would like you to indulge me and continue the discussion.

Pre-Cueing:

CLIENT: I can't believe you even brought it up!
THERAPIST: I can see this is uncomfortable for you. Ignoring
the problem, however, will not make it go away.

Making interactive assessments according to the complementary/symmetrical scheme allows therapists to make needed adjustments in their relationships with clients as they evolve. For example, picture a therapist who is quite assertive. She is confident, sociable, and comfortable taking charge of situations. Naturally, she brings this interactive style into her sessions. Enter a client who has had difficulty recovering from two unsuccessful marriages in which he suffered emotional abuse. He now finds it overwhelming to make any decision because he is so afraid of making another mistake. He presents himself as passive, tentative, and clinging. The therapist attempts to charm him, to win him over through her bubbly enthusiasm, but she becomes increasingly frustrated by his deference and dependence. He seems to draw comfort from her confidence but not to the point that he is willing to show any initiative on his own. The therapist makes a diagnostic determination of dependent personality disorder and begins a treatment plan for long-term treatment.

An interactive perspective, however, would focus neither on the therapist's style nor the client's presumed disorder. Attention would, instead, be directed to the relationship that developed between them. The therapist's interpersonal behaviors could be classified as leading, a style that is considered to be on the friendly side of the affiliative dimension, and on the dominant side of the control dimension. The client, however, is functioning in an extremely docile manner, creating a clearly complementary relationship. Unfortunately, then, the nature of this relationship prevents the client from adopting the very behaviors that his therapist is attempting to facilitate. In this example a complementary relationship pattern, while familiar and comfortable, is not helpful but instead limits the potential for change.

The importance of complementarity is also illustrated by a number of empirical studies. In several analyses of therapeutic sessions, patterns of complementarity have been identified after only one session (Quintana & Meara, 1990; Tracey & Hays, 1989). Other studies have found a relationship between early therapist-client complementarity and successful treatment outcome. In an analysis of the differences between successful and unsuccessful therapy cases, Tracey (1985, 1986) found that therapists who matched their interpersonal style to that of the client, choosing one that complemented the level of dominance/submission in the client, were most often successful in their treatments. Those relationships that were least successful were composed of dyads that displayed equal dominance and control in their interpersonal styles. In another study, poor therapy sessions were distinguished by symmetrical behavior while good ones were complementary (Friedlander, Thibodeau, & Ward, 1985). In an analysis of the role of interactional patterns in therapy, Tracey (1993) suggested that early complementarity may be important for the development of a therapeutic relationship. However, symmetrical interaction may be most important in the middle stages of therapy. He suggested that the symmetrical struggles may be the actual change-producing interaction.

The idea of complementarity is unique in that it helps to explain the seeming redundancy and similarity of the types of relationships that both clients and therapists engage in. When seen through the interactional lens, it makes sense that affiliative people seem to have large numbers of friends who are also affiliative. Similarly, it makes sense that controlling individuals draw submissive partners into relationships.

One interesting exercise is to examine your own interpersonal/therapeutic style to determine which kinds of clients are most responsive to what you do. It is also intriguing to look at the patterns of those therapeutic relationships that have not worked out well for you, most likely those that have been symmetrical in structure. Of course, the more flexibility and willingness you have to change your interactive style according to what is best for a given client, the more likely it is that the resulting relationship will prove helpful.

Therapeutic Interactional Patterns

One of the great advantages of positing an interactive dimension within the therapeutic relationship is that we can view our therapist's role and "problem" behaviors in an entirely different way. We need no longer think of ourselves as devoted healers who are predominantly therapeutic instruments. Instead, we can consider ourselves as individuals whose personalities and interpersonal styles participate decisively in the therapeutic relationship, perhaps even more than the theoretical models we espouse would predict. A new paradigm emerges for us, one that is specifically anchored in relational participation and that addresses itself to formative and ongoing experiences derived from the evolving relationship in each given therapeutic situation. Consciously or inadvertently, the very act of participating in a therapeutic relationship influences, alters, and directs the client and the therapist.

Symptoms also take on new meaning. Clients who have certain characteristics (stubborn, manipulative), symptoms (depressed, anxious), or behaviors (self-defeating, passive) are unsuccessful in getting what they want. Traditional approaches focus on the individual attributes that keep clients from accomplishing their goals in life. From the interactional perspective, however, client problems exist within the context of social relationships. Maladaptive behavior is synonymous with inflexible interpersonal behavior. For example, those clients who rigidly adhere to one strategy in responding to all interpersonal situations, or who are insensitive to feedback that their actions have been less than constructive, are likely to have difficulties. They may also encounter trouble when there is an incongruence between the content and the underlying messages of their communications.

Symptomatic behaviors may also be seen as a reflection of clients' efforts at impression management. In a review of strategies that clients use to control the relationship with their therapists, Friedlander and Schwartz (1985) noted the prevalence of facework, a strategy in which the client denies responsibility for his or her predicament ("It's not my fault; I was traumatized as a kid"; "My mother is the problem. If only she would leave me alone, I could get on with my life"; "I just never do very well when I am under this kind of pressure. I can't help it"). The complementary response is a feeling of sympathy in the therapist.

Relationship Positioning

Our ability to influence clients emanates not only from our personalities and interventions alone, but from the position and role that we assume in our interactions with clients. If we choose a dominant role, we will likely structure the session, control the content and pace, recommend certain therapeutic tasks, and decide how much is enough. Interactional positioning may also be used as an intervention. We may purposely adopt a passive role in order to encourage more dominant behavior by the client. In either case, the position taken by the therapist is often met with a counterproposal from the client. We often call this interactional counterproposal "resistance."

But resistance is hardly a description of one person's behavior in a relationship. Rather, this label is sometimes more the result of the therapist's frustration over unmet expectations than of the client's behavior (Kottler, 1992a). It is thus helpful to conceive of resistance as the client's counterproposal regarding what is preferred in the relationship (Claiborn, 1986). Whereas opposition is the client's disagreement with the content of what is being communicated, resistance is a negative reaction to the entire underlying structure of the interaction. While opposition can be recast as feedback concerning the current course of action (including the appropriateness of our interpretations and the metaphors we are using), resistance is a rejection of the way the relationship is defined. As such, major renegotiation is needed to find a position in which we can be influential and yet be acceptable to the client.

When a client disagrees vehemently with something that we are offering (a suggestion, an interpretation, a directive), we at first assume that we are dealing with a form of opposition that is perhaps a legitimate response to some ineptitude or insensitivity on our part. We take that feedback gratefully and try again. If, however, there is an ongoing pattern of defiance beyond a few episodes, we have evidence there is resistance to the relationship as a whole. In such instances, it is likely that fairly dramatic changes will become necessary in the therapeutic position that has been taken. A therapist, for example, is confronted with an adolescent who refuses to speak under most any circumstances. At first he assumes it is because the young man is offended with something he said, or the way he said it. He tries again, several times, with similar results. The therapist then decides to alter the role that he has taken, abruptly changing to a one-down position in which he reluctantly defers to the boy. The adolescent takes the bait and becomes quite feisty and more disrespectful in their subsequent encounters but involved—an active participant. Now the therapist must struggle with the type of involvement the client is engaging in. Taking a more dominant role, the therapist again attempts to renegotiate with the boy a relationship definition that they can both live with. Thus, once the issues of hostility and friendliness (complementarity) are resolved, the boy becomes quite eager to cooperate.

The Paradoxical Nature of Interactional Change

In the following example, Tom Sexton sums up some of rigors of dealing with the interactional patterns.

I first noticed my discomfort after about three months of working with Linda. What had been a rocky beginning developed into a complacent process. Initially, she believed that because I was a man I could not possibly understand her perspective. In many ways, she was right—her divorce and her difficulty in balancing home and career were very foreign to my personal experience. However, as she further described the pressures she felt, I could easily relate to her predicament of feeling overwhelmed. I have felt that way many times. It became clear to her from the accuracy of my responses to her, that I really did understand much of what she was experiencing. A closeness developed that seemed to bind us together. However, as we continued our relationship, the sessions became very predictable; we seemed to be making little progress beyond this point. Although I continued to challenge and confront her perception of events in her life, these interventions seemed to have little immediate impact.

It was at this point that I consulted a colleague regarding Linda's case. After forty-five minutes of my explaining, analyzing, and moping, my colleague just laughed and responded, "How can you expect her to change if you make it so easy for her to remain the same? You are so predictable that you no longer make any difference; you no longer introduce anything new into the therapeutic relationship." What he suggested made sense, but it presented me with a dilemma. I enjoyed the comfort we had established in our relationship and so did Linda. We had both worked hard to come to a mutual understanding. My colleague was now suggesting that we disrupt that stability. . . . I wasn't sure if I was prepared to do that.

As was described in Chapter One, the therapeutic relationship is inherently paradoxical. Within a context of comfort and safety, we often attempt to provoke risky behavior. Thus, in spite of her best efforts, the client finds that her usual strategies do not work in the relationship. Since the therapist does not permit the client to control the relationship, the client has two options:

accept the conditions that are being offered or drop out of the relationship. If the client elects to stay, then she must develop new relationship patterns. Paradoxically, the healing relationship feels less safe and more frustrating even as healthy change occurs.

Therapeutic relationships are also paradoxical in the way control and power are exercised. The ultimate goal of any therapeutic interaction is an increased sense of control and responsibility on the part of the client. Yet according to the principles of complementarity, when the therapist leads, the client follows, taking a docile and submissive position. Thus, paradoxically, the road toward enhancing client control is reached by way of the therapist's giving up control.

Most of us would agree that in order to influence the client toward change, we must provide different or discrepant information. However, if what we provide is too different, the client will not be open to taking it in. Therefore, we must walk a fine line between controlling the relationship definition and providing enough comfort so that the client will not leave. This paradox goes even more deeply into some of our cherished beliefs. Many of us believe that the longer a client and therapist work together the better they get to know each other, and thus the better they work together as a team to promote change. Yet, from an interactional perspective, long-standing relationships may not be as helpful as we have traditionally believed—unless they change over time, continuing to emphasize differences. Without change, there is no influence, and no healing.

Therapeutic Relationships as Social Constructions

So far, the elements posited to describe the interactional dimension of therapeutic relationships have been presented as somewhat discrete, yet they fit together under the larger conceptual framework of *social constructivism*. This philosophical perspective explains the process by which people come to describe, explain, or otherwise account for the world (including themselves) in which they live. For the therapist, in offering the following assumptions, it offers a unique philosophy from which to think integratively about the interactional dimension of the therapeutic relationship.

The therapy relationship is a co-constructed social interaction. The most basic assumption of social constructivism is that interactional patterns gain meaning *only* when considered within the context of the particular relationship in which they occur. In turn, relationships gain meaning because of the broader cultural and social context in which they exist. The significance of this view is that we ought to be placing more emphasis in our work on what things mean rather than how they are caused.

The therapeutic relationship evolves dynamically. Through the course of dialogue, a co-constructed meaning of the problem and a co-negotiated definition of client and therapist roles begin to emerge. Regularities of behavior and co-generated definitions of the nature of the relationship then influence future interactions by encouraging certain therapist and client behaviors while discouraging others. Therapist behaviors such as empathy, self-disclosure, and interpretation have therapeutic value only within this co-constructed relationship, not because of a predetermined template. The outcome of a relationship represents neither the intentions, beliefs, or meaning of either the therapist or client but rather a *synthesis* of the intentions, beliefs, or meaning of both (Angus, 1992).

From this social constructivist perspective, a working alliance can be viewed as the desired outcome of the process of co-construction. The heart of the working alliance will be the collaborative agreement concerning goals and subsequent tasks in therapy, and collaboration will be based on a synthesis of client and therapist expectations, beliefs, and knowledge. In fact, the working alliance may actually be a measure of the degree of client and therapist agreement concerning the co-construction of the relationship.

Language is the medium of social interaction. A long-held adage holds that language mirrors reality. The social constructivist perspective assumes, to the contrary, that language and the social dialogue in which language occurs, *constructs* reality (McNamee, 1992; Wittgenstein, 1953). For Gergen and Kaye (1992), it is by virtue of how language is used in the co-construction of explanations about self, others, and events that meaning is developed in relationships. Since the basic premise of social constructivism is that meaning is created in partnerships, the role of language becomes crucial in any social interaction. Also, since human interactions are, by their nature, language-generating systems, they are consequently meaning-generating systems (Anderson & Goolishian, 1992).

There are two specific ways in which language is important. First, words, or vocabulary, are vehicles that carry implicit meaning. As meaning-laden symbols, words may stimulate affective and cognitive experiences. Language may thus create an idiosyncratic brand of knowledge, because these symbols are based on a distinctive set of social assumptions and beliefs (Maturana & Varela, 1987). Language as a symbolic medium is also what individuals use to develop narrative explanations about their lives and cultures and about the relationships that are their reference points for understanding and generating meaning. Narratives, the very fabric of our story-centered work, are language-based explanations of phenomena that occur within individuals (by way of talking to oneself), in relationships with others (by way of conversation), and among members of a culture (by way of cultural mores, myths, and values). Once developed and internalized, narratives become the basis of knowledge regarding self and the world. White and Epston (1990) postulate that it is the distinctions drawn in conversational language that make the social discourse process important. The types of distinctions drawn determine what properties are attributed to events and, consequently, the meanings of those events. Because these distinctions serve as the basis of individuals' knowledge of the world, they promote behaviors that are congruent with the narrative and discourage behaviors that are not.

Second, language is important because the development of narratives is inherently social, a process performed in conjunction with others. Language is not, however, used merely for verbal exchange but also to shape patterns of relational activity. Language use is an active process of adopting certain relationship positions and behavioral stances in regard to the issues identified in the narrative (Epston, White, & Murray, 1992). As the client and therapist deal with issues considered important, a narrative develops that distinguishes certain features of the events. Based on this mutual creation, certain behaviors or interactional sequences become more logical than others. For the therapy relationship, it is the manner in which those conversations promote or limit relationship development that is of primary concern (McNamee, 1992).

Language influences social interaction through its influence on cognitive processes. The contention that human action is influenced not by the reality of the world but the way in which that world is perceived is an operating assumption not only of social constructivism but also of a number of other systems, such as the cognitive therapy of Aaron Beck and the rational emotive therapy of Albert Ellis. Cognitive psychology traditionally focuses on the premise that understanding is the result of a person's perceptual system and that "reality" is primarily a projection of those cognitive structures.

By encouraging a shift of emphasis away from the individual to the interactions that take place, the social constructivist perspective also supports the principle that individuals are active participants in the interpretation, meaning generation, and proactive selection of the physical and social contexts in which they operate (Mahoney, 1991). The dialogue between client and therapist is the mechanism that influences the mental representations and organization of information that are the basis of personal knowledge.

Toward Integration

It is the interactional patterns that develop in relationships that form what we ordinarily think of as the authentic and projected dimensions of therapy. These patterns take on a life of their own, encouraging some actions, discouraging others, fluctuating between periods of stability and chaos.

The previous chapters have laid the personal, cultural, conceptual, and multidisciplinary foundations of the healing nature of relationships. The aim has been to present ideas that challenged, stimulated, and disoriented you, and caused you to recast your views of how you operate with your clients, especially when you feel yourself being pulled into a black hole. The intention in Part Three is to draw inferences from these threads and dimensions in order to create specific guidelines for clinical application during sessions. After describing how the integrative model presented in Chapter Five can be employed to make sense of what is going on at various stages in the therapeutic process, Part Three offers suggestions for functioning differently in relationships with clients.

Part Three

Clinical Challenges

Chapter Ten

The Nature of Healing in Relationships

Parts One and Two have detailed how four distinct threads characterize therapeutic relationships. It is the personal thread that represents those aspects of people relating to one another that benefit both therapist and client. When the cultural thread is added to the personal thread, it becomes clear that healing relationships are neither modern nor solely Western phenomena, but have occurred throughout history and across diverse cultures. The theoretical and empirical thread, with strands from a multitude of disciplines, describes a multidimensional model of the therapeutic relationship, in which the authentic dimension, the projected dimension, and the interactional dimension intertwine to form a healing alliance. These dimensions compose the conceptual thread.

Conceptual descriptions in any field are exceedingly more useful when they are accompanied by clinical applications. Thus, although information from a variety of sources has already been integrated in the previous sections, this exploration of the therapeutic relationship can hardly be complete until it has also examined the clinical dimension in order to discover how the concepts described may be put into practice. It is the therapist who must successfully navigate the complex interpersonal interactions with clients. It is the therapist who must pull these threads together into a useful package that works. Thus, it is this last, but essential, clinical thread, that binds the others together.

This chapter has two agendas. First, drawing upon each of the first four threads, it will integrate what this book has posited about the healing nature of the relationship into a series of clinically applicable principles. Second, given these principles, it will show how the model outlined in Chapter Five provides a new map for the therapist to follow in successfully negotiating effective therapeutic relationships that incorporate all the common dimensions.

Guiding Principles

Taken from all we have covered previously, the following eight summary statements best represent the clinical thread and form the guiding principles for what we do with our clients:

Principle one: the healing nature of relationships is universal, while the practice of healing is culturally specific. It is of more than passing interesting that the basic characteristics of Western therapeutic relationships, as revealed by empirical methods, are also found in the relationships developed by healers in other cultures, for example, in the jungles of Peru, Africa, or Malaysia. Not only are there some striking parallels in our methods as compared to those from other cultures but there are also some instructive differences.

The healer, or *brujo*, who lives and works in the Andes of Peru, who has developed his strategies over thousands of years from his Incan ancestors, employs a number of methods that seem strangely familiar. First of all, he begins treatment with a format similar to our group therapy, as participants journey together to a remote mountaintop setting. There they form a circle of bonds with their healer and with one another. Confidences are exchanged. Secrets are shared. Intimacy and trust develop over the course of the long night.

Next, the *brujo* carefully constructs a complementary relationship with each client, relating to him or her as an expert who has been further endowed with higher powers. He looks deep into each person's eyes, as if he really can catch glimpses of the soul lurking within. After listening closely to each individual's plight—which may include everything from sexual dysfunctions and dysthymia to family problems or chronic pain—the healer then prescribes treatments with authority and great drama. Compliance to his recommendations is assured, since the belief of his clients is that divine intervention can be for better or for worse, and one would not wish to anger the spirits even more by refusing to comply.

The *brujo*'s practices are but one way to illustrate the universal nature of healing encounters. One of the unique characteristics of the relationship between client and healer in some cultures is that it is viewed as a shared journey. Client and healer enter the spirit world together. They both endure hardships (strenuous dancing or sleep deprivation), trials (vomiting and purging), and shared experiences (drinking hallucinogens or meditating). During this shared journey, clients do not feel alone in their misery and bewitchment. Not only are they are offered nurturing by their brethren and the healer but also their fears are specifically allayed through special chants and dances. These methods almost always work, since they will continue, if necessary, for hours on end, until the client agrees that he or she feels cleansed.

In our Western version of therapy, we reinforce similar ideas of a shared journey when we use the pronoun "we" to encourage the idea that we are in a partnership with the client ("*We* need to look at this together"), because our clients feel so alone in their misery, often without much intimacy or companionship. Figuratively, the therapeutic relationship is one in which we offer to take their hands and guide them to find a way out of their maze of confusion. Such interventions as self-disclosure strengthen the perceived similarity between client and therapist, communicating on a profound level that "I was once like you but I found a way out. So can you."

In our culturally specific manner, we unite with our clients and welcome them into the journey of change. The witch doctors of the Amazon may use a form of ritualized hypnotic induction procedures. We do something quite similar when we welcome our clients, infusing a sense of confidence while capitalizing on the placebo effect ("You came to the right place"; "I can help you"; "Trust me and we'll figure this out"; "You probably feel better already"). Given sufficient patience on the part of the client, and sufficient flexibility and inventiveness on our part, treatment continues until the client agrees that goals have been met. (This, of course, does not necessarily mean they were met; simply that the client reports feeling better.)

Principle two: the activities of the healing encounter are a series of culturally specific rituals that enhance the power and influence of the healer. The *brujo* wears special clothes that attest to his stature in the community. His consultation chambers may boast a stuffed condor, the ultimate symbol of power. His vast array of healing implements—swords, skulls, potions, pharmaceutics, herbs—lends testimony to his mastery of the spirit world.

We also begin our work on a culturally specific stage. In our offices, diplomas and book-lined walls create an atmosphere of wisdom and expertise. We begin our sessions with rituals that may not specifically resemble the *brujo*'s chants and incantations but that also offer hope, comfort, and structure. Clients are requested to fill out forms. They are invited to tell their stories. As we take notes, nod understandingly, provide preliminary guidance, we are already establishing ourselves as knowledgeable experts in clients' eyes.

Regardless of the specific culture, the healer knows and does mysterious things to work his magic, rarely explaining himself. He may enhance his prestige and expertise in others' eyes by passing a small rodent over the client's body, sacrificing it to examine its internal organs, and then confidently proclaiming the exact location in the client's body where the infestation has taken place. These diagnoses are always correct since they cannot be refuted. We also present ourselves in a manner that enhances our influence. We appear understanding, expert, trustworthy, and attractive. We structure sessions according to a process that is known to us but usually mysterious to the client. We offer hypotheses or interpretations regarding what may be taking place in a client's life, hypotheses that cannot be directly confirmed. The client feels relief in hearing a plausible explanation for a mysterious ailment that, heretofore, was frightening because its etiology was unknown.

Thus, we might say, "The reason why your panic attacks seem to strike you with no warning in the most unpredictable of circumstances is because you have ignored more subtle signs your body has been giving you that the stress level in your life is too high. This is your body's way of saying slow down." Only the least intimidated and mystified of clients will ask us, "So how long have you been having conversations with people's bodies in which they speak to you and tell you why they are doing what they are doing?"

More subtle actions also magnify our therapeutic mystique. We might place a clock in a strategic location so that we can appear to always know what time it is without looking (clients often assume we have some built-in time mechanism, just as birds have a navigation system that leads them with unerring accuracy to their winter vacation homes). Similarly, we may appear to be able to read the client's mind by offering interpretations or reflections of feeling that are exactly on target ("How did you know that I had been abused as a child? I barely gave you any background"). We smile enigmatically and shrug, but we know full well that it is our vast clinical experience with hundreds of similar cases that allows us to hypothesize and make predictions with surprising accuracy. We do all of these things not to be deceptive or manipulative, of course, but to create the healing relationship that is likely to be most constructive.

Because of the healer's unavoidable special cultural role, the therapeutic relationship is definitely not one of equals. The healer stands aloof, apart from others, even as she joins them in their chants, songs or vision quests. Within her community at large, she is endowed with special status and privileges. To a Peruvian healer, reputation is everything. Many clients will travel great distances and pay the equivalent of a month's wages in order to be granted and audience with a particular *brujo*. Similarly, the greater the prestige that clients ascribe to our position as professionals, the more likely they are to give weight to what we have to say and to comply with what we request of them.

Principle three: the personal connection promotes changes in both the client and the helper. The very nature of human interaction sat-isfies important human needs. Both therapists and clients gain a sense of kinship, a shared personal history, and a connection that may satisfy both personal and possibly biological needs. Thus, ther-apy is not simply a matter of techniques, treatments, or the result of some special power of the helper. It is a personal connection that nourishes and encourages change in all those involved. The impor-tance of the personal connection between any two people is evi-dent in the individuals' reports of immense personal help received from bartenders, hairdressers, lawyers, and others. In fact, as previ-ously noted, some empirical literature suggests that, indeed, ama-teurs at times do admirable work. All have had experiences supporting the notion of the personal bond that promotes healing. Each of us has known times when an encounter with someone who is not a practitioner has provided the support, perspective, or infor-mation that seemed to assuage a burden in life.

Principle four: healing relationships have reciprocal influence. It is not only the client who changes in a therapeutic relationship. The environment of this encounter is so potent that effects radiate in all directions, affecting not only the significant people in the client's life but also the therapist. It is impossible to spend time with someone in such an intimate, emotionally charged, and honest exchange without being changed by the process. As practitioners we are touched by the lives of the people whom we attempt to influence. There is not a single session we are ever part of that we do not later reflect considerably on, mulling over what happened and what it means for us as well as the client. The interactive nature of our work is such that we become part of the systems that we attempt to change. Even more intriguing (and frightening) is how our own families may become sucked in as well. Things that our clients do and say to us continue to reverberate inside our heads and hearts, for better or worse, impacting the ways we think about ourselves and others, influencing how we act in the future.

Principle five: the therapeutic relationship is a process; it is a means to an end. Unlike other close personal relationships, those that are healing are designed to be transitional. The ultimate goal is not to create intimacy for its own sake but to help clients change. The objective is to make the relationship unnecessary in the shortest period of time. Without this principle, therapy becomes a relationship without boundaries and without direction. While the terminal nature of therapeutic relationships may seem artificial, disturbing, and sometimes even uncomfortable, there is something important about this principle that makes healing possible. Much of the influence and change in the client-therapist interaction may actually be dependent upon that interaction's temporary status. It may be that some of the power of therapy comes from its freshness, its specialness and uniqueness, and the precious nature of its limited tenure. This helps explain why much of the research literature on outcomes indicates that clients receive most of their help in the first several sessions.

Principle six: every therapeutic relationship is multidimensional. To say that the therapeutic relationship is complex is, to say the least, an understatement. (The central section of this book has been devoted to identifying the many dimensions of the relationship that are operative at any given time.) These multiple layers and levels of interaction can be baffling, particularly when you are caught in the middle of them. The proposed multidimensional model of the relationship (see Chapter Five) accounts for the common elements in all therapeutic relationships. Rather than representing any single theoretical perspective, this integrative model depicts both unique and invaluable features from many different perspectives. The authentic dimension is the direct and uncontaminated side of the relationship. It can be represented by the notions of genuineness, empathy, and regard that are typically associated with facilitative conditions. This dimension is additionally explained by the social psychological forces of attraction, commitment, and influence. The projected dimension recognizes those unseen ghosts from the past that to one degree or another have an impact on the nature of the relationship. Powerful interactional patterns, based on the authentic and projected dimensions, come to define, promote, and limit the relationship. Once established, these interactional patterns seem to take on a life of their own. Finally, when all of these components are combined in an effective manner, the therapeutic relationship evolves into a *healing alliance*.

Principle seven: every therapeutic relationship is unique. While therapeutic relationships have common dimensions, each relationship is unlike any other. Part of the uniqueness evolves from the shared interaction that occurs in therapy. Through conversation, a narrative is built in which the therapist and client come to explain the client's concern and the nature of their relationship. This story is influenced by events of the authentic encounter as well as the projections of both therapist and client. Once constructed, the narratives carry certain interactional guidelines that strongly influence the course of the relationship. It is the specifics of these narratives that give each therapeutic relationship its uniqueness.

Although social constructivism is discussed in many disciplines, in the therapeutic relationship it takes on special meaning. For example, early in their relationship, therapist and client need to develop a shared explanation of the nature and etiology of the problem. It is not so crucial that the explanation be "true" as that both believe the same explanation. One of the therapist's major tasks, in any culture, setting, or profession, is to facilitate this common narrative and shared belief about how and what to do. To the Peruvian witch doctor, there is a supernatural rather than an empirical basis for most illness, a belief that is also shared by his clients. They agree that emotional distress is caused by sorcery of some sort—the envy of others, bad luck, or "bad air" that emanated from the spirit world of the dead. They also agree that only "white" magic can combat evil. For our Western relationships to work, as well, there must be agreement on the cause of the problem and the mechanism by which a cure will take place. If the client believes his agitation and panic will only lessen with mediation while the therapist is sure that cognitive restructuring is the answer, there is not likely to be a successful outcome to treatment.

Principle eight: the healing alliance is dynamic and changes over time. Relationships in general and the therapeutic relationship in particular are developmental. We have all seen that our early relationships with clients are quite different than those after a long working collaboration. In addition, numerous empirical studies have indicated that therapeutic relationships are not static, but change, vary, and progress as the participants journey through the psychotherapeutic process. In our field, it is the stages of therapy that are most often denoted in the therapeutic journey. The result is a glaring omission in the plethora of conceptual and theoretical pieces: a lack of attention toward identifying the manner in which the relationship changes over time. For the practitioner, such knowledge is critical if we hope to alter what we do according to what is most likely to work at any given moment in time.

Navigating Therapeutic Relationships

This was Connie's first session with her therapist, Nawall. She had been experiencing a great deal of ambivalence regarding her relationship with her husband. Connie entered Nawall's office with a considerable amount of trepidation; she was concerned that, if she told Nawall too much, the therapist would certainly side with Connie's husband. All through the first hour, Connie wondered if Nawall could be trusted (*Does she understand me? Does she care?*). Nawall was equally cautious. She was also involved in her own form of systematic scrutiny of the process, assessing what was going on, calculating what the client could handle. It was as if they both were walking on eggshells. The questions that bombarded Nawall's mind were the same ones she had when she thought about most of her clients (*When have I demonstrated enough empathy? I know there is something from her past that is influencing our interaction, but when is the right time to confront her with this? I have been very accommodat-*

ing with Connie, but I wonder if it is time to be more proactive? Should different "facilitative conditions" be offered as the relationship progresses to the middle and latter stages?).

Throughout the next four weeks, Nawall and Connie became more familiar with one another and their relationship changed in numerous ways. Both began to feel as if they were more able to take risks, with Connie being able to divulge more and Nawall becoming more confrontive. Nawall was initially interested in fostering some dependence, hoping to increase the bond between them. As therapy progressed, however, Nawall became more interested in guiding Connie toward increased autonomy and independence, gradually decreasing the strength of the alliance. As this example illustrates, the four dimensions of the therapeutic relationship (authentic engagement, projected images, interactional patterns, and healing alliance) evolve in a manner that is *both* epigenetic and reciprocal. On one hand, the dimensions change as therapy progresses, and each stage of the relationship prepares the way for what is to come next. A solid authentic engagement and sorting of projected images leads to a set of interactional rules that facilitate a healing alliance. On the other hand, changes in any one dimension also influence each of the other dimensions reciprocally. For example, as interactional dynamics are negotiated, the authentic relationship also improves and the projected images become less influential, which leads to a more stable working alliance.

Investigations allow the conclusion that these epigenetic and reciprocal changes can be identified. While each relationship is unique in its content and not every therapeutic relationship always changes in exactly the same way, there appears to be a common progression of changes that occurs over time. It is not a matter, however, of each dimension within the relationship simply dissolving as each therapy stage is concluded. Therefore, in the descriptions of the five developmental stages of the relationship that follow, the dimension that is highlighted is the one in which the *primary* work is occurring, not the sole dimension that is

involved. Moreover, these five stages are somewhat arbitrary distinctions, made for purposes of illustration, in a process in which
clear demarcations do not exist in actual practice.

Preliminary Stage

The relationship between therapist and client may begin with
something as innocuous as a telephone conversation that sets up
an appointment. In other situations, the first contact may occur
with a handshake or greeting. Whatever form those first moments
take, the development of the relationship begins in those moments.
Even if the preliminary stage is not marked by monumental revelations and consists mainly of small talk and social pleasantries, it
has a fundamental impact. As Figure 10.1 illustrates, the authentic dimension is critical at the time of initial impressions, while the
other dimensions are relatively less important. Projected images,
while meaningful, are not the primary area of relating; the interactional patterns have yet to evolve; and the healing alliance is
nonexistent. At this point, it is extremely difficult to project
whether therapy will be helpful or not.

In the authentic dimension, both the client and therapist begin
to feel the force of attraction. It may be related to physical characteristics, client perception of therapist credibility, or behaviors of
the clients that indicate they are motivated to work. In addition,
as the following example illustrates, even at this early point, clients
are quickly developing perceptions regarding the therapist's ability
to help. The constructs of attraction and social power are significant at this point in the process and influence the evolution of the
relationship.

Shawn worked as a construction foreman, while Susan, his
wife, was a homemaker. They came to Janet for help in rectifying
what Susan labeled a "communication problem" in their relationship. Susan had made the call to make the first appointment. Janet
always made her own appointments, so after receiving Susan's

Figure 10.1. Preliminary Stage.

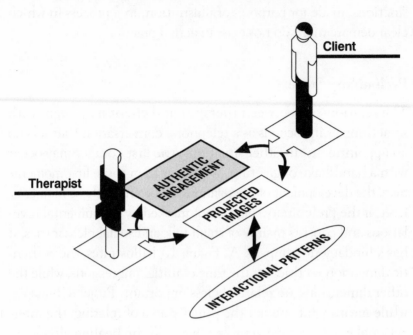

message, she returned their call later that night, after her last client. Susan was initially impressed at Janet's warm but businesslike attitude, her prompt response, and her interest in their situation. Susan felt hopeful after this first contact, because Janet had stressed that the introductory session was designed to ascertain if all parties felt that they could work together. Susan knew that her husband had reservations, and she liked Janet's not just assuming that everything was set.

Shawn was a reluctant participant at best. In his and Susan's discussions regarding therapy, he expressed no desire to go in and have the "doctor" analyze and diagnosis him. He argued that he had never liked stuffy offices and didn't enjoy sitting and talking. He also was not sure how some "intellectual" could ever understand a down-home kind of guy like him. Shawn was afraid that, because he was not very articulate, the therapist would certainly favor Susan and side with her. However, in their first few minutes of contact in Janet's office, Shawn began to relax. He could not put his finger on it but something in Janet's style was reassuring. She looked him in the eye and shook his hand as she met him. She asked him direct questions, and seemed down to earth. He still had doubts, but he decided that at least he was willing to try.

Beginning Stage

After the initial contact, the formal part of the therapy usually commences with a preliminary discussion of the client's presenting concerns and the gathering of appropriate background information. At this stage, the authentic dimension persists in its significance. The client continues to evaluate the trustworthiness and credibility of the therapist, and the therapist assesses and forms clinical impressions about the client. These initial impressions are both confirmed and altered as the relationship progresses. This is the stage of rapport, in which client and therapist come to know each other.

In the structure of our Western form of therapy, it is at this point that the clients tell their stories. This continuation of their self-disclosures is facilitated by the empathic, genuine, and compassionate responses of the therapist. At this early stage, the depth of the authentic dimension is fully developed, as both therapist and client strive to connect. As therapy progresses both therapist and client come to know each other more closely. This is reflected in the curiosity that many clients exhibit concerning their therapists' interests, temperaments, and life-styles.

It is at this stage that the projected experiences of the past begin to emerge (Figure 10.2) as the client begins to project onto the therapist those expectations that originated in past relationships. The client's conflicted relationship patterns usually become activated when the emotions of "unfinished business" bubble to the surface through the therapist's methods. Therapists, as well, react with their own projected images. Furthermore, much of the struggle over what

Figure 10.2. Beginning Stage.

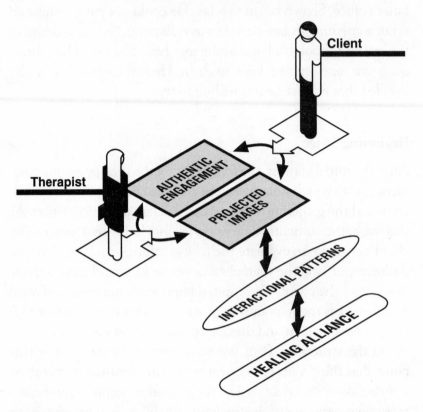

the interactional definition of the relationship will be takes place as these projected images from the past emerge.

As we well know, the advent of the projected dimension is not necessarily a negative occurrence. However, it can be detrimental to the therapeutic process if the therapist ignores these ghosts. The arrival of transference signals the opportunity for client insight and understanding of relationship patterns as they are unfolding. These transference issues are normal, to be expected, and when placed on the table, as shown in the following continuation of the previous example, help promote the progress of therapy.

Shawn had begun to experience some difficulties with authority figures at an early age. He and his father often disagreed about the most trivial of matters. This theme of discord and antagonism transferred to Shawn's relationships with friends and bosses. Shawn tried to work hard at getting along well, but it always seemed that his superiors would end up criticizing and humiliating him. In retrospect, he had seemed to anticipate a similar reaction from Janet. Therefore, when she would respond to one of his statements, he would be sure to correct her, just so she would not get too uppity. And to Shawn's surprise this seem to work, for instead of holding her ground and arguing, she stood corrected and even apologized for misunderstanding him. Shawn was not actually aware of his subsequent behavior, but he found himself baiting her into being critical of him. Finally, in a tense moment, Shawn began to scream angrily at Janet and accuse her of only listening to Susan. Janet did not respond with animosity; instead, she began to discuss Shawn and Susan's patterns of communication. The discussion led to Shawn's expressing a conviction that "offense is the best defense— or hit somebody before they hit you." Janet used his angry responses to her as examples of his relationship patterns. Shawn began to realize that what he wanted from others (respect) was not what he was actually asking for (animosity).

As the example illustrates, the interactional patterns begin to emerge at this stage. While not the primary focus of the work, the participants' preliminary definition of what will constitute their new therapeutic relationship begins to take shape. As a result of his or her distinct background and experiences, each client enters therapy with an individual set of expectations. Clients hope to get their therapists, as individuals hope to get anyone with whom they are entering a relationship, to behave according to the clients' pictures of what therapy should be. At this point, the future of the relationship resides with the therapist. If the therapist does not follow (at least to some extent) the client's definition of the relationship, therapy may soon end. It is the complementarity between therapist and client that is the hook, or the glue, that helps the client get through these early and tense times.

Middle Stage

It is in the middle stage that interpersonal interaction becomes of paramount importance (Figure 10.3). At this juncture, the initial agreement and established complementarity between the therapist and client begin to change as conflict increases. The interactional stability established in the previous stage is now disrupted, and instability is introduced. It is at this stage that the therapist becomes aware of the client's previous relationship patterns, since they are unfolding before the therapist's eyes. The therapist no longer accepts the client's typical style but, instead, tries to expand the definition of what is possible between them. In this middle stage of the relationship, the therapist has two primary goals. First, it is necessary for the therapist to identify when the client's interactional style is impeding the progress of therapy. Often, the therapist makes this identification primarily through monitoring the ways that he or she reacts internally and interpersonally to what is taking place. The therapist may feel bored, irritated, or even angry with the client. He or she may feel impotent or helpless. Second, once the client's eliciting behavior is identified, the therapist needs to alter his or her own behavior in such a way as to change the level of complementarity in the relationship. By changing behavior, the therapist destabilizes the relationship and introduces a degree of conflict. Change begets change. The therapist's change will force the client to alter his or her behavior as well.

This is the stage in which premature termination is most likely to occur. It may be that the client's interactional style is extremely rigid, and the client cannot adapt to changes initiated by the therapist. It may also be that the therapist changes too much too quickly and asks the client to stretch beyond his or her ability. It is a bit like walking a tightrope, the therapist must introduce enough difference, but not so much that an extreme client reaction is provoked (for example, feeling set up, abandoned, or betrayed).

As therapy with Shawn and Susan reached this stage, Janet was

Figure 10.3. Middle Stage.

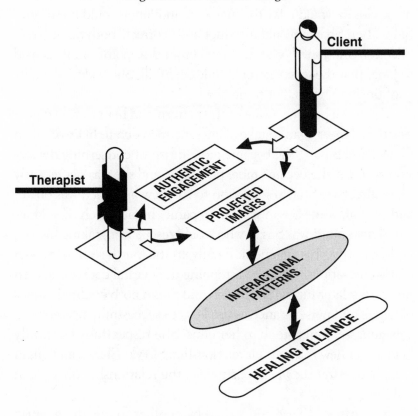

becoming increasingly uncomfortable. She knew that initially she had to connect with Shawn and that if she did not hook him any attempt at marriage counseling would fail. In retrospect, she believed that she had been very successful at satisfying his initial expectations and helping him fit into the structure. Her dissatisfaction centered around the pattern that seemed to have developed in the sessions. Without Janet's intending it, Shawn had taken the role of the expert regarding his relationship with Susan. While the various stories the couple told were different, the pattern was essentially the same. Susan and Shawn would come in, and before Janet could initiate her treatment plan, they would tell her about some monumental fight, event, or conflict that had occurred during the week. Susan would relay the incident, and Janet would listen carefully. Then Shawn would interrupt and "correct" both Susan's recollection and Janet's clarifications. From that point on, it seemed to Janet that the sessions would slide downhill. She had tried mildly confronting Shawn, but to no avail.

Once she became aware of the pattern and her growing dissatisfaction, Janet began to take a different approach to her work with Shawn and Susan. She became more insistent concerning the session agendas, she became more proactive, and she was significantly more directive. Shawn's reaction to the new approach was one of withdrawal, while Susan seemed to panic. In fact, each time Janet cut Shawn off, it was Susan who would rescue him, taking his side and supporting his argument. Finally, in the fourth session, Shawn and Susan seriously discussed stopping the marital counseling with Janet. In a later interview, Shawn and Susan both credited Janet's patience and perseverance as the keys to successfully overcoming this impasse. Janet stuck to her guns. She respectfully but firmly held to her new role in their relationship. Slowly, Shawn and Susan complied. After six weeks of struggle, the relationship once again stabilized.

Sometimes we are concerned by conflict in our therapeutic relationships, but the interactional dimension suggests why this conflict and dissatisfaction can lead to healing. Up to the time of this middle stage, therapist and client have been working toward developing a mutual understanding and an accepting relationship. However, in this stage, the therapist must now introduce discrepant information, play a different role, or confront the client in such a way that changes in client patterns can be instituted. In any of these cases, the therapist takes a new interactional position with the client and disrupts the balance that has been established in previous stages.

As Figure 10.3 illustrates, the healing alliance begins to grow in this stage. As client and therapist work through their conflict, their bond is intensified and fortified. As their interactional struggle stabilizes, it is the client's goals that become most important. If these interactional changes are worked through, the relationship can start to become one in which both participants are working on a commonly defined and understood problem. Their energy can then be invested in agendas directly related to client change. This change continues to take place in the dimension of interaction, but it is the healing nature of the relationship that is most operative.

Ending Stage

In the final stage, the labors of previous steps are rewarded. This is the time that often feels magical. The feelings associated with the healing alliance are intoxicating, and sometimes it is difficult for both the therapist and client to acknowledge that the relationship will inevitably end. Where before there was struggle and uncertainty, now there are set interactional patterns and the comfort level between the client and therapist is at its peak. This is a stage of relationship stabilization (a return to high complementarity), a stage of work, a stage that is goal directed and intentional. As Figure 10.4 illustrates, this is the stage of the healing alliance.

Closing Stage

For Janet, in the ending stage, Shawn and Susan became one of those cases that seemed to be on automatic pilot. It just seemed as if everything began to fall into place. She suggested communication skills exercises that were quickly and easily adopted. She focused on conflict management, and it became almost second nature to them. When she brought up their sexual relations, things seemed to become tense, but using new skills, they were able to work through the conflicts. More and more, Janet felt as if she were a team member, now just facilitating their growth. The goal, from the first contact, has been the healing alliance; now the therapist

Figure 10.4. Ending Stage.

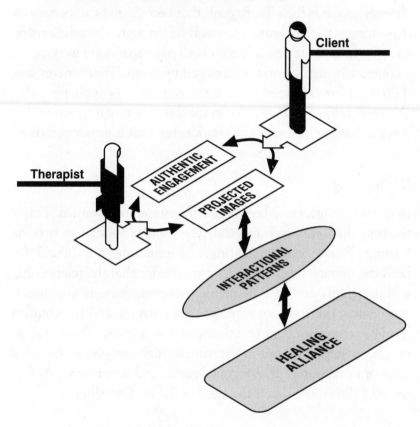

and client must work toward closing their relationship. As the end approaches, the relationship evolves to one of wrapping up business and saying good-bye. Unlike other close relationships, where the goal is to keep and maintain the level of intimacy, in therapeutic relationships the attachment must come to a close. The outgrowth of this developmental progression is a relationship that is more casual and egalitarian.

Ending is about loss as well as gain. Say what you will, but there is grief work to be done as any relationship comes to a close, especially one as intimate as that between client and therapist. Clients feel ambivalent about letting go. We do as well, although we rarely articulate the extent to which we have trouble saying good-bye, as Jeffrey Kottler does here:

> If the truth be told, I feel angry most of the time a client leaves. Once the announcement has been made that the client will not be returning, I do my best to appear proud and supportive, yet inside I also feel hurt, even abandoned. I want to say: "Well, then, go if you like! I hope you have someone to fill your vacant spot in my schedule."
>
> This is immature and unprofessional, I freely acknowledge. Certainly this primary response represents my own needs for intimacy and unresolved relationship issues of my past, yet I have talked to enough clinicians to know that my reaction is not unique. The loss upon ending therapy is indeed felt by *all* the participants.

We have the training, experience, and hopefully, inclination, to work through our ambivalence about ending in such a way that clients can follow our lead. We attempt to integrate, for ourselves, as well as for our clients, a reconciliation between sadness and exhilaration, fear and hope, closeness and distance, past and future. We try hard to end the relationship gracefully so that clients may follow this pattern in such a way that they will no longer avoid intimacy for fear of the loss that may occur.

It is in closing that the authentic dimension is once again prominent (Figure 10.5). The therapist and client have come full circle, beginning predominantly in the authentic dimension and now concluding there.

During their last two sessions, neither Susan nor Shawn had a great deal to say. They had successfully incorporated into their marriage a number of communication rules that, both reported, made dramatic differences in their level of satisfaction. The sexual relationship between them had improved, and the number and level of their conflicts had decreased. This closing stage more closely approximated social conversation rather than therapeutic work.

Figure 10.5. Closing Stage.

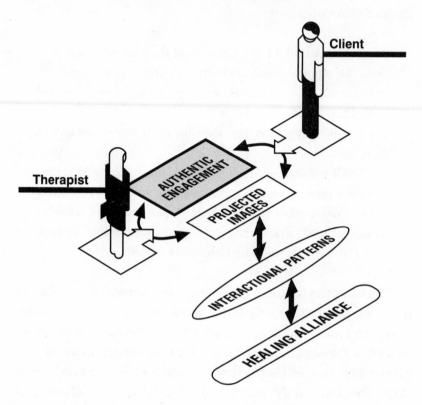

Janet talked some about herself. Susan and Shawn talked about their recent desire to have a baby. When Janet suggested terminating therapy, all three agreed that there was a feeling of loss but concluded that it was time to stop.

Toward Applications in Clinical Practice

The most important elements of each of the threads that form the therapeutic relationship come together into a set of principles that can guide the therapist. Much of the information provided in this chapter is an integration of those principles, which are intended to be atheoretical and culturally universal and to contain the essence of that which is healing in therapeutic relationships. These principles are intended to be the foundation of the final and essential clinical thread.

This chapter has also illustrated a further crucial aspect of the therapeutic relationship: its dynamic and changing nature. Whatever model of the relationship stages you prefer, at each stage, different dimensions of the relationship become important. It is the authentic and projected dimensions that are first prominent. Then the conflict of the interactional stage results in dissatisfaction but also needed changes. Finally, the work of the healing alliance moves toward accomplishing goals.

Up to this point, the discussion has purposefully stayed away from specifically proposing the technical manner in which relationships can be used to produce client change. The next chapters provide these specific guidelines, indicating, first, ways to use these relationship dimensions advantageously and, second, descriptions of what happens when changes do not occur.

Chapter Eleven

Using the Relationship Advantageously

While we are no doubt interested in refining our conceptual understanding of therapeutic relationships, of equal importance to us is translating the principles described in Chapter Ten into a number of practical ways in which we can employ this powerful human connection advantageously. Although as clinicians we often report that the therapeutic relationship is helpful, we do not usually consider the exact methods by which the relationship assists our therapeutic work. Yet this human connection can serve as a vital tool within the process of therapy in a number of ways.

Some Uses of the Therapeutic Relationship

The therapeutic relationship is an instrument that has many uses, which will be examined in turn. It may function as:

A diagnostic aid

An interpersonal engagement

A personal support system

A basis for social influence

A means to finishing old business

A path to intimacy

A problem-solving collaboration

A new interaction experience

An enforcement of boundaries

A new construction of reality

Most of these therapeutic functions are employed by the majority of practitioners some of the time, although each of us places more emphasis on some applications over others. In part, we base our choices on certain client variables: the presenting complaint, the client's expectations and stated preferences, the client's personality and interpersonal style. In addition, our decision how best to use the therapeutic alliance is based upon factors related to our own theoretical position, conceptual models, and personal preferences. Thus, a therapist who is not especially comfortable structuring a relationship upon clearly defined parameters and strict rules of engagement will not often use the model that requires these techniques unless it is clearly indicated (as for severe personality disorders). Likewise, a practitioner who shies away from professional relationships that are informal, spontaneous, and intimate exchanges, based upon genuine expressions of feelings between client and therapist, is not going to choose the model that requires these techniques.

If the therapeutic relationship truly has the components identified in previous chapters, it may be that all these uses of the relationship are important if lasting client changes are to occur. The suggestion here is that we must be flexible, using all these dimensions of the relationship at some time during the course of therapy. At least this is the authors' hope—that as our profession continues to evolve, as we increasingly come to understand the nature of the therapeutic relationship, we can use as many different facets of this alliance as possible in order to help our clients make constructive changes in their lives.

A Diagnostic Aid

Regardless of your individual orientation, whether psychodynamic, cognitive-behavioral, humanistic, or systemic, it is likely that you attend to your relationships with clients as clues to the issues they are struggling with. The therapeutic relationship thus represents a sample of behavior, not unlike client performance on any assessment instrument or observation of client actions in real-life predicaments. In some ways, there is no more fertile environment in which to learn how a client deals with interpersonal intimacy and conflict than the encounter that takes place between client and therapist. Anchin and Kiesler (1982) also see this encounter as a primary source of diagnostic information. Each of us employs an interpersonal style that he or she brings to new relationships. Naturally, clients enter therapy with the same interpersonal styles that they use in their social worlds, styles that evoke complementary sets of responses in the therapist.

One assessment orientation thus takes the form of identifying the parallel pattern that emerges in such client-therapist interactions and exploring how it affects the presenting issues. Another area of assessment, suggested by Cashdan (1982), focuses on the relationship as an initial glimpse into the maladaptive strategies that may be at the center of the client's problematic social relationships. In this view, individuals can develop either adaptive strategies (those that are mutual, reciprocal, and beneficial to all participants in a relationship) or maladaptive strategies (those that exploit, benefit only one relationship participant, and bind individuals into unsatisfactory long-term interaction). *Pathology* is then defined as a function of maladaptive interpersonal strategies rather than intrapsychic dynamics. These dysfunctions are particularly apparent within close personal relationships, especially with respect to the four maladaptive strategies (power, dependency, martyrdom, and sexuality) that may be particularly important in diagnosing client presenting concerns. For each of these styles, the therapist will notice the complementary roles of feeling powerless, dependent, martyr-like, or sexually seductive.

For example, during her second meeting with a Hispanic man in his early thirties, an African-American female therapist noticed some discomfort on his part in talking about some of the intimate details of his conflicts at work, about which he was seeking help. Sensing some tension related to their ethnic differences, the therapist was at first reluctant to bring up the issue, questioning whether the discomfort was more her problem than his (during their first session she felt he had been condescending and unnecessarily aggressive). Given that his presenting complaints were related to conflicts with others at work, especially an African-American female supervisor and several co-workers who were of cultural backgrounds other than his own Mexican-American heritage, the therapist began to wonder if the tension she was feeling might not be evidence of what he had been describing was taking place at work. Just as she felt the impulse to "put him in his place," to spar with him in a competitive way to prove she was his equal, perhaps people at work with whom he was in conflict were feeling similarly threatened.

She decided to check out her hypothesis by sharing with him what she observed about their own interactions. He then became even more aggressive, apparently confirming her observations (although other possibilities also occurred to her, since she realized she might have been aggravating him through defensive actions on her own part). With patience, and a certain amount of struggle on the part of both, a degree of trust between them did develop to the point at which the client felt safe in admitting that, indeed, he did feel animosity toward others outside his culture, especially those in positions of power over him (such as supervisors and therapists). The key to understanding his dysfunctional patterns, and subsequently changing them, was thus identified most clearly by using the therapeutic relationship as a diagnostic aid.

Much the same process takes place in a number of ways when we ask ourselves the following diagnostic questions about a relationship and, if our results seem valid, then direct a number of questions towards the client.

Relationship Diagnostic Checklist

- What is the cultural context for the client's experience?
- What is going on in our relationship that parallels other conflicted encounters taking place in the client's life?

- What is the client doing that is getting in the way of my knowing, understanding, or becoming close to him or her?
- How are the life themes and past difficulties in the client's life being played out during our encounters?
- How does the pattern already established appear limiting?
- What recurrent issues between us might represent dysfunctional or fully functioning behavior on the part of the client?
- What interactional role and relationship position does the client take in our therapeutic relationship?
- What interactional therapist role is being evoked in me by the client?
- How has my credibility been compromised?
- How has my humanness been withheld or diluted?

Combs, Avila, and Purkey (1971) once postulated that it is the therapist's "self" that is the most important instrument in assessing, understanding, and treating clients. This book contends that it is probably more appropriate for us to move beyond using our internal perceptions as the sole primary mode of assessment and to start making assessments by using the interactive phenomenon, the relationship *between* therapist *and* client, which offers some of the most valuable information about the client's characteristic functioning, not only about present problems but also about unresolved issues of the past.

An Interpersonal Engagement

As previously mentioned, successful therapeutic relationships must develop and change as the therapist and client come to know each other and establish a stable interactional pattern. It is the initial involvement that determines if the relationship will ever progress to the later stages in which change may occur. Thus, as every clinician well understands, it is of major importance that we help the client feel involved and invested in the relationship, not as a spectator but as an active participant. The social psychological perspective suggests that involvement and commitment in relationships result from the perception by the client of a potentially rewarding encounter (when compared to others available at the same time). The client anticipates that we have something to offer and that becoming involved with us will somehow be beneficial. This initial attraction is a matter of hooking the client by establishing conditions under which we can be perceived as significant others. Consider the example of Rebecca, a therapist who senses that she had only a few minutes to make contact with the surly, pockmarked adolescent scowling at her. She wonders if it is already too late; perhaps she has hesitated too long, trying to get her bearings and to give him time to adjust to his obviously unpleasant situation. Now, he is impatiently tapping his foot and playing with the delicate things sitting on the table. Is he deliberately provoking her to see if she will stop him? Feeling she has little to lose in an already unstable relationship that is teetering toward rapid extinction, Rebecca abruptly jumps out of her seat, startling the young man from his scowl (momentarily replaced by a look of panic): "Come on," she says. "Let's get out of here. I know a place where we can sit and talk while we get some milk shakes. You *do* like milk shakes, don't you?" A glorious smile erupts on the teenager's face. Contact made.

Saltzman, Luetgert, Roth, Creaser, and Howard (1976) conducted a series of studies that illustrates the importance of engagement as part of therapeutic encounters. After the third session, the clients who dropped out, as compared to those who continued, felt that their therapists did not respect them as individuals and had little understanding of what they were experiencing. Further, they said that the relationship did not feel any different from others and was not thought about much between sessions. These studies illustrate that, within a relatively short period of time, both therapist and client either become engaged in the interaction or begin the process of dropping out. It is also clear that the engagement process is a mutual one. Both therapist and client have expectations that must be fulfilled. If those expectations are not met in some way, engagement does not occur and therapy is not successful.

A Personal Support System

There are some who demean therapy as a waste of time, an exercise in self-indulgence, or nothing more than purchased friendship. Other cynics, who hold regard only for their own brand of treatment to the exclusion of all others, would nevertheless agree with the first group that if therapy primarily does one thing for people, and that one thing most consistently, then what it does is to provide a temporary support system for the client.

The whole process of therapy may be likened to a kind of safety net, a place for people to find consistent support for changes in their lives that they wish to make. Even if it was Carl Rogers who so enthusiastically and poetically lauded the benefits of the therapeutic relationship as a source of support and positive regard, almost every practitioner before and after him has noticed how nurturing, motivating, and encouraging a truly supportive relationship can be. No matter how supportive the client's relationships are with friends or parents, conflict and disagreement are integral parts of these connections. No matter how loved and accepted clients feel by their relatives and peers, they well know that this regard is hardly unconditional. The professed unequivocal love parents feel toward their children comes with a number of strings attached. The support offered by friends is invaluable but, similarly, is contingent on one's acting within acceptable parameters.

In the therapeutic relationship as well, there are certainly conditions, parameters, limits, and contingencies. But what is unique about this kind of relationship is that, as therapists, we have no vested interest in any particular outcome, other than the welfare and best interests of the client. We have few hidden agendas or secret motives. The affection and regard that we express, while certainly predicated upon the client's acting appropriately, nevertheless are more unconditional than those found in other relationships in that we will treat the client with continued respect and support as a person no matter what crime, sin, or destructive act that client has committed. Friends and parents may also feel this way, but their own interests, preferences, and concerns become entangled in whatever it is that they offer. It is only in a therapeutic relationship (with doctors, lawyers, or other helping professionals) that client support is unequivocal and an explicit part of contractual obligations—certainly not support for anything and everything the client says or does, but support in the form of the helper's being a consistent advocate for the client's healthy goals.

Turner, for example, looked like a shell-shocked casualty of war when he first walked in his therapist's door. In a sense, he had been defeated in battle, taken prisoner, tortured, and then set loose a broken man. Turner had been working for the same company for eighteen years when it closed its doors and booted him out on the street, not only without his old job or the prospect of a new one but stripped of his pension and, most of all, his dignity. Turner was despondent, depressed, without hope. His family and friends, trying to do the best they could, encouraged him to find work elsewhere. He appreciated their help but also sensed (or imagined) that they were tired of his moping around and were worried about how his misfortunes would affect them. Turner became embittered and difficult for others to be around.

During the several months Turner was in treatment, his therapist dutifully wrote detailed case notes, treatment plans, and progress summaries, describing all the interventions that he employed and the techniques and structures he used to help Turner. But during reflective moments, when the therapist considered what he had really offered that made the greatest difference, he had to admit that he was rather uncertain that anything was more important than the support he provided. His efforts to provide leads for possible jobs were certainly appreciated. When he reflected Turner's feelings, confronted his exaggerations of disaster, interpreted underlying issues, or summarized core themes, he also observed that these clinical skills were helpful. He did not wish to underestimate the value of the role-plays they created in anticipation of possible interviews, or the structuring efforts he introduced to help Turner regain control of his life. But he could not help but agree with Turner's final assessment during their last session:

> You know, I do appreciate everything you've done and all. I could see how hard you were trying—the things you told me to do and stuff. And I thank you for your ideas, telling me things I should do that I knew I had to do. But, you know, what I think helped me the most was just knowing that no matter how bad things got, I could count on you. My wife, my kids, some of my buddies stuck by me too. I just never felt all right about burdening them. But you, I knew this was your job, so I didn't think that I had to hold back. I could just let myself go and know that you would catch me if I was in any danger. Even when I did take some hard falls, you were there to help me up and get me going again. Your support means everything to me.

Turner could be describing any number of therapeutic ingredients that made the most difference to him, even though he calls them support. It is hard to deny, however, the often-compelling features of any healing relationship in which the therapist's consistent support gives clients the courage, determination, and persistence to follow through on some very tough decisions.

A Basis for Social Influence

Since therapy is a process designed to help clients change, it is by definition an exercise in influence. People are not influenced by what they already know. Instead, the critical elements in change are the discrepancies between ideas individuals already believe and other ideas perceived as useful but different. Of course, if a discrepant idea is too different, it is likely to be rejected; if it is too similar to what is already believed, it will have little impact.

Many of us are quite uncomfortable with the social power we wield as therapists. Some practitioners may even deny that we have the ability or the position to influence clients, believing instead that we are but mirrors that reflect clients' own intentions. Of course, this is hardly true, since unscrupulous practitioners may manipulate individuals into doing a number of things that are not strictly within their freedom to choose. Certainly, if we are honest with ourselves, we will admit that we do impose our will with a greater frequency than we like to acknowledge on the people we see. This influence is evident in the studies that document the extent to which clients' values, and even mannerisms, come to resemble those of their therapists over time. It is hardly a coincidence that we hold, for example, the value that more education is better than less, and lo and behold, most of our clients end up going back to school to better themselves. Our roles require that, for each and every client, we believe that we know what is best for that client and what that client needs to do to straighten out his or her life. We hope we guard against explicitly influencing clients to become what we think they should be, but the reality remains that we do use the leverage of our relationships with clients to guide them in specific directions.

A number of therapists have disclosed examples of how they use this leverage.

> Taking risks is a common theme in my work with clients. I spend most of my time trying to encourage people to overcome their fears, to end destructive relationships or risk beginning new ones.

> When a client is engaging in some actions I consider anyone would agree are pretty stupid, I do everything I can to get him [or her] to stop. This is true if someone is about to do something

life threatening, but [is] also the case when [a] client is about
to quit a job or leave a marriage without thinking through the
consequences of these decisions.

There is a time that is reached in every therapy case when clients
and I both realize that nothing will change unless they are prepared to do some . . . things other than what they are already
doing. This is the most critical point. I use whatever resources
are at my disposal to get the client to get up off his or her butt
and to act.

Chief among the resources mentioned by this last therapist is
the leverage of the relationship, the resource that empowers us to
influence clients to think in alternative ways, to make clearer decisions, to feel differently about their plights, and most importantly,
to act more constructively in the situations where it matters most.

A Means to Finishing Old Business

We have come to expect that certain ways that clients relate to us
are based more on client associations that link us to past relationships than they are responses to us as individuals in the present. It
is, therefore, standard operating procedure for most of us to monitor closely the degree to which clients are acting out unfinished
issues with significant others versus responding to the present
moment ("Is this client angry at me, or at someone I represent?").
The therapeutic relationship as projection is thus not solely within
the province of psychoanalysis, and most of us recognize the value
of helping clients understand that they have unfinished old business, that important relationships from the past continue to haunt,
if not influence, the ways they relate to others in the present. In the
context of therapy, where we make an effort to present ourselves as
neutral advocates who are not using the relationship to meet our
own needs and where many personal markers are, therefore, absent,

clients are even more likely to project assumptions and characteristics that are not based in present reality onto us.

When Catherine, a therapist specializing in weight loss management and healthy life-style programs, began her behavioral treatments, she never imagined the extent to which relationship issues would affect the success of her outcomes. Time and time again, she observed that clients who were most noncompliant seemed to carry over some grudge that influenced their interactions with her. Rather than functioning with Catherine as part of a client-therapist team working toward a common goal, certain clients appeared to enjoy secondary gains from eliciting frustration and disappointment in her. It was as if they were not seeing her as a professional trying to help them as much as a controlling authority figure who was withholding affection. It became clear to Catherine, even within the context of her behavior management programs, that unless she addressed resistances as they were being played out in her client relationships, there was little hope of creating long-term life-style changes.

The ways in which Catherine, or most any clinician, uses the therapeutic relationship as a means to complete unfinished business, will depend on the particular pattern that has emerged. Interpreting the phenomenon directly is, of course, usually the preferred intervention. Catherine might say, "I notice that you seem to enjoy, with an almost perverse delight, reporting that you didn't lose any weight this week. It is as if you are not talking to me at all, but responding to me as if I were your mother, nagging you to do something that you resented." In theory, anyway, the client gains insight into the dysfunctional patterns, completes the unfinished issues, and then ceases using the relationship to act out. In reality, especially under today's time-limited mandates, which may restrict treatments to less than a dozen sessions, we often no longer have the luxury to launch major archaeological digs into the past. Pragmatic concerns may restrict our efforts, so that we focus only on centering the alliance on the treatment goals at hand. We may recognize that the client has some unfinished business, label it as such for the client's benefit, but then work around those issues to target the problem at hand.

Operating under just such limitations, Catherine agreed to work with one obese gentleman for the six sessions contracted with his employer. Whereas it quickly became apparent that his overeating was directly related to unresolved issues with his mother, Catherine chose not to share this insight with him in standard interpretive style. Instead, using dynamic aspects of their therapeutic alliance to form a strategic intervention, she structured their relationship in such a way that it even more closely paralleled the mother-son interaction. In no time, the client vented his anger about the way he was being treated, declared that he no longer needed a mother, or mother figure, to tell him what to do, and then promptly announced that losing weight was a matter of commitment anyway. He would do what he knew he needed to do, and then *he* would determine where they would go next.

After a symbolic protest, Catherine gave in to his declaration of independence, hopeful that he would not only meet his life-style goals but also generalize this new resolve toward relating to his mother differently. While she never had the opportunity to follow up on the success of his efforts to change his relationship with his mother, Catherine did note that he took a more active role in the therapeutic partnership and eventually achieved a significant weight loss.

A Path to Intimacy

There are few relationships that are more intimate than that between therapist and client. People will tell us things they would never even tell themselves, much less anyone who was not a therapist. With the utter privacy, confidentiality, and safety that are built in to the therapeutic relationship, clients are offered opportunities to take interpersonal risks that they would otherwise not venture upon. Perhaps even more so than with lovers, friends, or spouses, individuals are able to reach a type of closeness with us in which they do not have to question hidden agendas or personal motives that are not in their own best interests. After all, therapists are paid for their time specifically in order to maintain professional boundaries that assure security. Where else can a person interact with someone who will provide complete, total, undivided attention; always appear in a good mood, as well as demonstrate boundless patience and good will; guarantee to be available at predetermined times; and exude warmth, caring, and compassion, irrespective of whether the person did what he or she said he or she would do? No wonder intimacy is such an easy by-product of therapeutic relationships.

Whether you believe that therapy provides the ultimate experience in controlled intimacy or not, it certainly simulates a kind of closeness in which the client is unlikely to be neglected, rejected, abused, or taken advantage of. Given the client's less than satisfactory previous encounters with intimacy, the therapeutic relationship supplies the client with an opportunity for getting close without getting burned. Once the client gets a taste of how good it feels to be nurtured, understood, and cared for, it does not take long for a hunger to grow for other experiences that are more reciprocal and "real."

Fred, for example, had lived through a sequence of dismal attempts at intimacy with women. After three failed marriages, two unsuccessful live-in arrangements, and at least a dozen subsequent short-lived dating relationships, he swore off love in the future. He was just not destined to find a compatible partner—or so he told himself and his female therapist.

Fred's mistrust and suspicion of women definitely entered into his interactions with his therapist. In fact, he could be caustic, if not downright hostile, at times. Their relationship was marked by a series of skirmishes and conflicts, explosive crises that the therapist could never seem to predict consistently. The trust between them was tenuous, as was the little progress that had been made in improving his interpersonal functioning. Trust became *the* issue between them. Fred accused the therapist of not really caring about him, of just pretending interest because it was her job. Unable to deny the charge, she nevertheless attempted to address his concerns about being valued. Perhaps as a function of time spent together more than any particular intervention on her part, Fred did come to feel close to his therapist. This intimacy resulted in the vulnerability that both of them expected would develop as a consequence. Now that he finally trusted her, what good would it do, since soon their relationship would end?

Unwilling to face life without the prospect of closeness to a lover, Fred began venturing out once again. He was even able to articulate that, now that he had experienced a truly healthy relationship with a woman for the first time in his life, he knew what he was looking for. The image he was searching for, unfortunately, was someone like his therapist, someone who would take care of him. Thus, instead of creating relationships as he had before in which he was thoroughly in control, he tried the opposite, with equally unsatisfactory results. It took him quite a while (several years) to find a middle ground. Even though he has yet to find a life partner, Fred has shown sufficient resilience and determination to keep trying for the pure pleasure of being close to someone, even if for a finite period of time. He will never forget that his relationship with his therapist taught him that he was capable of relating to a woman as a coequal, a prospect that he savored for the future.

The therapeutic relationship can also produce the experience of intimacy within the context of a genuine encounter between two people. This encounter contains elements of the spiritual, the mystical, and the magical. Whatever happens defies explanation, at least with the rational mind. There is some sort of transformation that takes place in the lives of *both* participants in the relationship as a result of the connection that is created. This kind of relationship may not be experienced or acknowledged by all practitioners. Even among those who recognize that genuine encounters do take place in the therapeutic setting, such a phenomenon is quite rare. By definition, this is a special kind of human engagement, one that takes place when two people are operating on the same exact wavelength. The client feels understood as at no other time in his or her life. Yet, because this is an interactive experience, the therapist also feels the close connection.

Howard (1975) speaks of the "flesh-colored cage" in which individuals reside, potentially a place of infinite peace and solitude yet also a form of solitary confinement. No other person will ever truly know the unique experience of another. There are no words one can say, images one can create, pictures one can draw that can ever bridge the schism between self and others. Existentialists are fond of addressing the essential isolation and alienation of the human experience, of attempting to connect with clients in such a way that a temporary feeling of intimacy is created. It is assumed that this "felt experience" can act as a catalyst, allowing destructive energy held inward to be expressed in more self-enhancing ways. Whether you buy this philosophy or not, most practitioners can recall a time in which a client relationship developed that felt quite special. This was a "pure" alliance, devoid of erotic complications. It was as if for a moment, an hour, or even a string of several sessions, the two of you were completely open and honest with one another, not as professional and client but as human beings. This is not to say that under these conditions, the therapist abandons his or her professional role, or lapses into self-indulgence; rather, the alliance is expanded to include the uniquely human qualities of both partners in the relationship.

A Problem-Solving Collaboration

Filter out the magic and the mystery and what is left is an agreement between two parties to work together for a period of time in order to accomplish predetermined goals. The therapeutic relationship can thus be viewed as a kind of negotiated contract that exists only to facilitate action toward an agenda. It has no purpose other than as a means to an end. There are those who have considered the therapeutic alliance itself to be a sufficient condition for change, but many others view it as useful at best and potentially destructive at worst. It is, after all, an *artificial* connection. We might act (or even be) genuine, authentic, all-accepting, caring, and empathetic during sessions with clients but quickly turn the other way when we see certain ones on the street, we may have a professional interest in their well-being yet know that several in our caseload are not folks we would gravitate toward, or even tolerate, outside the walls of our offices. In all fairness, many of our clients would not seek us out as confidants if it were not for the elevated status created by the trappings of our profession—those books, diplomas, and environments that make us appear more wise, attractive, and expert than we really feel.

Moreover, as suggested previously, one of the characteristics of healing is that an authentic encounter between therapist and client is directed toward specific goals and tasks. Bordin (1979) proposed that it was the collaborative and consensual nature of therapeutic goals and tasks that marked effective working alliances. Some recent research (Horvath & Symonds, 1991) supports this contention, finding that almost 40 percent of outcome variance can be attributed to the strength of the collaborative working alliance (p. 148). The following example shows how this goal-directed relationship can function.

Florence walked into the session with a clipboard. On it she had created a brief list of exactly what she wanted to accomplish:

1. Sleep less.

2. Do more.

3. Not drink so much.

4. See my grandchildren more.

When the therapist attempted to collect background information, she politely but firmly informed him that she knew where she came from. Why was it necessary for him to know?

"Why, to get to know you better, of course. Otherwise, how can I help you?"

"Young man, I have no wish to know you, or to have you know me. I just need your assistance on a few matters."

The therapist pouted for awhile but eventually realized that perhaps Florence was entitled to have the benefit of the doubt. She seemed to know what she wanted, and she knew just how to get it. After three sessions that she considered quite satisfactory, even though he did not know what to make of them, she took her clipboard, with each item checked off, and returned from whence she came. Their relationship, if it could be called that (and he had his doubts considering how frosty it had been), had existed only as means to exchange information. Although quite unlike anything he had experienced before or since, the therapist had to acknowledge that Florence had met her goals and left a happy customer.

The relationship between Florence and her therapist was instrumental to accomplishing her stated goals. Therapist and client developed an efficient way of relating to one another that allowed them to move briskly from one topic to another and from beginning to later stages in the therapeutic process—although the therapist marveled that even after spending three hours talking to the lady, he still knew very little about her. Maybe she was right—it was none of his business.

A New Interactional Experience

So, what do you think that I should do? If I end this relationship, I might end up being alone for the rest of my life. I mean, maybe it's better to have something, even if it's not all that terrific, than to have nothing at all? But if I stay in this relationship, then aren't I just relying on him to take care of me instead of growing up? What should I do? Come on. Don't play games with me. You know me, and my situation, what do you think would be best? I know that you want me to be different—I know that you want me to stand up to him and tell him what I think. I don't know if I can do that! I know I need to, but I don't want to.

Even if clinicians are not strong subscribers to systemic think-ing, they still may recognize ways that their relationship with a given client may be used to make structural changes in the client's other interactive patterns. The client whose remarks were just quoted related to her therapist in much the same way she inter-acted with her spouse—deferential, dependent, and resentful toward his control. She asked for advice and then hated herself for giving away her power, thereby provoking feelings of ambivalence toward those she has begged for assistance. As is common in such circumstances, direct influence proved fruitless. The more the ther-apist urged her to be assertive, the more passive and dependent she became. When he interpreted this pattern in their relationship that so resembled her marriage, she vehemently denied such was the case and became even more despondent.

Instead of continuing the direct action, the therapist elected to use his relationship with this client as a means to change her other relationships with the men in her life (her husband, father, older brother, and male partners at work). Applying the strategic maxim that if something is not working one should try something else, usu-ally the opposite of what has already been done, the therapist restructured the relationship in such a way as to exaggerate this client's self-defeating behavior. He took on a more authoritarian, dictatorial role, a task quite difficult for him to complete, given his propensity toward diffusing responsibility for client choices. The rela-tionship became even more like others that the client was used to. Slowly and progressively, he programmed opportunities for her to assert herself, but rather than overtly encouraging her assertive efforts (a strategy he had tried unsuccessfully before), he exaggerated his efforts to control her. The client felt too intimidated to stand up to him directly during their sessions, but she began to report instances in which she was becoming more assertive at home and work.

The husband eventually called, wanting to join his wife and the therapist for a session to find out what was causing her to be so "belligerent." During this joint consultation, the therapist used his close, dependent relationship with the wife to spark reactions in the husband. The wife was now perfectly positioned to be the strong one during this encounter. She mediated a dispute between these two powerful men in her life, thereby establishing herself as being even more capable than they were. Further structural changes soon followed in which her overly dependent relationship on the therapist became a platform from which she could make realignments in her other relationships. Soon the therapeutic alliance, too, took on a more egalitarian flavor, culminating in the announcement that she no longer "needed" further sessions.

In this example, the therapeutic encounter became one in which the client had to play a different interactional role than she ever had before. Within the interactional dimension, the therapist took a relationship position that "forced" the client to be more assertive, that "required" behavior change. By insisting that these new interactional roles become part of their relationship, the therapist helped to create a new interactional experience.

An Enforcement of Boundaries

The therapeutic alliance is a relationship quite unlike any other: warm, respectful, engaging, permissive, it is also marked by some fairly strict rules and boundaries. Say anything you wish, dear client, but stay on track, keep focused on the subject at hand, use the language we have rehearsed, and oh yes, make sure to stop at the appointed moment when the session is over.

Some might cynically offer that the boundaries and conventions of the therapeutic relationship are established more for our comfort, convenience, and protection than for the client's. Freud, after all, put his patients on the couch out of his field of view not only because it facilitated their free association but also because he was sick of people staring at him all day. Likewise, there is nothing magical about the fifty-minute hour as a preferred length of treatment, except that it fits quite nicely as a scheduling interval—for the therapist. Innovators such as the French analyst Jacques Lacan, who determined the length of sessions—five minutes to two hours—according to the needs of his clients, took more heat for that adaptation than for any of his more outrageous changes in analytical methods. It was considered sacrilege to play with the invariant length of sessions. How could therapists ever plan their days?

Yet many of the boundaries installed in therapy are indeed for the safety and benefits of clients. Nowhere is this more evident than in cases of severe personality disorders—individuals who act out interpersonal pathology by trying to manipulate, control, or otherwise subvert intimate encounters. To create a "holding environment" in these cases, clinicians establish a set of therapeutic restraints that are consistently enforced to maintain socially appropriate behavior. Whereas with other clients, the relationship is an exercise in freedom, a complete indulgence in permissiveness and free self-expression, with severely dysfunctional individuals, the indulgent relationship will only become more rather than less pathological. These individuals crave limits, just as some rebellious children are crying out, "Stop me before I hurt myself." In these circumstances, the boundaries of the relationship become more important than the freedom that is possible in other contexts.

One therapist describes the value the relationship had as a "container" for inappropriate behavior this way:

When Marsha first walked in, I was delighted by her wit and charm. Here was a woman who knew just what she wanted and just how to get it. "An ideal client," I remember was my first impression. If only all my clients were so self-directed. Since Marsha clearly knew what she wanted from therapy, and what I could do to be most helpful, I allowed her to structure the sessions. Actually, this is my preference in general, since I emphasize self-responsibility in my work. Most of my relationships with clients are constructed as informal exchanges in which I follow where clients lead, even if they believe that I am the one directing the show.

I first became aware that I was in trouble, and the therapy was doomed to fail unless I made some drastic changes, when I noticed the extent to which Marsha would test the limits of what she could get away with. She came five minutes late to a session and then asked if we might extend the end a bit to finish what she was saying. Cheerfully, I readily complied. She asked for extensions on her payment contract to the agency, even though her fee had already been established at a token level. She called me at home a few times, ostensibly to reschedule an appointment time or clarify a point raised in the previous session. Before long, I finally realized what I was dealing with.

I sure had my work cut out for me trying to establish some limits to our relationship after I had already been so flexible and permissive. Nevertheless, I did announce that some changes would be made in our relationship (I chickened out and used as an excuse a change in agency policy). Marsha fought me every step of the way. She challenged any attempt to restrict her control. She acted out constantly, testing the limits of what I would tolerate. At this point, I was willing to indulge her in very little; I had learned my lesson previously.

Marsha and I worked together for some time. We talked about a number of issues and dealt with several themes in her life, among them her need for control in relationships. I am convinced, however, that most of what I did for her was to be the good parent she never had. I was kind to her but consistent and firm. I cared for her, but refused to tolerate her acting out. I told her exactly what I would do, and I *always* followed through on my promises. Our relationship became a safe haven for her, a kind of playground with high walls and even her own monitor to make sure she would not hurt herself, or anyone else. It was within these walls that Marsha learned how to relate to me, and from these humble beginnings, to reach out to others.

A New Construction of Reality

Recent theoretical and philosophical advances in our field have proposed a view of the therapeutic relationship dramatically different from the traditional one. Many are now suggesting that the social interaction among individuals is the source of the values and meanings those individuals hold. A major feature of this perspective is that individuals' beliefs regarding themselves, their relationships, and the events of the world are based in the narrative explanations, or schemas, that they construct by way of social interaction (Gergen, 1989; Lax, 1992; Sarbin, 1986). These schemas allow them to organize and represent seemingly diverse and unrelated experiences and events as meaningful wholes (Epston, White, & Murray, 1992). In addition, the schemas provide a structure from which they make decisions about appropriate behaviors.

Given this perspective, change may be achieved by way of narrative revision (see Anderson & Goolishian, 1988; Cyone, 1986). For example, Missy is asked by her therapist to describe how she ended up in her current predicament—unemployed, homeless, and physically ill. She tells a story of events, as she recalls the sequence—her husband became more abusive physically and emotionally; she began drinking more to dull the pain; her work performance suffered to the point that she was fired; her health further declined, as did her financial resources; the bank took her house; her husband left. And here she is. As the therapist poses certain questions, asking for further detail and clarification, Missy's narrative is already changing a bit. The therapist then offers some of his own interpretations of the same events, co-constructing with Missy a still different version of the events. Eventually, they agree on a modified story that is different from the original version—Missy is now the active protagonist instead of the passive victim.

Russell and Van Den Broek (1993) suggest that narrative revision is a process that has two stages. First, a rival narrative must be presented and differentiated, and be considered by the client as a legitimate representation of the events. This occurs within the interpersonal conversation of the therapeutic relationship. By way of the therapist's elaborating meaning, reframing, and seeding questions regarding the explanatory power of the initial narrative, a client may become more open to considering another perspective. Therapists may focus on the validity of the content or the structural relationship among the components of the narrative. Second, the rival narrative must be perceived as more accurate and coherent than the previous narrative and thus able to subsume that narrative. Rival narratives must present a subjective sense of accuracy and ring true to the client.

For Epston, White, and Murray (1992) new realities are created through a process of reauthoring one's life stories. This approach aims to assist clients to separate their lives from life stories that may be impoverishing and limiting, and to encourage these clients to reauthor stories in such a way that preferred outcomes are more likely. Through reauthoring, the meaning of relationships, people, and events is revised as the story changes. With meaning revision comes a new view of the world.

The Relationship as Change Agent

This chapter has presented various ways in which the relationship between client and therapist can be used to promote change. In essence, the suggestion is that therapy *is* the relationship and that change occurs only within that interpersonal encounter.

If we think about the process of therapy, we will notice that very few tangible items, techniques, or events really take place. All we really do is talk. It is the social interaction that is the only tool we really bring to therapy to help clients with their various concerns. In some magical way, that relationship, conducted by way of conversation and dialogue, has the potential to have meaning well beyond mere words. It has the potential to draw clients in, influence them, promote the intimacy they may be missing, shape the role they may play in life, and often help reconstruct their conceptions of reality.

However, in spite of our best intentions, therapeutic relationships are not always helpful and healing. Because they are such powerful vehicles by which to promote change, they may cause as much damage as positive change. This is true not only for the clients, but also for the practitioners, who appear to be in charge. The next chapter discusses instances when therapeutic relationships fail to work.

Chapter Twelve

When Therapeutic Relationships Don't Work

Like the thinking behind the old saying, "give a kid a hammer and he hammers everything," the thinking in our field has sometimes taken a therapeutic ingredient or intervention that seems to be helpful with some clients and has generalized it as being useful with everyone all of the time. Thus, we have seen fads from primal therapy to encounter groups come and go as, at first, they are hailed as the miracle cure for all that ails you, and then, once disillusion sets in, they slowly fade from view.

The better part of this book has been devoted to citing case after case and study after study that demonstrate quite clearly the benefits of the therapeutic relationship within the context of psychological healing. Yet there are exceptions to any rule, and there are certainly instances in which the therapeutic relationship is something less than helpful and may even be harmful to certain clients. There are limits to what even the most universal of our tools can do to be therapeutic, just as the most broad-based antibiotics will not work with every patient and every set of symptoms.

Therefore, this chapter discusses those instances when the therapeutic relationship is not especially helpful, when it does not work very well, and when it even interferes with reaching client goals. It is crucial that we be able to recognize when the therapeutic relationship is not working or when it is interfering with treatment objectives. During such times, we must make adjustments in the kind of relationship that has been constructed or, in some cases, adjust our clinical style so as to minimize the ineffective process in favor of other approaches.

251

Knowing When the Alliance Is Not Working

Central to any of our attempts to be helpful is our careful monitoring of what we are doing and the impact it is having. This is true not only in regard to the treatment plans we create and the interventions we select but also in regard to the relative importance of the therapeutic relationship. There are some clients we see for whom we are fairly certain that much of what we have to offer falls within the context of the alliance that has been created. This might be true for a young child who revels in the loving freedom that we provide. It could be the case with a client with a borderline disorder for which firm limit-setting is the primary mode of treatment. It might also be true for someone feeling quite anxious, who needs some support in order to initiate some changes. These clients fall at one end of the treatment continuum illustrated here.

Relationship Helpful	Relationship Irrelevant	Relationship Harmful
←		→
Supportive or Confrontive Encounters	Task/Goal Focus	Referral

Yet further along the continuum are those clients who do not require the therapeutic alliance in order to meet their objectives. They may indulge our need to banter and engage in social interaction but basically this is mildly pleasant to them at best and a waste of time at worst. Finally, at the other end of the continuum are those clients who are not only unresponsive to our attempts to build a therapeutic alliance but who are harmed by this endeavor.

How do we know when the therapeutic relationship we have created is not working? Our first task, of course, is to make a determination that it is, in fact, the relationship that is the problem rather than other factors. Negative outcomes may be the result of several other possibilities: we may experience a lapse in judgment or skill, attempt to do too much or take too much responsibility for client change, be too timid and reluctant to offer structure when needed, or mistime interventions, or there may be other factors unrelated to relationship issues (Kottler & Blau, 1989). Nevertheless, when there is trouble in therapy, quite often we tend to look first at the quality of the therapeutic alliance. We are inclined to ask ourselves the following questions (as we asked questions to complete the relationship diagnostic checklist in Chapter Eleven) in our attempts to figure out what is going on:

- How is the relationship proceeding differently from what I would normally expect?
- How are boundary issues being violated or played with in the relationship?
- In what ways is the client manifesting self-defeating behaviors in the relationship, behaviors that are characteristic of those described in his or her other relationships (avoidance, dependence, manipulation, and so forth)?
- What is the client doing to sabotage the quality of our alliance?
- Have I lost my flexibility in the relationship?
- What transference issues seem to be triggered by our interactions?
- Which of my own personal issues are being sparked by what is taking place (countertransference)?
- Is the pace of the relationship too slow or too fast compared to what the client can effectively handle?
- Who is working behind the scenes to sabotage the progress we are making?
- What interactional patterns may be preventing change?
- How is this impasse similar to others that I have encountered?
- What can I do differently to restructure what is taking place?

These questions help us to clarify that, indeed, there is something out of balance in the relationship. And there are yet other potential problems: for example, when by all appearances we have developed a wonderful alliance with a client yet there are still few noticeable changes in client behavior. However, in this chapter, the focus is on those situations in which the relationship is not working and that failure to function well is stifling other progress.

Forms of Relationship Resistance

There are a number of terms that we often use when therapy is not working in the ways that we hope and expect. Foremost among them are all the permutations of what is commonly known as *resistance*, that is, when the client is, for some reason, obstructive, noncompliant, or uncooperative. There are quite a number of different perspectives on this phenomenon, depending on who is seen as primarily responsible for its occurrence (Seligman & Gaaserud, 1994).

In the traditional psychoanalytic view, resistance is seen as the client's attempt to avoid threatening material. Yet when clients appear uncooperative, their behavior may also be a situation-specific response to a perceived threat (Brehm & Brehm, 1981; Dowd & Seibel, 1990), to a perception that the therapist is an illegitimate social influencer (Heppner & Claiborn, 1989), to therapist bungling or misjudgment (Fisch, Weakland, & Segal, 1982), or to a family's attempt to maintain homeostasis (Anderson & Stewart, 1983). The behavior may result from a cooperative failure on the part of therapist and client to collaborate effectively (Lewis & Evans, 1986). Resistance may even be viewed as a creative form of cooperation that is just different from what the therapist expects, or as a naturally occurring aspect of change (see Chapter Nine).

Unlike resistance in therapy, which has been generally defined as the client's deliberate avoidance of important issues (Miller, 1990) or obstruction of progress in the process (Otani, 1989) and in making personal changes (Dyer & Vriend, 1973), relationship resistance is a situation-specific form of opposition that is essentially interpersonal and systemic. Manifesting itself apart from any particular issue or presenting problem, it is an interactive effect that results from miscommunication, misunderstanding, incompatible goals, and other difficulties inherent in the ways the client and therapist relate to one another. While this form of resistance may be (and usually is) related to the avoidance of making changes or taking risks, or to otherwise obstructing therapeutic goals, it is centered primarily in experienced frustration and an expressed dissatisfaction in the quality of the partnership that has been established.

Relationship resistance may take many specific forms including the following.

Client does not comply with treatment. This is the most directly observable indicator that there are problems in the relationship. The client repeatedly refuses to do what is expected, presumably not out of laziness or fear but as a statement of defiance toward the therapist. When a client does not do what is expected, or what he says will be done, one of the first places we look to explain the trouble is to some dynamic occurring between us and the client.

Client's symptoms are getting worse. A second indicator that there may be relationship difficulties is the client's failure to improve as a result of our efforts. Certainly such deterioration could be the result of a misdiagnosis, poor treatment plan, or bungled execution of interventions, but often we will tinker first with the variable that is least intrusive. If we resolve the failure to improve by making a few adjustments in the way we relate to a client, or the way we structure the relationship between us, that is much preferable to starting all over with a whole new treatment plan.

Client discloses dissatisfaction with the way things are proceeding. Some clients will simply tell us directly that they are not pleased with the way they are being treated. This may not at all be an attempt to manipulate or control but honest feedback from a dissatisfied customer. Such input may come in the form of client observations about our being too passive, being overly dogmatic and rigid, not offering enough structure, being evasive, appearing withholding, or acting manipulative—we have all heard these comments at one time or another. Before we shrug them off as mere attempts to play games with us, we should consider whether some relationships do not work because we are not addressing what the client requires.

Therapist senses or observes that the relationship is not working. This last sign that something is wrong can occur when everything appears just fine but some intuitive observation on our part leads us to believe that things are not what they seem. The client may appear to be quite cooperative, and may even report that she is quite satisfied, yet we sense some inauthenticity, some deception, something that does not quite fit appropriately. The relationship may not be working very well because it is built upon dishonesty and manipulation.

Why Relationships Do Not Work

The reasons why the therapeutic relationship may not work can be grouped into four categories of variables that overlap considerably (Kottler & Blau, 1989; Kottler, 1993): variables related to the client, variables related to the therapist, variables related to the interactive process between the two parties, and extraneous variables that interfere with or undermine the therapeutic efforts.

Maybe It's the Client

It is often easier to discuss this topic—that is, what the client is doing or not doing to make our lives difficult—than the others presented here. In cases involving the client's behavior, we can more easily sidestep responsibility for the impasse ("It is not my fault; it is the client who is the problem. If only he was more cooperative or more highly motivated, less hopeless, resistant, or disturbed, I could do my job properly. But under these conditions, nobody could do this any better than I could").

There a number of reasons why something in the client may be short-circuiting the relationship. Organic factors may play a part— clients with attention deficits, neurological problems, or degenerative diseases may lack the capacity to respond appropriately in a relationship. Their cognitive functions or information processing may be impaired in such way that they have problems with memory, speech, motor control, or any one of a hundred other variables that are important when individuals relate to one another.

The client may also simply not be motivated or all that interested in cooperating with the therapist's agenda. Even if the client has genuine interest in making life changes, she may still have a bit of reluctance to get along with a therapist who may be perceived as a threat or someone not worthy of attention. This obstructiveness may be deliberate and intentional (resistance) or part of an unconscious attempt to sabotage the therapy. The individual may fear intimacy on any level or have some hidden agenda that is incompatible with what the therapist has in mind. Certain attitudes the client may adopt can also be a problem, especially those in which she comes across as argumentative, hopeless, overly compliant, or obstructive.

Even more basically, the client may simply have unrealistic expectations for what the relationship can do. If a client anticipates a miracle cure and expects that he will not have to do much to make that cure happen, problems will inevitably occur. Finally, the client may exhibit personality traits (narcissistic, hysterical, borderline) that make it difficult to establish a therapeutic alliance. In each of these instances, the relationship does not work very well (or as well as we would prefer) because of some factor that lies within the client's behavior, interpersonal style, personality, intentions, or physiological mechanisms.

Consider the problems exhibited by Felicia, who had pleaded with her therapist to offer some relief, saying, "I will do anything you ask of me. I just can't stand this situation any longer." Yet, in spite of her dramatic pronouncement, Felicia seemed to quite enjoy her apparent misery, at least those aspects of the secondary gains that allowed her to feel in control. As long as the relationship with her therapist remained at a standstill, she was able to revel in a sense of power. Furthermore, the skirmishes and bickering that became the norm for their interactions, sufficiently distracted both of them from getting to the heart of what Felicia most feared. To further doom this encounter, Felicia exhibited evidence of an attention deficit disorder that made it difficult for her to concentrate. She held a number of expectations about therapy that, while erroneous, would not be surrendered. No matter how hard the therapist worked on this case, the relationship was not going to solidify until a number of preconditions were taken care of.

There are many specific ways that a client can undermine a relationship. These are the most prevalent methods.

Withholding Communication. This is essentially a passive form of sabotage. In the most basic form of withholding communication, the client simply refuses to speak or responds with monosyllabic grunts, like the adolescent client in the following example:

THERAPIST: I notice that you don't have much to say.
CLIENT (*Shrugs*).
THERAPIST: What would you like to do with our time?
CLIENT: Doesn't matter.
THERAPIST (*Waits four minutes, determined not to keep pushing*).
CLIENT (*Averts eyes. Shuffles feet*).
THERAPIST: Is this how you want to spend our time together?
CLIENT: No.
THERAPIST: What then?
CLIENT (*Mumbles under his breath*).
THERAPIST: Excuse me?
CLIENT: Nothing.

Nothing indeed. This adolescent is determined to control the relationship by dictating the terms. He may not have had much choice whether to attend sessions or not, but by golly, he will be fully in charge of what he chooses to reveal.

This sort of relationship, involuntarily matched, in which both parties are stuck with one another, can be tedious to an extreme. The therapist is challenged to break through the reluctance, to open things up by trying to win the client's cooperation. Since often this goal is not feasible or realistic, the therapist has little choice except to abandon the treatment effort altogether or redefine the relationship in such a way that the client will be motivated to cooperate. This may involve moving away from a relationship-oriented therapeutic approach, de-emphasizing aspects of intimacy and trust that might be threatening, and instead concentrating on objectives that are unrelated to what we normally think of as a therapeutic alliance. The adolescent in the previous dialogue might be invited to draw pictures, play cards, play a game, go for a walk, sit silently, pretend to be someone else, do homework, anything that he is willing to do within the parameters of a nonrelationship (that is, a relationship that does not seem like one in the usual sense of the word). This particular adolescent spent almost six months in sessions with his therapist, never speaking about anything that was remotely personal, consciously withholding as much direct communication as possible, relating only within the confines of a card game. Yet progress was reported by his parents, and the truly amazing thing is the degree of progress that can occur in cases of nonrelationship therapy. Of course, the therapist and client did create a relationship of sorts with one another, one that allowed the young man to control the extent to which he revealed anything about himself.

Restricting Content. This form of relationship resistance is somewhat more sophisticated than the previous one, requiring as it does a degree of creativity and skill in addition to persistence. The client attempts to sabotage the relationship and keep the therapist from getting too close by controlling the content of what is discussed without appearing to be overtly obstructive. A number of variations are possible. The client may focus on *making small talk* ("How about those Yankees! And they said there was no chance they could stay in the pennant race. Did you see the game last night? No? It was pretty amazing. Eighth inning. Two outs. And . . . No. No. Wait a second. I got to tell you what happened . . ."). Or the client may engage in *intellectualizing* ("I see what you mean. But the fact of the matter is that even if I am unwilling to face things, I am cognizant of the reasons why. I think it was Nietzsche who said . . . No, I'm not trying to avoid anything; I just think it is important to explain the reasons underlying my decision. The test of any clear thinker is . . ."). Clients may also restrict content by resorting to *rambling* ("So there I was, stuck in the elevator, without a clue as to what to do next. I tried the phone but it wasn't working. I tried the alarm button but nobody seemed to hear me. Besides, the noise was driving me crazy. It reminded me of the time I was aboard a ship and . . . Did I tell you that story? I did? Oh, well, where was I? Oh, yeah, so then I sat on the floor for awhile . . .").

In each of these instances, the client is interested in a carefully constructed relationship with the therapist in which the risk of intrusion or authentic engagement is minimized. The intent is primarily to withhold communication by a more indirect means than staying silent. These forms of manipulation are relatively benign compared to others that can be considerably more challenging to counteract.

Being Manipulative. There are many therapists who believe that therapy is essentially a battle over who will be in control. The relationship is a battleground in which skirmishes for control are fought and negotiations take place. Depending on the particular resources and weapons at their disposal, clients may seek to destroy the relationship by undermining any progress that takes place, seducing the therapist to keep her off balance or discounting the value of the connection.

Violating Relationship Rules and Structure. Violating the basic rules and structure of the relationship is another tactic clients use to keep the relationship from working. When the client starts to feel close to the therapist, the client may punish the therapist (and herself) by delaying payment, missing appointments, coming late, or intruding on established boundaries. Individuals who do not feel that they deserve to enjoy intimacy with anyone or to experience personal success desperately need the therapeutic alliance to fail. If it should work, if the client learns that it is indeed possible for her to feel affection, respect, and caring for someone without being destroyed in the process, then she will no longer have an excuse for avoiding other relationships in her life. It is far easier to make sure the relationship with the therapist does not work.

This overview of client contributions to difficulties in the relationship would be incomplete without a reminder that all problems in relationships are, by definition, interactive problems, in which both parties bear responsibility for the predicament. While this idea has merit, we often have trouble putting it into practice because of our belief that certain clients are so difficult to deal with that it really is all their fault that things are not going as we would prefer and expect. So often when a therapeutic relationship does not work, the first thing that occurs to us, privately or as a complaint to colleagues, is something along the lines of: "I can't believe this person is so ornery! No wonder nobody else can deal with him. Why can't he just do what I ask of him? Why must he give me such a hard time?"

Indeed, a number of the folks we see do manifest fairly extreme disorders of personality and thinking, distortions of reality, restricted or flamboyant affective expression, exaggerations of reaction, or counterproductive and self-defeating behavior patterns. We label these people as character disordered, psychotic, sociopathic, borderline, hysterical, or narcissistic, or we group them together as resistant and obstructive.

While it is important not to minimize the effects of disordered thinking or pathological processes in clients' sabotaging of therapeutic and other relationships, there is no doubt that certain clients come to us with hostile intent, rigid defenses, seething anger, seductive intentions, or uncooperative attitudes and manipulative strategies. But we also ought to keep in mind the warning mentioned earlier: the client's resistant behavior is only one facet of the relationship problem; the other component is what we think, feel, and do in response.

Maybe It's Us

There are as many reasons why something in the therapist could be interfering with the effectiveness of the alliance as there are reasons for interference among clients. This is especially the case when the therapist's needs are not being met, expectations are not explicitly stated, and interactional roles are not agreed upon. Take, for example, a therapist named Monty, who had a strong need to feel appreciated by his clients. Like most of us, he preferred to hear some degree of gratitude for his efforts, especially when he really extended himself. To make matters worse, Monty tended to pout when he did not get his way. Not only was this noticed by his wife, children, and a few close friends, but many of his sensitive clients also picked up on this tendency. Monty also tended to become punitive during those times when he felt unappreciated. He would withdraw or become rigid and less yielding in his style.

When one of his clients criticized the work the two of them had been doing, Monty responded in kind, attempting to place blame away from himself. His manner became gruff and defensive. In subtle and sometimes more direct ways, he looked for methods to put the client in a one-down position, a strategy that did not exactly endear him further to the client. When the client eventually fled the sessions, Monty smugly thought to himself, *If you can't stand the heat, it is better to go elsewhere.*

Just as the client may have unrealistic goals for the treatment, so too may the therapist. If the clinician demands something of the client that she cannot respond to or is unwilling to comply with, problems in the relationship will frequently occur. This is but one of an infinite number of personal issues for the therapist that could circumvent progress. There may be aspects of the therapist's personality (arrogance, narcissism, dogmatism) or attitudes (racist, sexist, seductive) that are off-putting, just as there may be in the client's personality. Countertransference may be operating, so that the therapist responds to the client not as she is but as she appears to be through distorted filters.

When the therapist misdiagnoses what is going on, misjudges the timing of an intervention, makes a poor choice as to which interventions are employed, poorly executes a therapeutic skill, confronts a client prematurely, or misses the mark repeatedly during interpretations or reflections, relationship problems are also likely to occur.

Difficulties may also occur in the relationship when the therapist is not aware of distortions and interactive projections that are taking place. Either participant in the relationship can start this ball rolling. The client, let us say, starts to feel censured and disapproved of by the therapist. Some of these feelings begin immediately after the therapist vehemently disagrees with a course of action the client has initiated, but most of the intensity of the client's reactions is actually lingering from previous encounters in which he had felt similarly criticized by other authorities in his life (older sister, father, boss, and so forth).

As the client withdraws, becomes more reticent and withholding, and starts to pout, the therapist starts to feel irritated in an exaggerated way. Part of this counterreaction is a genuine human response to disappointment; another part of it, however, is motivated by experiences in the therapist's own life, some with clients who responded to her in this way previously, some of rejection in other relationships with men. As is so often the case in these runaway interactive sequences, neither the therapist nor the client is quite aware of why each is irritated with the other. In this example, the interactions were related to the projected dimension, but the example could have just as easily have presented a runaway interaction related to the authentic dimension. In either case, the relationship has some problems, and until the therapist and the client are able to identify what these might be and respond to each other in different ways, not much productive work is going to take place.

Jay (1991) gives the example of an interaction that took place between a Holocaust survivor and her therapist. After hearing the client talk in great detail about her despair, her pessimism, and her profound mistrust of anyone or anything, the therapist insisted that the client had an indomitable spirit that prevailed over catastrophe. Missing the point completely because of countertransference issues triggered by the client's plight, the therapist, like everyone else in the client's life, could not hear nor understand what she was really saying. "The woman's story was no fable about the soul's struggle through the profound lessons of adversity, but a far darker tale, not just about the transient, historical catastrophe that swept her up, but about the terrible, hidden truth of human nature that the Holocaust forced her to see. Having witnessed the horror of the world in all its nakedness, she recognizes the futility, even the impossibility, of hope" (Jay, 1991, p. 20).

This is but one example of so many situations that occur every day in our professional lives, situations in which we seem unable to respond optimally to the client in the relationship. It is at that point that the client may begin to appear hostile or reticent or withdrawn or may exhibit any of the other forms of relationship resistance. The therapeutic relationship is not likely to work well as long as these dysfunctional interactive patterns continue.

We should already know this, just as we know how important it is that we closely examine our personal reactions as well as our professional assessments throughout any client interaction. When we examine both, we engage in a parallel thought process like the following.

Professional Assessment	Personal Reaction
What are the ways that this relationship is not working?	*How am I overreacting to what is taking place?*
How might I alter my working diagnosis?	*How have I distorted the picture?*
What interventions have been most and least helpful?	*What am I doing to drive the client away?*
What might I do differently?	*What in me is getting in the way?*
Who has an interest in sabotaging the relationship?	*How am I making things worse?*
How is the client avoiding issues through the resistance?	*What am I avoiding or unwilling to explore?*
What outside resources can I access (colleagues, research)?	*How can I learn from this encounter?*

Parallel questions such as these help us not only to get a better handle on what might be going on in the relationship that is counterproductive and what the client is doing (or not doing) to resist or obstruct the process but also to focus on our own role in this interactive pattern.

Maybe We Don't Want to Know

We are all vulnerable to certain blind spots. Take work with trauma victims as an example. Here, problems in the alliance may easily interfere with our helping clients to heal their wounds. In a description of therapeutic variables that are most significant when treating victims of severe trauma, Jay (1991) points out that often the experiences such people have lived through are so awful that nobody, not even their therapists, really wants to hear the truth, because it would attack the very foundation of their beliefs about the fairness of the world and goodness of humanity. A Holocaust survivor, disaster victim, abused child, or former prisoner of war attempts to describe his or her experience of what took place and how he or she is different and most people respond with gentle words of encouragement, as they would to a child ("Now, now, don't worry. Everything will be all right. You just have to put this behind you and get on with your life").

Of course, the trauma victim can never fully recover from the effects of the experience—most of all because others do not want to hear about it. Other people find the experience too tedious to consider, or too horrifying because then they must contemplate that it could also happen to them. Enter a therapist, whose job is primarily to hear and understand what the client is experiencing. Yet we professionals, as well, struggle with trauma victims who need to tell their stories, for what they have to say directly contradicts many of the values we consider most sacred: hope, optimism, faith, trust, and the underlying order of things.

Maybe It's the Interaction

Since relationships are interactive phenomena, it is clear that any difficulties that exist will quite often result from some process variables between both parties that are interrupting the quality of communication. When the client and therapist have incompatible personalities, when their respective communication styles do not complement one another very well, when they have symmetrical patterns of relating that escalate tensions, when their personalities just rub each other the wrong way, the relationship between them will not work well without considerable effort from both of them.

Margie, for example, was a therapist who liked to think she could work with most anyone. As a private practitioner for many years, she had honed her skills in being able to connect and hold onto clients with a variety of personalities, complaints, and backgrounds. Working now in a leadership position in a mental health center, Margie prided herself on being flexible enough to take on the most challenging cases. She preferred to see these clients as complex puzzles to be solved. Wynn, a new client at the center, felt a desperate need to be validated as a person. For her whole life, she had felt like one tiny part in a large machine that was being operated by unseen forces. When Margie first introduced herself and began the initial assessment, Wynn felt as though she were under a microscope, being scrutinized as a mutated organism. The more questions that were asked, the more reticent she became. Wynn felt that Margie was being rude and cold. Margie, in turn, perceived her client as uncooperative and resistant. Each felt the other was at fault, when actually there was a problematic interactive process developing that is typical of many relationship conflicts.

Limitations in our treatment approach, unrelated to anything that we or our clients are doing, can also present problems. If the client requires some form of access to affective or cognitive processes and the style of treatment focuses exclusively on another area, there will be a mismatch between client needs and the service provided. When the client expects things from us in the relationship that we are unwilling or unable to deliver, the relationship will not work very well. The client may need the therapist, for example, to provide continual, specific feedback in order for the client to continue to feel understood and motivated to disclose. The therapist, however, may not be able to respond as often, or as in depth, as the client prefers. There is thus an incompatibility between their respective intentions, resulting in both parties' feeling frustrated. An impasse in a relationship may be due to the therapist's expectation about what every relationship ought to be. We have often heard that a therapeutic relationship must be warm and caring, yet that particular interactive pattern may not always be effective. When Dawar first walked into his therapist's office, it was immediately apparent how nervous he was. His eyes darted around the room looking frantically but unsuccessfully for a comfortable place to rest. His hands washed themselves so continuously the therapist worried they might start to bleed. When Dawar spoke, it was with a halting cadence that betrayed not only his ethnic origin but also the clipped tones of someone who was trying to keep things firmly under control.

The therapist, trying to put Dawar at ease, turned up the warmth and empathy a notch ("I see that this is very difficult for you"). The therapist was employing his normal approach, seeking to build a relationship with his client built on the usual ingredients of trust and acceptance. Yet the harder he tried to put Dawar at ease, the more nervous Dawar became. Finally, it was apparent that things were not going to work out; Dawar was ready to bolt for the door.

The therapist was puzzled by what was taking place. All his usual and favorite methods were proving to be useless at best and at worst maybe even harmful to his client. Indeed, Dawar seemed even more distraught than when the session first began. He confirmed the therapist's suspicion that not only would he not be returning for any more sessions with this therapist but that he was certain he would not consult anyone else either. This therapy stuff was just not his cup of tea, and he would have to make do as best he could.

Fortunately, the therapist was flexible enough to abandon his usual way of working. Since all seemed lost anyway, he decided to spend the last few minutes of the session asking Dawar under what conditions he would be willing to work on his problems with a helper. Surprisingly, Dawar was quite articulate about what he had in mind. He wished to keep things on a businesslike arrangement— no probing questions, no expectations that he would have to reveal personal things about himself or his family. He candidly expressed that he had little interest in knowing anything about his therapist, nor did he care to have the therapist know him either. When the therapist spluttered a reply, wondering how, then, he could be helpful, Dawar answered: "Let's just keep this simple. I'll tell you what I wish you to know and what I want from you. I would like you to listen carefully, and then offer me some sound advice as to what I might do."

The therapist realized that no matter how foreign this type of relationship, or nonrelationship, was to him, it was the only way in which his client was likely to respond. He was also surprised to find that this simple arrangement appealed to him as a change of pace, although he was skeptical whether he could do this kind of work without making the alliance the centerpiece of the therapeutic effort. Nevertheless, they proceeded along for a few sessions. Dawar left a satisfied customer. And the therapist realized that they had been able to accomplish the stated goals outside the context of the therapist's traditional therapeutic relationship.

Some might argue that it is impossible to have a nonrelationship with a client, that even the alliance created with Dawar is one type of relationship. Yet, nevertheless, this relatively sterile contractual arrangement proved helpful to the client, precisely because the therapist was willing to acknowledge that the usual ingredients of therapeutic relationships were counterproductive in this particular case. In fact, it may be that a practitioner's rigid expectations about what an interaction has to be can produce an impasse in the therapeutic relationship.

Maybe It's Someone Else

Some elements that interfere with the therapeutic alliance are those that are usually out of our control. During the third interview with an adolescent girl, her therapist discovers a host of reasons why client motivation has been minimal when the client says, "My mom tells me to come here. Actually, she makes me come. But every week after our session she pumps me for information. What did I tell you? What did you say to me? When I tell her this is private, then she makes fun of me and calls me crazy. You ask me why I don't seem to care about this therapy. How would you feel if you were told that as long as you have to come here it means you are nuts?"

As is evident from this example, extraneous factors may include family members or significant others who are working behind the scenes to sabotage the client's progress. The client may also lack other support systems that would reinforce progress during sessions. Or the client may have completely unrelated crises occurring—the death of a loved one, physical problems, financial troubles—that interfere with the relationship.

As brief review of the factors that can contribute to relationship problems illustrates, most difficulties stem from some form of client resistance that is sparked by internal, external, or interactive processes that are also related to the therapist and others in the client's life. Being able to identify clearly why a relationship is not working is crucial if we are to do anything about changing the client's dysfunctional pattern. Much of our current effort is usually centered around assessing the particular form of client resistance that pollutes the quality of the alliance. Since so many of our clinical strategies involve making adjustments in the ways we respond to the client, it is extremely important that we understand clearly exactly what form of client resistance is taking place, and what functions it serves. However, the contention here is that it is not possible for us fully to understand the client's obstructive behavior unless we consider how it is being inadvertently exacerbated or encouraged by our own behavior.

Tools Other Than Relationships

The relationship is but one of the many therapeutic ingredients that are involved in helping others work through personal difficulties. There are times when adjustments can be made in the relationship to correct for deficiencies, especially if the practitioner has the flexibility to make needed changes in structure, style, and pace. However, although relationships have much value in promoting healing and change, there are times when other tools are considerably more useful. The therapeutic relationship, like any force and process that we employ, does not work for all clients all of the time. Therefore, practitioners, especially those who think of their approach as relationship oriented, are urged to consider if there are specific times when what they are doing is more for their own comfort than it is for their clients' good.

Thus, this chapter ends on a note of caution. As powerful and universal as relationships may be as the promoters of healing across cultures, disciplines, situations, and theoretical approaches, they have their limitations. There are times when specific kinds of relationships work better than others, even with the same client or clients with similar presenting complaints. Just as therapeutic relationships contain several threads—the cultural, empirical, conceptual, and personal—so too does the process of therapy include other active ingredients that take precedence in certain situations.

Yet the relationship is indeed the most prominent mode of healing, the one that unites most clients and practitioners in a healing alliance. The extent to which we can harness its force selectively and flexibly, in order to use it in a variety of ways, will determine its power as a vehicle for promoting lasting change, not only in our clients but in our own lives.

Chapter Thirteen

The Future of Relationships in Therapy

Synthesis and *integration* are the watchwords of the future. No longer can therapists afford to be narrow and parochial in their thinking, limiting their allegiance to a single theoretical approach to therapeutic relationships. Neither is it feasible to expect that therapists can continue to identify themselves as phenomenologists or empiricists, practitioners or researchers, generalists or specialists. The future of the profession of psychotherapy will be found in weaving together the different threads presented throughout this book— the personal perceptions and experiences of the participants in the relationship, their respective cultural backgrounds, the conceptual foundations that are interdisciplinary and integrative in their approach, and the empirically derived evidence, to substantiate therapists' clinical beliefs.

In this closing chapter, the three of us who have written this book out of our own experiences and investigations look toward the future of relationships in the profession. We make some predictions. We anticipate what clinicians might encounter and what they will need to prepare for. Throughout this book, we have relied, to a certain extent, on the anecdotal and conceptually derived knowledge of others as well as on the empirical literature and our own experiences. It is our hope that this foundational knowledge will restrain our vision so that we can be relatively conservative, initially at least, in what we anticipate will take place in the field of psychotherapy. Following this exercise, our theme will turn once again to the personal perspectives with which we began this book.

Clinical Thread

Some may argue that the future of the therapeutic relationship is somewhat questionable. Almost every day, a new gene is discovered that may be related to depression, anxiety, or any one of many other emotional problems. Even within the helping field, what seems to draw the most attention are those innovations in technique that are relatively independent of the relationships therapists develop with clients. For example, eye movement desensitization and reprocessing (EMDR) is gaining attention as an example of a new therapy that emphasizes technical precision over human connectedness. In treatments of posttraumatic stress disorders, quite a bit of anecdotal evidence and a few controlled studies appear to indicate that EMDR can significantly decrease haunting memories in a few sessions (Butler, 1993). Perhaps an even a more dramatic example of an instance in which the relationship is not a significant factor is the use of drug therapies for treating emotional difficulties. Although few would dispute the value of a solid collaboration between patient and doctor in ensuring compliance to treatment, it is the chemical, not the practitioner, that alters the clients' moods. Following Kramer's impassioned book (1993) lauding Prozac as the new miracle drug of the nineties, nonmedical practitioners are beginning to question their future roles as healers. Might you and we soon become obsolete, replaced by pills, behavioral engineering, imagery reprogramming, or even computers? Will the therapeutic relationship be usurped by technology?

We doubt it. The same cries of protest were heard when behavior modification proponents threatened to put relationship-oriented therapists out of business, but practitioners have learned that these dichotomous approaches are hardly competitive but collaborative; each makes the other more powerful. The same is true of the application of chemical and technical treatments—they will always take place in a human context. Thus, the relationship between the client and the professional will continue to play a critical role.

We have argued throughout this book about the importance of

the therapeutic relationship, but what does the future hold concerning *specific* applications? In essence, the clinical application of the therapeutic relationship is still in its infancy. A look at the research about the rudiments of establishing a close relationship with a client reveals a dearth of studies in the last ten years. However, we suggest that, in the future, an integrative perspective will thrive: techniques and relationships will be viewed as inseparably intertwined, and client change will be tied directly to various dimensions intrinsic to this relationship. As a result of this perspective, there will be a blossoming of relationship-based clinical innovations. Examples of empirical questions that will be addressed include: How may language influence the close feelings generated in the authentic dimension? How is it that metaphors and co-created explanations may influence these close feelings? Can the profession develop instruments to identify relationship schemas so that this information will be more readily available to the clinician? What are the effects of different types of empathy?

Practitioners tend to have global notions about the relationships they create. They are also especially good at establishing effective relationships, even though they have yet to figure out reliable methods to harness this powerful force. So often they take the establishment of the relationship for granted, until they have a difficult time with a client, and the relationship blows up in their faces. Our prediction is that the future holds a new interest on the part of practitioners in identifying more specific relationship-oriented interventions.

Conceptual Thread

The conceptual future will be marked by a blurring of differences between the theoretical approaches to therapy. We forecast that the next generation of theoreticians will focus their attention on the development of conceptual maps that bridge the gap between various theoretical and disciplinary arenas. Some writers, such as

Alvin Mahrer, James Prochaska, Arnold Lazarus, Larry Beutler, and Perry London have already proposed general models of psychotherapeutic change. The future will be marked by meta-models that tie various dimensions together into a coherent whole. Furthermore, we submit that the therapeutic relationship will come to play a predominant role in these integrative models.

The conceptual thread will continue to emphasize models that are multidimensional, like the one we have proposed. This thread will also strive to understand the reciprocal and interdependent nature of the various dimensions of the relationship. How does the authentic dimension influence the interactional dimension? What interactional patterns lead to the development of a strong healing alliance? The goal in addressing these and other questions will be to provide a guide for practitioners in their efforts to construct relationships that are optimally effective for each client and clinical situation.

Empirical Thread

The future of the empirical thread will be marked by flexibility and inclusion rather than rigid adherence to the demarcations of professions and fields within the therapeutic community. In other words, the empirical thread will become a multidimensional and multidisciplinary thread. This means that the ways in which therapists test out therapeutic behaviors will change.

It is curious that therapists practice their craft by understanding and helping the individual, while their inquiry methods are constructed according to universal or group norms. Indeed, Levine, Sandeen, and Murphy (1992) suggest that therapists are faced with a dilemma in conducting therapy, because that therapy is conducted at an idiographic level, while the therapist's base of knowledge is from psychological research conducted and organized at a nomothetic level. Outcome research is conducted on treatments for a particular disorder or set of client difficulties to determine the relative effectiveness of the treatments. The findings typically indicate that one treatment is superior to another, but virtually never show uniform effectiveness for all subjects receiving a given treatment. Furthermore, diagnostic entities have a number of well-known limitations, and many clients do not fit neatly within existing categories. Hence, the current dilemma is how to apply this kind of nomothetic information when the results may not be accurate for the idiographic situation or specific client with which the practitioner is working.

It seems that research based on modern research assumptions often produces more exceptions than generalizable rules. However, Gergen (1992) suggests that such results should not be surprising, given the fact that the empirical approach decontextualizes the very process it attempts to understand and consequently loses all significant meaning. Therefore, a postmodern (Gergen & Kaye, 1992) or narrative (Rennie & Toukmanian, 1992) approach has been proposed as a new model upon which to base systematic inquiry. The approach calls for a science of understanding based on the assumptions that the observer and object of observation are inseparable, that the nature of meaning is relative rather than absolute, that phenomena are context based, and that the process of understanding is inductive, hermeneutical, and qualitative (Rennie & Toukmanian, 1992). Thus, rather than search for generalizable rules and laws of nature, the focus of inquiry shifts to the constructive and contextualized reasons for action and the constructive interaction between active learning and knowledge in the context in which behaviors occur (Mahoney, 1991).

Cultural Thread

We have mentioned repeatedly that culture provides the context for any therapeutic relationship or healing ritual. We have incorporated information from a variety of cultures found in Africa, South America, and Asia and the Pacific Rim, and among the indigenous peoples of North America. Even this scope is not broad enough. The principles we have discussed are influenced by our own cultural heritages and, in the future, we hope to expand and improve on the principles by infusing more information from diverse sources.

One of our contentions is that healing takes place in many different ways in cultures other than the therapist's own and that therapists can learn from this. We suggest that therapists' battle cry should be, "Let us continue to learn from others." There are a multitude of lessons from others that most therapists in this country have not yet begun to explore (for example, the ways of the Buddhist monk, the midwife from Tanzania, or the gang member from East St. Louis).

Furthermore, therapists need to broaden their definition of the therapeutic relationship. It does not always have to be up close and personal. It can encompass a number of different roles for the healer—as coach, friend, wizard, or mediator with the spirit world. Different cultures have different expectations, and if therapy is something that is going to help people globally, then maybe therapists need to make some significant changes in the ways that they operate. They need to become more culturally literate.

Personal Thread

A primary theme throughout this volume has been the importance of the personal side of the therapeutic relationship. As authors, we found our collaboration appealing because each of us is so different in the relationships he or she creates with clients. These differences in our theoretical orientations and personal and clinical styles have been a source of conflict between us but, we hope, also a rich source of dialogue that has led to an integration of diverse points of view. In spite of our attempts toward compromise, there are still significant differences in the ways we think about the healing relationship, and we believe that our differences are reflective of the struggles and diversity within our profession as a whole. Here then are our personal individual statements about our views of the healing relationship.

Jeffrey Kottler

I believe in magic. When all is said and done, I don't believe that we will ever truly understand the full complexity of what takes place between human beings during therapeutic encounters. The relationships between people do indeed have some identifiable characteristics, some of which are considered better than others. Furthermore, there are many things that we do know about how to create client alliances that are likely to be more helpful than harmful. Likewise, we can describe stages in this process, isolate variables that are often associated with positive results, and construct unified models that appear to contain the salient features of this phenomenon.

Even after all of the study that went into preparing this book, the conversations and debates we had with one another, the reading and reflective thought about the literature, the interviews conducted with practitioners, the reviews of my own clinical experiences, I still feel that there is an essence that is missing from our discussion. I must say that I feel quite tentative, even embarrassed, about disclosing this belief. I am setting myself up for ridicule, especially if you take me seriously. Well, I have been stalling long enough: I believe that the core of healing between human beings, whether in the context of friendship, therapy, or any other professional relationship is love. I don't mean love in the romantic sense, of course. I also don't wish to conjure up a simplistic image that could be part "unconditional positive regard," part spiritual connectedness, part genuine caring for other people.

I recognize that it is possible to help clients without loving them, or even liking them. I also have noticed times when relationships with clients have been anything but cordial, much less loving, and still some therapeutic benefit seemed to result. I have observed irrefutable evidence of the value of certain kinds of structures and interventions that take place in therapy, irrespective of this diffuse quality I am describing. I have great faith in what the empirical and conceptual foundation of my field has led me to think and do with respect to my clinical work (well, perhaps not *great* faith, since I doubt *everything,* but reasonable confidence anyway). I truly believe what my most articulate teachers, supervisors, colleagues, and clients have told me they think is happening in their relationships; I certainly know what has worked for me when I have been on the receiving end. Yet even with all of the theories, conjectures, testimonies, studies, and case examples presented throughout these pages, even with as complete a picture as seems to be emerging, what is missing for me is the magic of how wonderful it feels to be understood by another. Call it empathy, or positive regard, or yes, love, but what I am describing is the magical, transcendent state that takes place between human beings when they are making contact.

As far as I am concerned, paradox is inextricably linked to therapy, now and in the future. I respect the contradictory. I have learned to live with ambiguity. I do not think therapists can ever completely reconcile the polarities that are part of this profession— the need for structure versus freedom, the dependence in the relationship that facilitates independence, the deception couched in apparent authenticity, the forced spontaneity, the purchased intimacy, on and on the contradictions go.

Therapists can attempt to measure relationship variables all they like, to quantify elements present, to isolate factors, to control experimental conditions, to synthesize, integrate, to describe the phenomenon qualitatively. What will always be missing for me is that magical essence that defies description. It is a felt sense, a glow in the heart. It is magic.

Tom Sexton

I believe in stories. When all is said and done, I am not sure there is a "truth" to discover in the search to understand the essence of healing in therapeutic relationships. One's understanding of relationships, like one's understanding of almost anything else, seems to be as much a result of one's unique lenses as it is a matter of reality. *One person's transference seems equally to be another's interaction.* Thus, I believe that the search for the "truth" too often polarizes and divides therapists and clients.

Ultimately, I think that what is important is understanding the relationship that allows clinicians to successfully navigate their work with clients. I am increasingly convinced that if therapists are to develop maximum flexibility, they must develop models of the relationship that are *client-centered.* I am not suggesting a return to the Rogerian model of therapist-offered facilitative conditions. Instead, client-centered relationships are those created from within the context of the client's world. These relationships use the clients' stories, their meanings, and their system of explaining the world. The therapist enters this world, and looks, rather than at what is right (healthy communication, characteristic of optimal functioning), at what is functional, what is useful to the client within the cultural context in which he or she operates.

I think it is the stories that therapists create with their clients that are the essence of the relationship. Thus, *rapport* is a congruent story in which the therapist steps into the world of the client. *Satisfaction* is a relationship system in which client and therapist complement each other in role, function, and position. It is also through these stories that therapists facilitate change. In many ways, therapists are authors, helping construct stories that open doors and create new alternatives. Instead of viewing a therapy relationship as primarily affective, cognitive, or behavioral, the focus is on types of narrative explanation and the mechanism through which language is used by the therapist and the client to affect the co-construction process.

The switch from "truth" to the functionality of stories will have a profound effect on how therapists work. Methods of inquiry will have to undergo the paradigm shift we have suggested throughout this book. Therapists will have to realize that "objective" measurements represent the observer as much as the observed. The focus of inquiry will be on the mechanisms of narrative construction. Unfortunately, present methods of ethnographic and qualitative research are currently not up to the challenge of this type of inquiry. New methods are needed or therapists will be left with nothing more than subjective interviews that create the same illusions of "truth" I described earlier.

Clinical interest will be directed at the role of the therapist in reauthoring the narrative explanations. In particular, therapists will need to know how and when they will have most influence to facilitate constructive change in the way their clients make meaning in the world.

What is exciting about this position is that it opens up an entirely new world to inquiry and clinical action. This view paints the therapeutic relationship in a unique way that has the potential to help therapists make advances in their conceptual and clinical models. What is a bit threatening is that it also calls into question many present therapeutic values and traditions. Will therapists be willing to give up those models they were taught? Will they be able to stretch themselves and think differently? Can they stand the ambiguity created when they give up the generalized rules painstakingly developed over the last one hundred years? I think the future will be a time of unrest as the profession struggles over whether to adopt new lenses with which to view a familiar phenomenon.

Sue Whiston

I believe in empiricism. It is interesting that I am the only woman in our group, and I am the one arguing for the importance of research as the key to understanding the therapeutic relationship (so much for stereotypes based on gender!). I believe that for too long researchers have given minimal attention to investigating the therapeutic relationship in all its aspects. Many of the crucial techniques related to the therapeutic relationship are not being studied in our laboratories. A justification for this neglect is that the helping field attracts individuals who already have commendable interpersonal skills, and I believe that to a certain extent this reasoning is true, many practitioners have developed admirable relationship skills. Yet, I do not think this is enough. Some nebulous feeling that you are close to somebody does not mean a lot in these days of managed care. Therapists need additional studies that directly show the efficacy of the therapeutic relationship, studies that are convincing to insurance organizations and/or governmental agencies. I hope that the near future will bring clinicians more detailed information about how to train individuals in establishing therapeutic relationships and more specific information on methods for improving individuals therapists' healing alliances with clients.

I also want to stress that the unfolding of the therapeutic relationship does not rest solely with academicians, in fact quite the contrary. However, I do think the paradigm shift that we discussed earlier can only happen with a better marriage between therapeutic practice and scientific scrutiny. I must also admit (although this does not come particularly easily) that there is probably a portion of relationships that researchers will never be able to quantify. There can be a closeness in certain relationships that produces change and healing. My belief that this is so arose out of my actually experiencing a change in personal relations when I became involved in a relationship that was nurturing. The bond within this relationship had a profound effect on my life. As I end this book, I am more convinced of the power of the relationship than I ever was before.

In the End . . .

In the end it is still you, the practitioner, who must put to use the ideas we have presented here. The future of the therapeutic relationship depends, ultimately, on how you apply what you know to the real-life problems that confront you and your clients on a daily basis.

The threads of healing are interwoven in such a way that the therapeutic relationship is all that we have each described it to be—an empirically derived structure, a mutually negotiated narrative, and yes, a magical encounter. It is all of these together, and none of these alone.

References

Alexander, L. B., & Luborsky, L. (1986). The Penn helping alliance scale. In L. S. Greenberg & W. M. Pinsoff (Eds.), *The psychotherapeutic process* (pp. 325–366). New York: Guilford Press.

Anchin, J. C., & Kiesler, D. J. (1982). *Handbook of interpersonal psychotherapy.* Elmsford, NY: Pergamon Press.

Anderson, C. M., & Stewart, S. (1983, January/February). Meeting resistance in on-going treatment. *Family Therapy Networker,* pp. 32–39.

Anderson, H., & Goolishian, H. (1988). Human systems as linguistic systems. *Family Process, 27*(4), 371–395.

Anderson, H., & Goolishian, H. (1992). The client is the expert: A not knowing approach to therapy. In S. McNamee & K. J. Gergen (Eds.), *Therapy as social construction* (pp. 7–24). Newbury Park, CA: Sage.

Angus, L. E. (1992). Metaphor and the communication interaction. In S. G. Toukmanian & D. L. Rennie (Eds.), *Psychotherapy process research* (pp. 187–209). Newbury Park, CA: Sage.

Arredondo, P., Dowd, P. M., & Gonsalves, J. (1980). Preparing culturally effective counselors. *The Personnel and Guidance Journal, 58,* 657–661.

Ashby, W. R. (1956). *An introduction to cybernetics.* London: Methuen.

Bachelor, A. (1988). How clients perceive therapist empathy: A content analysis of "received" empathy. *Psychotherapy, 25,* 227–240.

Bailey, K. G. (1987). *Human paleopsychology: Applications to aggression and pathological processes.* Hillsdale, NJ: Erlbaum.

Bailey, K. G. (1988). Psychological kinship: Implications for the helping professions. *Psychotherapy, 25,* 132–142.

Bailey, K. G., & Nava, G. (1989). Psychological kinship, love, and liking: Preliminary validity data. *Journal of Clinical Psychology, 45,* 587–594.

Bailey, K. G., Wood, H. E., & Nava, G. R. (1992). What do clients want? Role of psychological kinship in professional helping. *Journal of Psychotherapy Integration, 2,* 125–129.

Bankart, C. P., Koshikawa, F., & Haruki, Y. (1992). When West meets East: Contributions of Eastern traditions to the future of psychotherapy. *Psychotherapy, 29,* 141–149.

Barkham, M., & Shapiro, D. A. (1986). Counselor verbal response modes and experienced empathy. *Journal of Counseling Psychology, 33*, 3–10.

Barrett-Lennard, G. T. (1981). The empathy cycle: Reinforcement of a nuclear concept. *Journal of Counseling Psychology, 28*, 91–100.

Barry, W. A. (1970). Marriage research and conflict: An integrative review. *Psychological Bulletin, 73*, 41–54.

Baruth, L. G., & Manning, M. L. (1991). *Multicultural counseling and psychotherapy*. New York: Merrill.

Bateson, G. (1958). *Naven* (rev. ed.). Stanford, CA: Stanford University Press.

Bateson, G. (1968). Information and codification: A philosophical approach. In J. Ruesch & G. Bateson (Eds.), *Communication: The social matrix of psychiatry* (pp. 168–211). New York: W.W. Norton.

Beck, A., & Katcher, A. (1983). Pets as therapists. In *Between pets and people*. New York: Putnam.

Benjamin, L. S. (1987). The use of the SASB dimensional model to develop treatment plans for personality disorders. I: Narcissism. *Journal of Personality Disorders, 1*, 43–70.

Bent, R. J., Putnam, D. G., Kiesler, D. J., & Nowicki, S. J. (1976). Correlates of successful psychotherapy. *Journal of Consulting and Clinical Psychology, 44*, 1–49.

Bergin, A. E., & Garfield, S. L. (1994). *Handbook of psychotherapy and behavior change* (4th ed.). New York: Wiley.

Bergin, A. E., & Lambert, M. J. (1978). The evaluation of therapeutic outcomes. In S. Garfield & A. Bergin (Eds.). *Handbook of psychotherapy and behavior change: An empirical analysis* (2nd. ed., pp. 139–190). New York: Wiley.

Beutler, L. E., Crago, M., & Arizmendi, T. G. (1986). Research on therapist variables in psychotherapy. In S. L. Garfield & A. E. Bergin (Eds.), *Handbook of psychotherapy and behavior change* (pp. 257–310). New York: Wiley.

Beutler, L. E., Machado, P. P., & Neufeldt, S. A. (1994). Therapist variables. In A. Bergin & S. Garfield (Eds.), *Handbook of psychotherapy and behavior change* (4th ed., pp. 229–269). New York: Wiley.

Binder, D. (1991, December 16). The power of puppy love. *People*, p. 102.

Bion, W. (1957). *Second thoughts: Selected papers on psychoanalysis*. New York: Jason Aronson.

Blanck, G., & Blanck, R. (1968). *Ego psychology: Theory and practice*. New York: Columbia University Press.

Blau, P. M. (1964). *Exchange and power in social life*. New York: Wiley.

Bloom, B. L., Asher, S. J., & White, S. W. (1978). Marital disruption as a stressor: A review and analysis. *Psychological Bulletin, 85*, 867–894.

Bordin, E. S. (1979). The generalizability of the psychoanalytic concept of the working alliance. *Psychotherapy: Theory, Research and Practice, 16,* 256–260.

Bordin, E. S. (1980). Of human bonds that bind or free. Presidential address delivered at the meeting of the Society for Research in Psychotherapy, Pacific Grove, CA.

Bourdillon, M.F.C. (1982). Pluralism and problems of belief. *Archives de sciences sociales des religions, 54*(1), 21–42.

Bowen, M. (1978). *Family therapy in clinical practice.* New York: Jason Aronson.

Bowlby, J. (1958). The nature of the child's tie to his mother. *International Journal of Psychoanalysis, 39,* 350–373.

Bowlby, J. (1969). *Attachment and loss.* London: Hogarth Press.

Bowlby, J. (1982). *Attachment and loss: Vol. 1. Attachment.* New York: Basic Books.

Boyden, T., Carroll, J. S., & Maier, R. A. (1984). Similarity and attraction in homosexual males: The effects of age and masculinity-femininity. *Sex Roles, 10,* 939–948.

Bradbury, T. N., & Fincham, F. D. (1990). Attributions in marriage: Review and critique. *Psychological Bulletin, 107,* 3–33.

Brain, R. (1976). *Friends and lovers.* New York: Basic Books.

Brehm, S. S. (1992). *Intimate relationships.* New York: McGraw-Hill.

Brehm, S. S., & Brehm, J. W. (1981). *Psychological reactance: A theory of freedom and control.* New York: Academic Press.

Brislin, R. W., & Lewis, S. A. (1968). Dating and physical attractiveness: Replication. *Psychological Reports, 22,* 976.

Burton, A. (1975). Therapist satisfaction. *American Journal of Psychoanalysis, 35,* 115–122.

Butler, K. F. (1993, November/December). Too good to be true. *Family Therapy Networker,* pp. 19–31.

Campbell, A., Converse, P. E., & Rodgers, W. L. (1976). *The quality of American life.* New York: Russell Sage.

Carson, R. C. (1969). *Interactional concepts of personality.* Hawthorne, NY: Aldine.

Cashdan, S. (1982). Interactional psychotherapy: Using the relationship. In J. C. Anchin & D. J. Kiesler (Eds.), *Handbook of interpersonal psychotherapy* (pp. 215–226). Elmsford, NY: Pergamon Press.

Charzonowski, G. (1982). Interpersonal formulations of psychotherapy: A contemporary model. In J. C. Anchin & D. J. Kiesler (Eds.), *Handbook of interpersonal psychotherapy* (pp. 5–45). Elmsford, NY: Pergamon Press.

Claiborn, C. D. (1986). Social influence: Toward a general theory of change. In F. J. Dorn (Ed.), *Social influence process in counseling and psychotherapy* (pp. 1–52). Springfield, IL: Charles C. Thomas.

Cogan, T. (1977) *A study of friendship among psychotherapists.* Unpublished doctoral dissertation, Illinois Institute of Technology, Chicago.

Combs, A. W., Avila, D. L., & Purkey, W. W. (1971). *Helping relationships: Basic concepts for the helping professions.* Needham Heights, MA: Allyn & Bacon.

Cormier, W. H., & Cormier, L. S. (1991). *Interviewing strategies for helpers.* Pacific Grove, CA: Brooks/Cole.

Cowen, E. L. (1982). Help is where you find it. *American Psychologist, 37*(4), 385–95.

Cray, C., & Cray, M. (1977). Stresses and rewards within the psychiatrist's family. *American Journal of Psychoanalysis, 37,* 337–341.

Curran, J. P., & Lippold, S. (1975). The effects of physical attraction and attitude similarity on attraction in dating dyads. *Journal of Personality, 43,* 528–539.

Cyone, J. C. (1986). The significance of the interview in strategic marital therapy. *Journal of Strategic and Systemic Therapies, 5,* 63–70.

Danzinger, K. (1976). *Interpersonal communication.* Elmsford, NY: Pergamon Press.

Dorn, F. J. (1984). The social influence model: A social psychological approach to counseling. *Personnel and Guidance Journal, 2,* 342–345.

Dorn, F. J. (1986). *Social influence processes in counseling and psychotherapy.* Springfield, IL: Charles C. Thomas.

Dowd, E. T., & Seibel, C. A. (1990). A cognitive theory of resistance and reactance: Implication for treatment. *Journal of Mental Health Counseling, 12*(4), 458–469.

Duck, S. W. (1983). *Friends for life.* Brighton: Harvester.

Dyer, W. W., & Vriend, J. (1973). *Counseling techniques that work.* Alexandria, VA: American Counseling Association.

Efran, J. S., Lukens, M. D., & Lukens, R. J. (1990). *Language, structure, and change.* New York: W.W. Norton.

Eisenthal, S., Emery, R., Lazare, A., & Udin, H. (1979). "Adherence" and the negotiated approach to patienthood. *Archives of General Psychiatry, 36,* 393–398.

Elwood, R. W., & Jacobson, N. S. (1982). Spouses' agreement in reporting their behavioral interactions: A clinical replication. *Journal of Consulting and Clinical Psychology, 50,* 783–784.

Epston, D., White, M., & Murray, K. (1992). A proposal for a re-authoring therapy: Rose's revisioning of her life and commentary. In S. McNamee & K. J. Gergen (Eds.), *Therapy as social construction* (pp. 96–115). Newbury Park, CA: Sage.

Eysenck, H. J. (1952). The effects of psychotherapy: An evaluation. *Journal of Consulting Psychology, 16,* 319–324.

Farber, B. A. (1983). The effects of psychotherapy practice upon psychotherapists. *Psychotherapy: Theory, Research, and Practice, 20,* 174–182.

Farber, B. A., & Heifetz, L. J. (1981). The satisfaction and stresses of psychotherapists' work: A factor analytic study. *Professional Psychology, 12*, 621–636.

Fincham, F., & O'Leary, D. K. (1983). Causal inferences for some spouse behaviors in maritally distressed and non-distressed couples. *Journal of Social and Clinical Psychology, 1*(1), 42–57.

Fisch, R., Weakland, J. H., & Segal, L. (1982). *The tactics of change: Doing therapy briefly.* San Francisco: Jossey-Bass.

Fischer, C. S. (1982). *To dwell among friends: Personal networks in town and city.* Chicago: University of Chicago Press.

Frank, J. D. (1961). *Persuasion and healing: A comparative study of psychotherapy.* Baltimore: Johns Hopkins University Press.

Frank, J. D. (1973). *Persuasion and healing: A comparative study of psychotherapy* (rev. ed.). New York: Schocken.

Frank, J. D. (1977). The two faces of psychotherapy. *Journal of Nervous and Mental Diseases, 164*, 3–7.

Frank, J. D., & Frank, J. B. (1991). *Persuasion and healing: A comparative study of psychotherapy* (3rd ed.). Baltimore: Johns Hopkins University Press.

Freud, S. (1958). The dynamics of the transference. In J. Strachey (Ed. and Trans.), *The standard edition of the complete psychological works of Sigmund Freud* (Vol. 12, pp. 98–108). London: Hogarth Press. (Original work published 1912)

Friedlander, M. I., & Schwartz, G. S. (1985). Toward a theory of strategic self-presentation in counseling and psychotherapy. *Journal of Counseling Psychology, 32*, 483–501.

Friedlander, M. I., Thibodeau, J. R., & Ward, L. G. (1985). Discriminating the "good" from the "bad" therapy hour: A study of dynamic interaction. *Psychotherapy, 22*, 631–641.

Garfield, S. L., & Bergin, A. E. (1986). Introduction and historical overview. In S. L. Garfield & A. E. Bergin (Eds.), *Handbook of psychotherapy and behavior change* (pp. 3–22). New York: Wiley.

Garfield, S. L., & Bergin, A. E. (1994). Introduction and historical overview. In A. Bergin & S. Garfield, *Handbook of psychotherapy and behavior change* (4th ed., pp. 3–18). New York: Wiley.

Gelso, C. J., & Carter, J. A. (1985). The relationship in counseling and psychotherapy: Components, consequences, and theoretical antecedents. *The Counseling Psychologist, 13*, 155–243.

Gergen, K. J. (1989). Social psychology and the wrong revolution. *European Journal of Social Psychology, 19*, 731–732.

Gergen, K. J., & Kaye, J. (1992). Beyond narrative in the negotiation of therapeutic meaning. In S. McNamee & K. J. Gergen (Eds.), *Therapy as social construction* (pp. 166–185). Newbury Park, CA: Sage.

Gill, M. (1982). *The analysis of transference.* New York: International Universities Press.

Glantz, K., & Pearce, J. K. (1989). *Exiles from Eden*. New York: W.W. Norton.

Gleick, J. (1987). *Chaos: Making a new science*. New York: Viking.

Goldstein, A. P., & Stein, N. (1976). *Prescriptive psychotherapies*. Elmsford, NY: Pergamon Press.

Gonski, Y. A. (1985). The therapeutic utilization of caines in child welfare settings. *Child and Adolescent Social Work Journal*, 2(2), 93–105.

Gornick, L. K. (1986). Developing a new narrative: The woman therapist and the male patient. *Psychoanalytic Psychology*, 3(4), 299–325.

Greenson, R. R. (1967). *Technique and practice of psychoanalysis*. New York: International Universities Press.

Gurman, A. S. (1977). The patient's perceptions of the therapeutic relationship. In A. S. Gurman & A. M. Razin (Eds.), *Effective psychotherapy* (pp. 503–543). Elmsford, NY: Pergamon Press.

Guy, J. D. (1987). *The personal life of the psychotherapist*. New York: Wiley.

Guy, J. D., & Liaboe, G. P. (1986). The impact of conducting psychotherapy on psychotherapists' interpersonal functioning. *Professional Psychology: Research and Practice*, 17(2), 111–114.

Guy, J. D., Poelstra, P. L., & Stark, M. J. (1988). Personal distress and therapeutic effectiveness. *Professional Psychology: Research and Practice*, 20, 48–50.

Haley, J. (1963). *Strategies of psychotherapy*. New York: Grune and Stratton.

Haley, J. (1973). *Uncommon therapy: The psychiatric techniques of Milton H. Erickson*. New York: Ballantine.

Hardesty, M. J. (1986). Plans and mood: A study in therapeutic relationships. *Studies in Symbolic Interaction*, 2, 209–230.

Harner, M. J. (1980). *The way of the shaman*. New York: HarperCollins.

Harwood, A. (1970). An introduction to Mwanabantu area. In *Witchcraft, sorcery, and social categories*. London: Oxford University Press.

Hayes, R. B. (1988). Friendship. In S. Duck (Ed.), *Handbook of personal relationships: Theory, research, and intervention* (pp. 391–408). New York: Wiley.

Heider, F. (1958). *The psychology of interpersonal relations*. New York: Wiley.

Heppner, P. P., & Claiborn, C. C. (1989). Social influence research in counseling: A review and critique. *Journal of Counseling Psychology*, 36(3), 365–387.

Horvath, A. O., & Greenberg, L. S. (1989). Development and validation of the working alliance inventory. *Journal of Counseling Psychology*, 36, 223–233.

Horvath, A. O., & Symonds, B. D. (1991). Relation between working alliance and outcome in psychotherapy: A metaanalysis. *Journal of Counseling Psychology*, 38(2), 139–149.

House, J. S., Landis, K. R., & Uberson, D. (1988). Social relationships and health. *Science*, 241, 540–544.

Howard, J. A. (1975). *The flesh-colored cage*. New York: Hawthorn.

Jackson, A. M. (1990). Evolution of ethnocultural psychotherapy. *Psychotherapy, 277*, 428–435.

Jacobson, N. S., McDonald, D. W., Follette, W. C., & Berley, R. A. (1985). Attributional process in distressed and nondistressed couples. *Cognitive Therapy and Research, 9*, 35–50.

Jay, J. (1991, November/December). Terrible knowledge. *Family Therapy Networker*, pp. 18–29.

Jilek, W. G., & Todd, N. (1974). Witchdoctors succeed where doctors fail: Psychotherapy among coastal Salish Indians. *Canadian Psychiatric Association Journal, 19*, 351–356.

Josselson, R. (1992). *The space between us: Exploring the dimensions of human relationships*. San Francisco: Jossey-Bass.

Kernberg, O. (1984). *Severe personality disorders*. New Haven, CT: Yale University Press.

Kiesler, D. J. (1966). Some myths of psychotherapy research and the search for a paradigm. *Psychological Bulletin, 64*, 114–120.

Kiesler, D. J. (1972). *The process of psychotherapy*. Hawthorne, NY: Aldine.

Kiesler, D. J. (1982). Interpersonal theory for personality and psychotherapy. In J. C. Anchin & D. J. Kiesler (Eds.), *Handbook of interpersonal psychotherapy* (pp. 3–24). Elmsford, NY: Pergamon Press.

Kiesler, D. J. (1984). *Checklist of psychotherapy transactions (CLOPT) and Checklist of interpersonal transactions (CLOIT)*. Richmond: Virginia Commonwealth University.

Klee, M. R., Abeles, N., & Muller, R. T. (1990). Therapeutic alliance: Early indicators, course, and outcome. *Psychotherapy, 27*, 166–174.

Klinger, E. (1977). *Meaning and void: Inner experience and the incentives in peoples' lives*. Minneapolis: University of Minnesota Press.

Kohut, H. (1984). *How does analysis cure?* Chicago: University of Chicago Press.

Kolb, D. L., Beutler, L. E., Davis, C. S., Crago, M. J., & Shanfield, S. B. (1985). Patient and therapy process variables relating to dropout and change in psychotherapy. *Psychotherapy, 22*, 702–710.

Kottler, J. A. (1990). *Private moments, secret selves*. New York: Ballantine.

Kottler, J. A. (1991). *The compleat therapist*. San Francisco: Jossey-Bass.

Kottler, J. A. (1992a). *Compassionate therapy: Working with difficult clients*. San Francisco: Jossey-Bass.

Kottler, J. A. (1992b). Confronting your own hypocrisy: Being a model for students and clients. *Journal of Counseling and Development, 70*, 475–476.

Kottler, J. A. (1993). *On being a therapist* (rev. ed.). San Francisco: Jossey-Bass.

Kottler, J. A., & Blau, D. S. (1989). *The imperfect therapist: Learning from failure in therapeutic practice*. San Francisco: Jossey-Bass.

Kramer, P. D. (1993). *Listening to Prozac*. New York: Viking Penguin.

LaCrosse, M. B. (1980.) Perceived counselor social influence and counseling outcomes: Validity of the Counselor Rating Form. *Journal of Counseling Psychology, 27*, 320–327.

Lambert, M. J., Shapiro, D. A., & Bergin, A. E. (1986). The effectiveness of psychotherapy. In S. L. Garfield & A. E. Bergin (Eds.), *Handbook of psychotherapy and behavior change* (pp. 157–211). New York: Wiley.

Lax, W. D. (1992). Postmodern thinking in clinical practice. In S. McNamee & K. J. Gergen (Eds.), *Therapy as social construction* (pp. 69–85). Newbury Park, CA: Sage Publications.

Lazarus, A. A. (1971). *Behavior therapy and beyond.* New York: McGraw-Hill.

Lazarus, A. A. (1981). *The practice of multimodal therapy.* New York: McGraw-Hill.

Leary, T. (1957). *Interpersonal diagnosis of personality.* New York: Roland.

Legrand, M. (1989). Traditional therapies and modern therapies: Differences and similarities. In L. Simek-Downing (Ed.), *International psychotherapy: Theories, research, and cross-cultural implications* (pp. 35–44). New York: Praeger.

Levine, F. M., Sandeen, E., & Murphy, C. M. (1992). The therapist's dilemma: Using nomothetic information to answer idiographic questions. *Psychotherapy, 29*(3), 410–415.

LeVine, P. (1993). Moria-based therapy and its use across cultures in the treatment of bulimia nervosa. *Journal of Counseling and Development, 72,* 82–90.

Levine, S. W., & Herron, W. G. (1990). Changes during the course of the psychotherapeutic relationship. *Psychological Reports, 66,* 883–897.

Levinger, G. (1979). Reviewing the close relationship. In G. Levinger & H. L. Raush (Eds.), *Close relationships: Perspectives on the meaning in intimacy* (pp. 137–166). Amherst: University of Massachusetts Press.

Levinger, G. (1980). Toward the analysis of close relationships. *Journal of Experimental Social Psychology, 16,* 510–544.

Levinger, G., & Snoek, D. J. (1972). *Attraction in relationship: A new look at interpersonal attraction.* Morristown, NJ: General Learning Press.

Lewis, W. A., & Evans, J. W. (1986). Resistance: A reconceptualization. *Psychotherapy, 23,* 426–433.

Lopez, F. G. (1993). Cognitive processes in close relationships: Recent findings and implications for counseling. *Journal of Counseling and Development, 71,* 310–315.

Lorr, M., & McNair, D. M. (1964). The interview relationship in therapy. *Journal of Nervous and Mental Disease, 139,* 328–331.

Luborsky, L. (1984). *Principles of psychoanalytic psychotherapy: A manual for supportive expressive treatment.* New York: Basic Books.

Luborsky, L., Crits-Christoph, P., Mintz, J., & Auerbach, A. (1988). *Who will benefit from psychotherapy? Predicting therapeutic outcomes.* New York: Basic Books.

Luborsky, L., Singer, B., & Luborsky, L. (1975). Comparative studies of psychotherapy. *Archives of General Psychiatry, 32,* 995–1008.

Luks, A. (1991). *The healing power of doing good: The health and spiritual benefits of helping others.* New York: Fawcett Columbine.

Lynch, J. J. (1977). *The broken heart: The medical consequences of loneliness.* New York: Basic Books.

MacLean, P. D. (1978). A mind of three minds: Educating the triune brain. In *Seventy-seventh yearbook of the National Society for the Study of Education* (pp. 308–342). Chicago: University of Chicago Press.

McNamee, S. (1992). Reconstructing identity: The communal construction of crisis. In S. McNamee & K. J. Gergen (Eds.), *Therapy as social construction* (pp. 186–199). Newbury Park, CA: Sage.

McNeill, B. W., May, R. J., & Lee, V. E. (1987). Perceptions of counselor source characteristics by premature and successful terminators. *Journal of Counseling Psychology, 34,* 86–89.

Maeder, T. (1989, January). Wounded healers. *The Atlantic Monthly,* pp. 37–47.

Mahoney, M. J. (1991). *Human change processes: The scientific foundations of psychotherapy.* New York: Basic Books.

Maturana, H., & Verela, F. (1987). *The tree of knowledge.* Boston: New Science Library.

Mellan, O. (1992, March/April). The last taboo. *Family Therapy Networker,* pp. 40–47.

Miller, M. J. (1990). On being attractive with resistant clients. *Journal of Humanistic Education and Development, 29,* 86–92.

Mitchell, K. M., Bozarth, J. D., & Kraft, C. C. (1977). A reappraisal of the therapeutic effectiveness of accurate empathy, nonpossessive warmth, and genuineness. In S. Gurman & A. M. Razin (Eds.), *Effective psychotherapy* (pp. 482–502). Elmsford, NY: Pergamon Press.

Moore, T. (1994). *Soul mates: Honoring the mysteries of love and relationship.* New York: HarperCollins.

Morse, J. M. (1991). Negotiating commitment and involvement in the nurse-patient relationship. *Journal of Advanced Nursing, 16,* 455–468.

Murchie, G. (1978). *The seven mysteries of life: An exploration in science and philosophy.* Boston: Houghton Mifflin.

Murdock, G. P., Wilson, L. T., & Frederick, C. (1978). World distribution of theories of illness. *Ethnology, 17,* 449–470.

Neihardt, J. G. (1961). *Black Elk speaks Lincoln.* Lincoln: University of Nebraska Press.

Neimeyer, G. J. (1984). Cognitive complexity and marital satisfaction. *Journal of Social and Clinical Psychology, 2,* 258–263.

Neimeyer, R. A., & Neimeyer, G. J. (1983). Structural similarity in the acquaintance process. *Journal of Social and Clinical Psychology, 1,* 146–154.

Neki, J. S. (1976). An examination of the cultural relativism of dependence as a dynamic of social and therapeutic relationships. *British Journal of Medical Psychology, 49,* 1–10.

Neki, J. S., Joinet, B., Hogan, M., Hauli, J. G., & Kilonzo, G. (1985). The cultural perspective of therapeutic relationship: A viewpoint from Africa. *Acta Psychiatrica Scandinavica, 71,* 543–550.

Nevels, L. A., & Coché, J. M. (1993). *Powerful women: Voices of distinguished women psychotherapists.* San Francisco: Jossey-Bass.

Orlinsky D. E., Grawe, D., & Parks, B. W. (1994). Process and outcome in psychotherapy—Noch Einmal. In A. Bergin & S. Garfield, *Handbook of psychotherapy and behavior change* (4th ed., pp. 270–378). New York: Wiley.

Orlinsky, D. E., & Howard, K. I. (1986). Process and outcome in psychotherapy. In S. L. Garfield & A. E. Bergin (Eds.), *Handbook of psychotherapy and behavior change* (pp. 311–381). New York: Wiley.

O'Sullivan, M. J., Peterson, P. D., Cox, G. B., & Kirkeby, J. (1989). Ethnic populations: Community mental health services ten years later. *American Journal of Community Psychology, 17,* 17–30.

Otani, A. (1989). Client resistance in counseling: Its theoretical rationale and taxonomic classification. *Journal of Counseling and Development, 67,* 458–461.

Page, R. C., & Berkow, D. N. (1994). *Creating contact, choosing relationship.* San Francisco: Jossey-Bass.

Patterson, C. H. (1984). Empathy, warmth, and genuineness in psychotherapy: A review of reviews. *Psychotherapy, 21,* 431–438.

Patterson, C. H. (1985). *The therapeutic relationship: Foundations of an eclectic psychotherapy.* Pacific Grove, CA: Brooks/Cole.

Paul, G. L. (1967). Outcome research in psychotherapy. *Journal of Consulting Psychology, 31,* 109–118.

Peacock, C. (1986). The role of the therapeutic pet in initial psychotherapy session with adolescents. In *Delta Society International Conference,* Boston.

Pedder, J. (1991). Fear of dependence in therapeutic relationships. *British Journal of Medical Psychology, 65,* 117–126.

Pogrebin, L. C. (1987). *Among friends.* New York: McGraw-Hill.

Pope, K. S., & Bouhoutsos, J. C. (1986). *Sexual intimacy between therapists and patients.* New York: Praeger.

Prochaska, J., & DeClemente, C. (1983). Stages and processes of self-change of smoking: Toward an integrative model of change. *Journal of Consulting and Clinical Psychology, 51,* 390–395.

Quintana, S. M., & Meara, N. M. (1990). Internalization of therapeutic relationships in short-term psychotherapy. *Journal of Counseling Psychology, 37,* 123–130.

Rambo, A. H., Heath, A., & Chenail, R. J. (1993). *Practicing therapy.* New York: W.W. Norton.

Rennie, D. L., & Toukmanian, S. G. (1992). Explanation in psychotherapy process research. In S. G. Toukmanian &. D. L. Rennie (Eds.), *Psychotherapy process research* (pp. 234–251). Newbury Park, CA: Sage.

Reynolds, D. K. (1976). *Morita psychotherapy*. Berkeley: University of California Press.

Richardson, E. H. (1981). Cultural and historical perspectives in counseling Indians. In D. W. Sue (Ed.), *Counseling the culturally different*. New York: Wiley.

Rogers, C. R. (1957). The necessary and sufficient conditions of therapeutic personality change. *Journal of Consulting Psychology, 21*(2), 19–57.

Rook, K. S., & Pietromonaco, P. (1987). Close relationships: Ties that heal or ties that bind? In W. H. Jones & D. Perlman (Eds.), *Advances in personal relationships* (pp. 1–35). Greenwich, CT: JAI Press.

Rubenstein, C., & Shaver, P. (1982). *In search of intimacy*. New York: Delacorte.

Ruesch, J., & Bateson, G. (1968). *Communication: The social matrix of psychiatry*. New York: W.W. Norton.

Russell, R. L., & Van Den Broek, P. (1992). Changing narrative schemas in psychotherapy. *Psychotherapy, 29,* 344–354.

Saltzman, C., Luetgert, M. J., Roth, J. Creaser, K., & Howard, L. (1976). Formation of a therapeutic relationship: Experiences during the initial phase of psychotherapy as predictors of treatment duration and outcome. *Journal of Consulting and Clinical Psychology, 44,* 546–555.

Sarason, S. B. (1985). *Caring and compassion in clinical practice: Issues in the selection, training, and behavior of helping professionals*. San Francisco: Jossey-Bass.

Sarbin, T. R. (1986). *Narrative psychology: The storied nature of human conduct*. New York: Praeger.

Schofield, W. (1964). *Psychotherapy: The purchase of friendship*. Englewood Cliffs, NJ: Prentice Hall.

Schullo, S. A., & Alperson, B. L. (1984). Interpersonal phenomenology as a function of sexual orientation, sex, sentiment, and trait categories in long-term dyadic relationships. *Journal of Personality and Social Psychology, 47,* 98–102.

Seligman, L., & Gaaserud, L. (1994). Difficult clients: Who are they and how do we help them? *Canadian Journal of Counseling, 28,* 25–42.

Sexton, T. L., & Whiston, S. C. (1991). A review of the empirical basis for counseling: Implications for practice and training. *Counselor Education and Supervision, 30,* 330–354.

Sexton, T. L., & Whiston, S. C. (1994). The status of the counseling relationship: An empirical review, theoretical implications, and research direction. *The Counseling Psychologist, 22*(1), 6–78.

Seyster, K. (1987). A lesson in therapeutic relationship. *Imprint, 34*(3), 56–58.

Shadley, M. L. (1990). Critical incidents: Life events for experienced family therapists. *Contemporary Family Therapy, 12,* 253–262.

Shapiro, D. A., & Shapiro, D. (1982). Meta-analysis of comparative therapy outcome studies: A replication and refinement. *Psychological Bulletin, 92,* 581–604.

Shaver, R. (1967). *Projective testing and psychoanalysis.* New York: International University Press.

Sheltzer, L. (1986). *Paradoxical strategies in psychotherapy: A comprehensive overview and guidebook.* New York: Wiley.

Singer, J. L. (1985). Transference and the human condition: A cognitive-affect perspective. *Psychoanalytic Psychology, 2,* 189–219.

Singer, J. L., & Kolligian, J. (1987). Personality: Developments in the study of private experience. *Annual Review of Psychology, 38,* 533–574.

Singer, J. L., Sincoff, J. B., & Kolligian, J. (1989). Countertransference and cognition: Studying the psychotherapist's distortions as consequences of normal information processing. *Psychotherapy, 26,* 344–355.

Sloane, R. B., Staples, F. R., Cristol, A. H., Yorkston, N. J., & Whipple, K. (1975). *Psychotherapy versus behavior therapy.* Cambridge, MA: Harvard University Press.

Smith, M. L., & Glass, G. V. (1977). Meta-analysis of psychotherapy outcome studies. *American Psychologist, 32,* 752–760.

Smith, M. L., Glass, G. V., & Miller, T. I. (1980). *The benefits of psychotherapy.* Baltimore: Johns Hopkins University Press.

Snowden, L. R., & Cheung, F. K. (1990). Use of inpatient mental health services by members of ethnic minority groups. *American Psychologist, 45,* 347–355.

Stiles, W. B., Shapiro, D. A., & Elliott, R. (1986). Are all psychotherapies equivalent? *American Psychologist, 41,* 165–180.

Strong, S. R. (1968). Counseling: An interpersonal influence process. *Journal of Counseling Psychology, 15,* 215–224.

Strong, S. R., & Claiborn, C. D. (1982). *Change through interaction: Social psychological process of counseling and psychotherapy.* New York: Wiley.

Sue, S., & Zane, N. (1987). The role of culture and cultural techniques in psychotherapy: A critique and reformation. *American Psychologist, 42,* 37–45.

Sue, S., Fujino, D. C., Hu, L., & Takeuchi, D. T. (1991). Community mental health services for ethnic minority groups: A test of the cultural responsibleness hypothesis. *Journal of Consulting and Clinical Psychology, 59*(4), 533–540.

Suttles, G. D. (1970). Friendship as a social institution. In G. J. McCall (Ed.), *Social relationships.* Hawthorne, NY: Aldine.

Tennov, D. (1979). *Love and limerance*. New York: Stein & Day.

Thelen, M., Fishbein, M. D., & Tatten, H. A. (1985). Interspousal similarity: A new approach to an old question. *Journal of Social and Personal Relationships, 2*, 437–446.

Thibaut, J. W., & Kelley, H. H. (1959). *The social psychology of groups*. New York: Wiley.

Thoreson, R. W., Miller, M., & Krauskopf, C. J. (1989). The distressed psychologist: Prevalence and treatment considerations. *Professional Psychology: Research and Practice, 20*, 153–158.

Thorne, F. C. (1950). *The principles of personal counseling*. Brandon, VT: Clinical Psychology Publishing.

Thorne, F. C. (1967). *Integrative psychology*. Brandon, VT.: Clinical Psychology Publishing.

Tillich, P. (1952). *The courage to be*. New Haven, CT: Yale University Press.

Torrey, W. F. (1986). *Witchdoctors and psychiatrists*. New York: HarperCollins.

Tracey, T. J. (1977). Impact of intake procedures upon client attrition in a community mental health center. *Journal of Consulting and Clinical Psychology, 45*, 192–195.

Tracey, T. J. (1985). Dominance and outcome: A sequential examination. *Journal of Counseling Psychology, 32*, 119–122.

Tracey, T. J. (1986). Control in counseling: Intrapersonal versus interpersonal definitions. *Journal of Counseling and Development, 64*, 512–515.

Tracey, T. J. (1993). An interpersonal stage model of the therapeutic process. *Journal of Counseling Psychology, 40*, 396–409.

Tracey, T. J., & Hays, K. (1989). Therapist complementarity as a function of experience and client stimuli. *Psychotherapy, 26*, 462–468.

Tracey, T. J., & Ray, P. B. (1984) Stages of successful time-limited counseling: An interactional examination. *Journal of Counseling Psychology, 31*, 13–27.

Truax, B. B., & Carkhuff, R. R. (1967). *Toward effective counseling and psychotherapy*. Hawthorne, NY: Aldine.

Tryon, G. S. (1983). The pleasures and displeasures of full time private practice. *Clinical Psychologist, 36*, 45–48.

Watkins, C. E. (1985). Countertransference: Its impact on the counseling situation. *Journal of Counseling and Development, 63*, 356–359.

Watkins, C. E. (1990). The effects of counselor self-disclosure: A research review. *The counseling psychologist, 18*(3), 477–500.

Watzlawick, P., Beavin, J. H., & Jackson, D. D. (1967). *Pragmatics of human communication: A study of interactional patterns, pathologies, and paradoxes*. New York: W.W. Norton.

Watzlawick, P., Weakland, J., & Fisch, R. (1974). *Change: Principles of problem formation and problem resolution*. New York: Gardner Press.

Weeks, G. R. (1989). An intersystem approach to treatment. In G. R. Weeks (Ed.), *Treating couples: The intersystem model of the Marriage Council of Philadelphia* (pp. 317–339). New York: Brunner/Mazel.

Wetchler, J. L., & Piercy, F. P. (1986). The marital/family life of the family therapist: Stressors and enhancers. *American Journal of Family Therapy, 14,* 99–108.

Whiston, S. C., & Sexton, T. L. (1993). An overview of psychotherapy outcome research: Implications for practice. *Professional Psychology: Research and Practice, 24*(1), 43–51.

White, M., & Epston, D. (1990). *Narrative means to therapeutic ends.* New York: W.W. Norton.

Winnecott, D. W. (1965). *The maturational process and the facilitating environment.* New York: International Universities Press.

Winstead, B. A., Derlega, V. J., Lewis, R. J., & Margulis, S. T. (1988). Understanding the therapeutic relationship as a personal relationship. *Journal of Social and Personal Relationships, 5,* 109–125.

Wittgenstein, L. (1953). *Philosophical investigations.* New York: Macmillan.

Yankelovich, D. (1981). *New rules: Searching for self-fulfillment in a world turned upside down.* New York: Random House.

Name Index

Subject Index

A

Aboriginal tribes, 70. *See also* Indigenous cultures

Acting out, setting boundaries for, 91, 244–247

Adaptive vs. maladaptive strategies, 227

Affective empathy, 124, 126

Affective experience, language and, 196–197

Affiliation, 79; in relationship negotiation, 186–190, 191–192

Affirmation, mutual, 101

African cultures: Bangwa, 39–40; healing relationships in, 74; Tanzanian, 69–70, 74

Age variables, 24

Algonquins, 24

Altered states of consciousness, 31

Amazon healers, 83–84, 203–204

Analysis, vs. contemplation, 73

Analyzing, in therapist's personal life, 58–59

Animalistic causation, 70

Animals, as healers, 33

Anthropology, 34

Appointments, client's missing of, 261

Asian culture, 39

Assertive behavioral style, 186

Assessment orientations, 227. *See also* Diagnosis

Attachment, 40, 77, 105; to therapist, 101

Attention deficit, 257

Attorneys, 36

Attraction/attractiveness, 95, 134–136, 142, 154, 155; empirical research on, 135; during preliminary stage, 211, 230

Attributions, 149–151; and therapeutic influence, 151–153

Authentic engagement dimension, 104–107, 113–128, 132, 207; changes initiated in, 106; client attributes/roles in, 104–105; in closing stage, 221; compassion and love in, 117–120; core conditions in, importance of, 115–116; cultural threads in, 105; empathy in, 120–127; genuineness in, 116–117; mutual self-disclosure in, 127–128; mutuality in, 114–115; personal threads in, 105; during preliminary and beginning stages, 211, 213, 229–231; respect in, 116–117; therapist attributes/roles in, 104–105, 106–107; within the working alliance, 128–130. *See also* Caring; Empathy; Facilitative conditions; Genuineness; Love; Social influence

Authenticity: multiple views of, 155–156; and working alliance model, 128–132. *See also* Authentic engagement dimension

Authoritarianism, in therapeutic relationship, 5–8

Autonomy, vs. self-control, 73. *See also* Independence; Individualism

B

Bangwa society, 39–40

Bartenders, 35

Beginning stage, of therapeutic relationship, 213–215; and costs/rewards, 144–145; and credibility, 140; empathy in, 103, 126; and impression management, 136–139; and initial

thread in, 277–278; empirical thread in, 276–277; personal thread in, 278–283

G

Gender: and empathy, 126; and projective dimension, 168; variables of, 24

Genuineness, 102, 105; and authentic engagement, 116–117; and experience of intimacy, 239–240; vs. projection, 10–14; and social influence factors, 142. *See also* Authentic engagement dimension

Ghosts. *See* Projected dimension

Global attributions, 150

Goals: content of, vs. agreement on, 131–132; therapeutic focus on, 240–242, 252

Grief work, in closing stage, 220–221

H

Healers: activities of, in cultures compared, 202–209; in Eastern cultures, 72–74; in indigenous cultures, 34–35, 67–69, 83–84, 202–209; in Western cultures, 35, 67. *See also* Medicine men; Shamans; Sorcerers; Therapists

Healing alliance, 110–111, 208; in middle stage, 218–219; in preliminary stage, 211. *See also* Working alliance

Healing relationships: cultural similarities and differences in, 83–85, 202–209; interdisciplinary perspective on, 34–37, 276; multicultural perspective on, 34–37, 65–86, 209; nature of, 201–223; nonprofessional, 33–34, 37; personal vs. therapeutic aspects of, 28–29; personal threads in, 37–42, 205–206; reciprocal influence in, 206, 210; as shared journey, 203–204. *See also* Personal relationships; Therapeutic relationship

Helper's high, 46

Hidden agendas, 11, 58–59, 257

Holistic treatment, 85

Hostile countertransference, 174–175

Hostility, in relationship negotiation, 186, 191–192

Human contact, need for, 37–38

Humanistic model, 31, 32, 92–93, 98, 105

Hunter-gatherer tribes, 41

I

Iban tribe, 83

Identity loss, therapist, 60

Impression management, 136–139, 142–143, 154, 155; during preliminary and beginning stages, 211, 213; symptoms as client strategy for, 191

Independence, client: cultural relativism in, 75–79; vs. dependence, 14–15. *See also* Autonomy; Dependence

India, culture of, 75–76; dependence in, 78–79

Indigenous cultures: community in, 41; healers in, 34–35, 67–69, 202–209

Individualism, in cultures compared, 39, 73, 74

Ineffective therapeutic relationships, 251–271; causes of, 256–270; client variables in, 256–262; client's restricting of content in, 259–260; client's violating relationship rules in, 261–262; client's withholding communication in, 258–259; diagnosing the existence of, 252–254; diagnostic checklist for, 253; extraneous variables in, 269–270; interactional process variables in, 266–269; relationship resistance in, 254–256; therapist variables in, 262–265; therapist's professional assessment of vs. personal reaction to, 265; with trauma victims, 265–266; and treatment approach, limitations in, 267–269. *See also* Resistance

Influence, therapist: cognitive approach to, 151–153; factors in, 204–205; interactional positioning approach to, 191–194, 242–244; using therapeutic relationship as basis for, 233–235. *See also* Social influence

Initial attraction, 134–136. *See also* Attraction

Intellectualizing, 260

Interactional model, 95–96, 99

Interactional patterns, 208; assumptions about, 179–183; in beginning stage, 215; complementarity and symmetry in, 186–190, 266; development of, 178; diagnosis using, 227–231; dimension of, 108–109, 177–198; in ineffective relationships, 263–264, 266–269; language and, 196–197; in middle